HAITI

BETWEEN PESTILENCE AND HOPE

THE PROGRESSIVE IDEALS FROM THE REVOLUTION OF 1804 SET THE PACE

HAITI

BETWEEN PESTILENCE AND HOPE

THE PROGRESSIVE IDEALS FROM THE REVOLUTION OF 1804 SET THE PACE

FRITZNEL D OCTAVE

Columbus, Ohio

Haiti Between Pestilence and Hope: The Progressive Ideals from the Revolution of 1804 Set the Pace

Published by Gatekeeper Press
2167 Stringtown Rd, Suite 109
Columbus, OH 43123-2989
www.GatekeeperPress.com

Website: www.fritzneloctave.com
email address: fritznel.octave@gmail.com

Library of Congress Control Number: 2022930377

ISBN (hardcover): 9781662923760
ISBN (paperback): 9781662923777
eISBN: 9781662923784

Contents

Acknowledgments

It takes a great team effort to realize something of that importance. I need to register my debt and gratitude to a number of individuals whose contributions and inspirations have made this project a success. First among them is my wife, Magalie, who had encouraged me to write this book. Without her encouragement and unconditional support, this laborious and time-consuming project would not be possible. Her brilliant advices and technical assistance have been invaluable. To my two children, Keandre and Nephtalie, I owe a special debt of gratitude for their understanding and sense of compromise, at times, when they could not count on my fatherhood duties. Guys, I love you deeply.

I have been blessed with great families, friends, and benefactors in my circle. Extraordinary people whom I love and admire. People who believe in hard work and good education, and whose faith in the future remains infinitely unshakable. These are things that continue to inspire my life with a greater sense of purpose.

I am grateful to my parents, Inove Octave and Rose Docilna Docius. I owe them everything for their effort, enormous sacrifice, and investment of all they had in their children's future. To my in-laws, Sodino and Rosette Morantus, I also express my gratitude for showing their patience, understanding, and unconditional love toward me. And this goes as well to the rest of my very large family on both sides, including my 12 siblings and their children, my aunts and uncles, and my infinite number of cousins whom I love and admire. I will be forever grateful especially to my cousins Mérieuse Octave Sanon and her husband Géthro Sanon, who helped shape my vision in life, to Germenie Octave Céant and her husband Elandieu Céant, and to Pastor Venès Octave and his wife Vania Octave, who received me in the United States in 2001 with open arms. To Fricienne Dortelus, Loreste Moise and his wife Souvenance Moise, Judge Marie Justine Moise, Bernadine Moise, Jean-Marcel Moise, Carline Moise, and Lonel Moise, whose invaluable supports allowed me to settle in Port-au-Prince during my difficult years in high school. Waltère Gallion Bien-Aimé, a reliable friend, and Madeline Paul and her husband Anovert Dérilus, an adopted family to us, also deserve my words of gratitude.

No words can fully express my gratitude and sentiments toward Jan Voordouw for his generosity and contributions in my early professional development through the Panos Institute. Additionally, despite his busy schedule with work-related projects and personal activities, he had spared some of his time to preface this book with enthusiasm. I am also indebted to my former colleagues Yves-Marie Chanel at Inter Press Service (IPS), Ronald Colbert, and Jean Lamy, who all taught me the practice of social responsibility and professional rigor in journalism.

My special mention is also addressed to my co-workers at American Income Life Insurance Company (AIL) for helping shape my career. I particularly owe a debt of gratitude to Tom Williams, State General Agent in Florida, David Zophin, president of AIL, my former Manager General Agents Earle Harris, and Kasali Kotun for giving the opportunity, training, coaching, and continuing support throughout my journey with the company.

Last, but not least, I need to acknowledge Gatekeeper Press for assisting me with a publishing service "à la clé". To the entire staff, I register my ample gratitude, from Rob Price the CEO for his understanding, collaboration, and commitment to quality and satisfaction, to my editor manager Yukiko Schlotter for her professionalism, her sense of agency and urgency, and to my cover design illustrator, Anna Szczypiorska, for her patience and dedication to excellence. I can't go without mentioning my editor Maria Arana for her hard work and professional rigor during the developmental edit process. She had pushed me to dig deeper into the story and provided me with intelligible suggestions and insights that have made this book a lot more informative and consistent with its tone and voice. I also register my thanks to my copy editor Talejah Todd-Hill who did an excellent job ensuring the technical quality of the manuscript, making sure that nothing fell through the cracks.

Dedication

Haiti Between Pestilence and Hope is dedicated to many institutions, organizations, and individuals including Haitians and foreigners whose works have contributed to help keep Haiti's hopes alive in spite of so many setbacks. This book is dedicated especially to the Haitian people; the millions of Haitians whose bravery, resilience, courage, perseverance, and determination in the ongoing struggle for changes and better living conditions have never ceased to amaze and surprise the world. We particularly remember the heroes of the slave revolution and independence whose illustrious works and progressive ideals remain the source of inspiration for ordinary Haitians, "True Haitians". Haitians from various fields of activities like Jean Léopold Dominique, Père Jean-Mary Vincent, Antoine Izméry, Odette Roy Fombrun, Ertha Pascal-Trouillot, Pastor Sylvio Claude, and Paul Dejean among many others who sought to put Haiti's collective above individual interests. Like Dessalines, some of them had paid the ultimate price. They died for daring to think that way.

Few foreign and local organizations and individuals of various backgrounds have contributed and continue working to make life better in Haiti. That's good news! We need a lot more than a few, of course. But without efforts from those entities and individuals the country would be a lot worse off, considering the type of performance from the local government. Below, we take the liberty to mention some people by name, yet dead or alive. The positive impacts of their contributions in community development projects, in many areas around Haiti, cannot be underestimated.

With that being said, we pay tribute to late Pastor Leslie G. Harris, a Jamaican born missionary, who dedicated more than 60 years of his life in the service of people in rural-northwestern Haiti, notably Môle

Saint-Nicolas, Jean-Rabel, Bombardopolis, and Baie-de-Henne. Many inhabitants of these regions will always remember Pastor Harris who died in Crève (Bombardopolis), Haiti, on October 8, 2019. When he arrived in the area in the mid-1950s, he found a population almost totally neglected or ignored by the Haitian government. Through his *Mission des Eglises Baptistes Independantes* (MEBI), he became one of the most important change agents in socioeconomic development, healthcare, and education to the population. A young missionary in Pastor Harris was introduced by American missionary and philanthropist pastor Wallace Sturnbull. Pastor Turnbull, on his part, had pioneered church planting, schools, community, and social developments in Haiti for over 70 years.

Haiti Between Pestilence and Hope is also dedicated to the memory of many others like late Dr. Paul Edward Farmer. An American medical anthropologist and physician, Farmer, who died on February 21, 2022, devoted most of his time to delivering quality public healthcare to the most vulnerable people around the world. In Haiti, he helped establish *Zanmi Lasante* through his philanthropic organization Partners in Health, which led several initiatives aiming at providing free healthcare to the people.

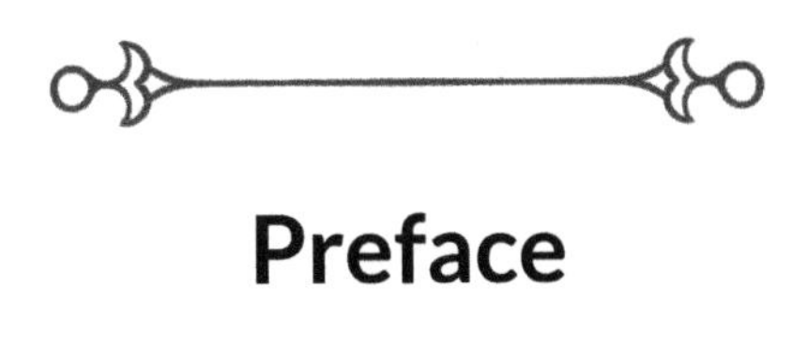

Preface

When I first met Fritznel D. Octave in the late 1990s, he was an active journalist with one of the radio stations in Port-de-Paix, Haiti. He also wrote for *Jounal Libète*. Fritznel was a curious young man who wanted to perfect his journalistic skills. At that time, I was setting up an NGO, the Panos Institute, that focused on supporting Haitian media and Haitian media workers to publish and broadcast underreported or emerging stories. Stories of hope and innovation within a context of socio-economic development and social justice. Panos helped people that were marginalized in one way or another to express their news and perspectives through the media. Street children, farmers and fisherfolks, people living with HIV and AIDS, sex workers, migrants, women in the media, or young people with innovative ideas featured in our productions. Politics was not underreported, so we shunned interviewing the usual newsmakers.

Fritznel quickly became a regular collaborator, bringing in a variety of stories from different parts of the country, for instance about the challenges of agriculture in the Central Plateau, management of the environment in Camp Perrin (south) and around Lac Azuéi (near the border with the Dominican Republic), among other social, health, and environmental issues. The hopes expressed by people who he interviewed: farmers, religious leaders, women, or representatives of local associations. He recorded the voices of ordinary people, in line with our motto *"Real People -Real Voices!"*

Fritznel was part of an active group of journalists that showed there was much more going on in Haiti than politics, disasters, and disillusion. That at least in some corners of the country, there was engagement with the poor and responsibility for progressive ideals.

It is only natural that Fritznel joined the long list of chroniclers of the history and politics of Haiti. What is special is the focus on the hopes and ideals that were planted in one of the great revolutions of mankind, the Haitian revolution. The revolution that followed the French revolution with its non-realized ideals: *"Liberté, Égalité, Fraternité."* He shows that there were many obstacles in trying to fulfil these ideals, both external to Haiti and internal. The book elaborates themes, such as betrayal, blame, lack of leadership, missed opportunities in the development of the country. But the book also indicates signs of hope, renewal, and thoughts on the way forward.

This is a friendly book, where a journalist talks to you and tells stories, stories about what happened, but also what people think really happened. It is a book about facts and perceptions. It explains the culture, the deep sense created by proverbs, among individuals or the population. It is also a book with some outspoken opinions, inviting debate and further reflection.

This is an honest book about a beautiful country, where the people, the culture, the history, and the landscapes capture your mind and imagination. A country with multiple crises at a time. A country where the vast majority of the people are not heard and still without having a say in their own destiny. But, hope is always there!

Jan Voordouw
Information for Development Specialist / Project Evaluator
March 2022

Introduction

So much news about what has been going wrong in Haiti, particularly the actions (brutality and avarice) of a minority of Haitians. So much has been reported about catastrophes and natural disasters. But we have not had enough reports about this wonderful place, and the amazing courage and humanity of the majority of people in Haiti. Most of Haiti's stories can be about its natural beauty and its extraordinary people who pioneered a revolution that led to the permanent abolition of slavery in the Americas.

Haiti's climate and landscape make it a very attractive place. Perhaps, that could have led to better actions. Actions that could have had more positive impacts on the country. In Haiti, the tropical climate produces seasonal rainfall for fresh air, picturesque vegetation, and agricultural activities. Haiti produces, perhaps, the most delicious fruits of all kinds among the Caribbean countries. It is particularly renowned for its mangoes. "Mango Madan Fransik", juicy and very tender, is well-recognized and largely exported to the United States. Temperatures in Haiti range from 70⁰F to 90⁰F, year-round.

The land is comprised of plains, hills, rugged mountains, coastal lines with beautiful beaches, excellent natural harbors and coral reefs, river valleys, and a large east-central plateau. The Haitian people are imaginative, creative, collectivistic, dependable, resilient, hard workers, caring, welcoming, and warm. Haitians strongly believe in education, which is a big deal. Families with limited resources do whatever it takes for their children to achieve success. And they take pride in that. That is why many young Haitians strive hard to earn degrees at universities in Haiti or in foreign countries.

Haiti has produced, and continues to do so in various domains, a number of great intellectuals and reasearchers such as Anténor Firmin and many others. In his work published in 1885, Firmin pioneered the fundamental challenge against the ideas of Arthur de Gobineau that some human races were "superior" to others.[1] Haiti gave birth to Jean-Baptiste Point Du Sable, the Black pioneer trader, who in the 1770s founded the settlement in the Midwest of the United States that later became the city of Chicago. Haiti also has love for the arts and theatre, a passion for music, dance, and sports (notably soccer, basketball, volleyball, and martial arts) among others.

This naturally beautiful country, where, paradoxically, both troubles and glory have led to its abundance of rich history, has been stuck on the road of perpetual transition, both visible and invisible. Haiti has been grappling with a present of great sorrow and an uncertain future. It has been trapped in a vicious circle where politicians and a tiny group of socioeconomic elites continue to dupe and damn the majority of ordinary citizens. There seems to be little to no way out for Haiti on the verge of its 220 years of independence.

For decades, Haitians have been living between fear, despair from uncertainty, and hope to see better days. Each time there is a tragedy, a disaster, a period of turmoil, or political and/or social turbulence provoking a moment of despair, people usually repeat again and again that the country cannot go down any further in its descent to hell. But the truth is that no significant and sustained efforts have been made by Haitians to change Haiti's fate. At every hard turn, Haitians think that they only need to find a way to survive through it, and then things will hopefully get better. The hell that people have been talking about for

---

1 Anténor Firmin, *The Equality of the Human Races* (University of Illinois Press, 2002). This English version was translated by Asselin Charles from the original French version "De l'Egalité des Races Humaines" published by Firmin in 1885 (Paris).

years, like a gigantic ocean, seems to be so infinitely deep. And Haiti, like a wrecked ship, has long been sinking deeper into it with the helpless captains and hopeless passengers on board looking down. So, how did we get here? It cannot be because of one or two things that went wrong. This book discusses Haiti's main problems, the related causes of those problems, and projects the hopeful impetuses for durable solutions.

During the last two decades, Haiti has experienced the severity of all symptoms stemming from its permanent pests. Among most phenomena called forth by the installation, the country has endured multiple contested elections, the assassination of a president, the proliferation of armed gangs, a health crisis, famine, natural disasters, and emigration. These were all compounded when in September 2021, border agents in Del Rio, Texas, began mass-expelling Haitian migrants seeking U.S. asylum. These migrants were desperate for better living conditions outside of Haiti. During its first year, the Biden administration deported more than 20,200 Haitian migrants. This growing number of deportations, covering the period between Biden's inauguration on January 20, 2021, and the end of January 2022, almost matched the recorded number of Haitians expelled to Haiti in the previous 20 years combined. During that period, the number of Haitian migrants deported by the U.S. authorities did not exceed 23,000.[2]

Many of these Haitian immigrants that the U.S. deported came by way of different South American countries after leaving the Caribbean country several years earlier. They had nothing to return to in Haiti. When the border agents decided to stop them after months of illegal

---

2 Tom Ricker, "Biden has deported nearly as many Haitians in his first year as the last three presidents – combined", quixote.org, Quixote Center, February 18, 2022. https://www.quixote.org/biden-has-deported-nearly-as-many-haitians-in-his-first-year-as-the-last-three-presidents-combined/

crossings, thousands were sheltering under a bridge near the Rio Grande River between Mexico and the United States. To get there, these Haitian migrants went through the journey of their life—a very long and perilous trek where they crossed several jungles in South and Central American countries. It took many of them weeks or months and all their savings before getting there. Hundreds of others, primarily women and children, did not make it that far. They unfortunately died of hunger, were devoured by dangerous animals in the forests, vanished while trying to cross deep rivers or oceans, and some were even killed by smugglers and human traffickers.

While Haiti's situation has been untenable for a while, the neighboring countries benefited greatly from the emigration of Haitian resources. Of course, some of them, particularly the Dominican Republic (D.R.) and the Bahamas, complain from time to time about the influx of Haitian migrants on their home soil. However, if the loss of human and financial resources constitutes a hemorrhage for Haiti, it has been a huge benefit to the other Caribbean counterparts, especially the D.R., which shares the island with Haiti. The Haitian elites, the working class, students, and thousands of other more fortunate individuals among the general population see in the D.R. a level of security, sociopolitical stability, and economic growth not comparable to the chaos that has presided over Haiti. We do not need to go any further than the economic downturn to glance at the negative effects of instability in Haiti. Financial reports made public by experts from both sides of the island revealed that the Dominican Republic recorded over US$70 million in money transfers alone to family members directly from Haiti during the first eight months of 2021.

In Haiti, people often say in their native Haitian language *lespwa fè viv* (hoping is to live) to express their belief in a better future despite their actual state of damnation.[3] They usually combine the old expression from popular wisdom *toutotan gen lavi gen espwa anba solèy la* with *toutotan mwen pa mouri mwen espere mete chapo.* Together, these two phrases mean as long as there is life, there is hope under the sun. Looking at what has become the nation of Haiti after more than two centuries of its independence, these adages have become more than an opium, more than just a way to escape from the harsh reality of daily living conditions. They provide faith, strength, and adrenaline to people. Above all, these proverbs are a source of strong resilience in times of many struggles, a sort of fuel in the locomotive of change. They help build an unbreakable belief system in Haitians, enabling them to always aspire to better days ahead even in the midst of dire situations and uncertainties. This maybe one of the reasons why the rate of suicide is relatively low in Haiti compared to other countries with similar difficulties or even better living conditions.

For most Haitians, "those who live are those who are constantly fighting," to borrow the words from *Les Misérables* by Victor Hugo, one of France's famed 19th-century essayists and poets. But their fight for a better life has been a terrifying roller coaster partly because change—progressive change—is rather difficult, especially when you do not

3 In reference to the language spoken by native Haitians (Ayisyen), we deliberately use the word Haitian as opposed to the word *Creole*. The term *Creole*, originally used by Europeans to make a distinction between people groups during the colonial era, does not apply to today's Haiti. If anything, Creole, as used in the context of Haiti, historically denotes a degree of inferiority to the French spoken mainly by the elites. The term Creole intends in its sociocultural connotation to diminish the value of efforts made by Haitians to develop an intelligible language in both its oral and written forms. In Haiti, very few people can speak French, which is the symbol and heritage of domination and exploitation. But everyone speaks Haitian (Ayisyen), which is an alternative to the culture of domination and exploitation.

have the right people in charge. It is a process that requires patience and continuity from one generation to the other. People cannot "microwave" their way to progress, nor can they "Amazon-Prime" their time to deliver major socioeconomic developments. More importantly, you cannot go from a long legacy of slavery, exploitation, division, corruption, discrimination, despotism, and domineering rules to a legacy of sound democracy overnight. Unfortunately, this is something that people often forget about. They seem to lose patience too quickly with a political process that involves the democratic construction of a society.

The Republic of Haiti, born of an extraordinary slave revolution, will celebrate the 220th inauguration of that revolution shortly. As seen from different perspectives today, Haiti can be compared to a man-made 220-year-old forest. For that long, that forest has been so ill-managed that its old trees—the institutions, systems, structures, culture, and habits altogether—derived from seeds sowed capriciously and maliciously to serve no good purpose at all, refuse to die, unroot, and fall down despite having been aged out and challenged by several big storms. Like it was the case for the slave revolt, an extraordinary common will and gigantic efforts are needed to orchestrate a complete cleanup. And that, only Haitians themselves can truly do.

Necessarily, the cleanup process passes through eliminating the bad trees. The old forest needs to be made anew under the sun of hope that brings unity, freedom, liberty, equality, and equity. To do so, the forest needs to be placed under new and better management. Those bad old trees that have continued to perdure for over two centuries need to be deracinated and burnt through their roots so that they get no chance to spring up again and continue to reproduce those undesirable fruits and seeds. They must be replaced by other types of plants, more endogenous trees with the potential for bearing enough good fruits with ideal seeds: behaviors, attitudes, and actions that are capable of renewing and inspiring different generations.

Due to the kind of media coverage the country often receives, some people tend to think of Haiti as a devastated land where misfortune always happens. This is an error. Of course, the country has problems. But those problems are often overestimated in comparison to the available resources and positive forces for change. Haiti still preserves its beauty and favorability to fertility and agriculture. Haiti produced generations of brilliant minds in the past. And the country still has the ability to continue doing just that. Wherever Haitians go, when given a window of opportunity, they excel at whatever they do.

In sum, there is no need to tear the whole location of the forest down to a point of making it uninhabitable and nonreproductive. Nor do we need to decimate its actual inhabitants whom we need to become better laborers for the common good. We do not need to cut ties with foreign laborers either. We merely need to intelligently monitor and manage their motives well enough. Let's wave goodbye to the old setting and get rid of all those bad old trees that have been either fruitless or producing rotten and poisonous fruits—those multiplying seeds that represent most of the behaviors and attitudes observed in the Haitian society. Those behaviors and attitudes stem from a long legacy of exploitation, foreign interventions, internal divisions, dupery, and impunity, among others. We will discuss this aspect with a more exhaustive list further in the book.

This is mostly a man-made disaster. Haiti did not need to be like this. In the 18th century, the country—then called Saint-Domingue under French colonization—was nicknamed the "Pearl of the Antilles" because it was the most wealth-producing colony in the entire Caribbean region. Around 1780, Haiti exported more than 60% of all the coffee and more than 40% of all the sugar consumed in Europe. The French Empire's exports from the Pearl of the Antilles to Europe at the time accounted for more than the exports that came from all Britain's West Indian colonies combined. Haiti was France's most precious colonial prize, although the more than 800,000 black slaves who produced the wealth in the colony saw very little to none of it. Today, we have a country with abject poverty, illiteracy, overcrowding, unreliable infrastructure, environmental disaster, enormous social and economic disparities, almost no rule of law, and very sporadic political stability.

As we stated previously, and this is a viewpoint developed into further detail throughout this book, Haiti's problems have been rather due to a cumulation of many issues influenced by both internal and external factors. Some of those issues are related to the country's general struggles with social, cultural, and economic realities. Others are rooted in political battles, some of which can be considered as good troubles mismanaged by ill-advised national leaders. Haiti is largely the legacy of slavery, revolution, insurrections, division, occupation, debt, corruption, environmental destruction (notably deforestation), exploitation, violence, and power struggles.

A bulk of Haiti's problem is mental—the psyche that was formed from the demons of the Willie Lynch doctrine designed to keep blacks in bondage. We need to defeat it, take ownership and responsibility. Above all, we need to cultivate accountability. We must end the culture of impunity and spurn any kind of violence against one another. Haiti does not need the continuous destruction of its already-meager resources, both materially and humanely. Rather, the opposite.

As good a trouble in our past political history, we defeated the brutal and physical form of the slavery system at the Vertières Battle on November 18, 1803, and proclaimed our independence on January 1, 1804. But our main issue remains that we have not yet defeated the "making of a slave" or Willie Lynch's methods. We need to do both.

William "Willie" Lynch was that British slave owner in the Caribbean who became famous for his methods of controlling slaves. He was invited in 1712 to the colony of Virginia in order to teach his methods to slave owners. Below is an extract of a speech that Lynch is said to have delivered on the bank of the James River in Virginia:

> *Your invitation reached me on my modest plantation of the West Indies, where I have experimented with some of the newest, and still the oldest, methods for control of slaves. Ancient Rome would envy us if my program is implemented. As our boat sailed to the south on James River, named for our illustrious king, whose version of the Bible we cherish, I saw enough to know that your problem is not unique. While Rome used cords of wood as crosses for standing human bodies along its highways in great numbers, you are here using the tree and the rope on occasions. I caught the whiff of a dead slave hanging from a tree, a couple miles back. You are not only losing valuable stock by hangings, you are having uprisings, slaves are running away, your crops are sometimes left in the field too long for maximum profit, you suffer occasional fires, your animals are killed. Gentlemen, you know what your problems are; I do not need to elaborate. I am not here to enumerate your problems; I am here to introduce you to a method of solving them. In my bag here, I have a full proof method of controlling your black slaves. I guarantee every one of you that, if installed correctly, it will control the slaves for at least 300 hundred years. My method is simple. Any member of your family or overseer can use it. I have outlined a number of differences*

among the slaves; and I take these differences and make them bigger. I use fear, distrust and envy for control purposes. These methods have worked on my modest plantation in the West Indies and it will work throughout the South.[4]

To consolidate his methods, Lynch used Christianity, people's physical appearance, skin tone, gender, sex, age, emotions, sizes, types of plantations, and status on plantations, among others as manipulative tools. He assured North American slave owners that "distrust is stronger than trust;" "envy is stronger than adulation, respect or admiration." He guaranteed slave owners that black slaves, after receiving his indoctrination, would carry on and become self-refueling for thousands of years.

Today's Haiti illustrates beyond measure the success of the Lynch doctrine in its application. We have a country where its citizens are perpetually distrustful of one another, and where all energies have been focusing on the pursuit of dupery and paralytic leadership. All seem to be driven, in no small part, by the abdication of leadership and damnation of the people. But for the optimists, there is still hope. Hope for a new day, a brighter future because Haiti still has the potential to rise up again. Potential that can be extracted from the better angel still living in the heart of each Haitian, from Haiti's natural resources, its beautiful landscapes, to its welcoming, resilient, magnificent, intelligent, mysterious, legendary, mythical, and hardworking people. We simply need to renounce the old practices of our past.

We need to instill in people a new way of doing things based on a new sociopolitical and economic contract stemming from the ideals

---

4 Willie Lynch, *The Willie Lynch Letter and the Making of a Slave* (Ravenio Books, 2011), p. 1-12.

of fairness, equity, good governance, and sustainable development. Additionally, we need to develop and adopt the understanding that inclusion is necessary. More divisions simply impede progress in Haiti.

All Haitians matter—rich or poor, intellectual or illiterate, old or young, urban, suburban, or rural inhabitants, industrials or peasants, religious or nonreligious, living inside the country or abroad. That was the Haiti envisioned by our forefathers at the dawn of 1804. Haitians need to reject what was wrong from their past, reconcile with what was glorious and right in that past, and definitely build on it for a better future. Most importantly, we also need to reconcile with ourselves as one people in order to stop the fast descent into hell.

Then, not just with one another as people, we need to develop a different type of relationship with our immediate environment when it comes to managing, protecting and reinforcing, planning, and developing resources. We must stop the continuity of history that makes the country a constant and heart-rending story where too many lives are gratuitously lost. Haitians need to truly embrace the idea that not changing the actual trajectory of events in Haiti is dishonoring the Revolution and Proclamation of Independence. A legacy that we need to work hard to reclaim and build on. Like the former U.S. President, the late Ronald Reagan, once said: "Freedom is one generation to extinction. In order to keep it, it needs to be fought from one generation to the other."

The new generations of Haitians and Haitian descents need to be enlightened by the truth about Haiti's history. And they need to carry on in changing the face of Haiti in order to force a different narrative about the country, not just by their words, but also by their actions. Haitians are among the greatest people on earth. After we destroyed the foundations of slavery and won our freedom, we had gone further in helping other nations worldwide. Below is a highlight of some of the most important interventions made by Haiti in support of freedom around the world:

Haitian soldiers fought alongside Americans in Savannah, Georgia, for U.S. independence. They fought again later in the Fort Charlotte Battle in New Orleans to help protect liberty and defend America's sovereignty.
Haiti provided arms, soldiers, and financial support to Simón Bolívar in his fight to free South America (Bolivarian countries).
Haiti provided arms, soldiers, and financial support to Greece for their independence.
Haiti provided Haitian passports to many Jews fleeing Europe during World War II in order to help save their lives.
Haiti welcomed many African Americans who escaped from the harsh reality of segregation in the United States, particularly in the South.
Haiti declared war against Nazi Germany and assisted New York with funds for the war efforts.
Haiti liberated the Dominican Republic from slavery.
Haiti helped create the United Nations Human Rights Council.
Haiti helped Libya win its independence.
Haiti did the same for Israel's independence. And the list continues . . .

Forget about the lies fabricated by certain imperial powers and their acolytes about the Haitian people, and particularly Haiti's war for independence, and actions taken afterward to preserve the revolution. Those lies, propagated by the Western world, are more than just excuses to explain France's defeat at the hands of the "indigenous army." They were orchestrated simply to benefit foreign empires' own desires and purposes. Those lies have served to minimize, belittle, and even be dismissive of the huge impact the Haitian Revolution had on the world, especially on the European canon in armed forces and political literatures. In the eyes of many at the time, it was unimaginable that former enslaved blacks allied with free people of color (mulattoes) could achieve such a mighty feat. Yet, the revolution was a huge twelve years of intense battles against slavery and colonialism that resulted in acts of extreme violence by both sides of the conflict, in which the Haitians had prevailed not just against France, but also Spain and England.

Far from being the end-all, this book proposes a different perspective on today's Haiti in its historical, social, economic, psychological, and political contexts. It invites you to look beyond the flashy and sensational reports in traditional news media about the country's struggles to have a broader understanding of what went wrong and continues to go wrong. Above all, it proposes some of the most important transformations, changes, and reforms needed in government and in society as a whole to construct a better nation-state for all Haitians, rather than the current hopelessly ineffectual state.

As a warning, this book is written not to please any domestic or foreign actor. It is written, rather, with the purpose of agitating the discourse for change in the narrative about Haiti. We would be thrilled if after reading it, this book irritated more than a few people. It must incense some people in a good way. If so, we would then have the satisfaction that things might change course in Haiti.

Far from being just about poverty, disasters, and political troubles, Haiti also has extraordinary strengths and beauty in its people and nature. The place has been suffering from the misdeeds of national stakeholders in complicity with foreigners whose plans have contributed mostly not to empower the people, but to accentuate their impoverishment and struggles with life in general.

Haitians, we have no more time to waste. We need to move quickly to take over and reshape our destiny according to the ideals of progress inspired by the Revolution of 1804. Those ideals set the pace for us to be able to run away from the pestilence that has made us look like a laughingstock in the eyes of many, and embrace the hope that we can believe in. Haitians—supported by true international friends—can write a different narrative than the one we all have become accustomed to. Haiti's history is there to prove that the country is capable of wonders through unity and with the right leadership at the helm. One unfavorable element after all has always been a lack of continuity in the direction of progress, which is a very big deal. For every step forward, Haiti seems to make millions of steps backward very quickly. While positive actions toward progress have usually been short-lived, the backward steps have been a lot more consistent throughout Haiti's history.

Chapter One

The Becoming of a Nation's Soul

When Saint-Domingue, as a French colony, called for its independence and became the nation of Haiti in 1804, things were not a "fait accompli." The new self-declared leaders were going to face many challenges. Perhaps they did not imagine how hard it was going to be to maintain that independence, both politically and economically. Overthrowing the slavery system to embrace freedom in its universal sense, the founders of the new nation-state were aiming to create the first black country in the Western Hemisphere, a strong and prosperous nation.

They had to forge unity guided by the ideals of freedom, liberty, self-determination, human dignity, prosperity, equity, and equality. With these ideals in mind, the forefathers of Haiti, who had little to no experience of governing, faced the difficult task of defining the rules, laws, structures, and a system of government capable of carrying their dreams forward.

In this chapter, we emphasize the importance of unity among Haitians and the struggles within the society to consistently hold onto it. We also outline the role that the country's founding fathers had played in establishing the conditions for revolutionary ideals and shaping the minds of Haitians for the reception of those ideals. Additionally, we point out the fact that Haiti's political system is deeply rooted into the history of autocratic governments and has merely evolved to accommodate the needs of imperial powers such as the United States, France, and England.

Haitian politicians often implement policies that favor the demands of these foreign powers in exchange for recognition and support to stay in power. In case of the U.S. for example, the demands are generally related to issues of national interest, such as immigration, drug trafficking, trade, strategic votes at the United Nations, etc. That political system based on infighting for individual dominance at the expense of collective well-being and common good, even though it had not contributed to the advancement of the Haitian Revolution, both in its design and purpose, continues today with just superficial changes and cosmetically sporadic stabilities. Deeper problems, laid at the very base of the society, have not been properly nor sufficiently addressed in order to be solved. From military autocracy to civilian dictatorship, and finally to a kind of transitional democracy, the struggles to define and establish a sound system capable of delivering the business for the people have undoubtedly remained. Therefore, the project of building a strong and prosperous nation-state continues presently to be undone. Haiti, as we know it today, is unequivocally the story of unfinished business.

1.1: The Dessalinian Ideals

One of the most highly regarded figures of the Haitian Revolution, Jean-Jacques Dessalines made Haiti the first country in the Americas to permanently abolish slavery; and he made it the second independent nation in the hemisphere after the United States. As the leader of the revolution, and after the kidnapping of Toussaint Louverture by the Napoleon military expedition in 1802, Dessalines vowed to keep the new nation free and independent. He declared his will to die as a free man instead of surrendering to slavery. He managed to influence and convince revolutionary troops from top to bottom to adhere to this universal principle of human dignity.

The ideal of freedom and individual liberty was translated in his desire to keep the sugar industry and plantations running and producing without slavery. He demanded that all black people work either as soldiers or as laborers on the plantations. Not as slaves, it was instead to defend the nation's freedom and to raise crops in order to sustain economic growth and prosperity. These aspects were so vital to maintain the country's independence, both politically and economically.

Early on, Dessalines understood the need to unite everyone behind his ideals. From the fierce war for independence to his coronation as Emperor Jacques I of Haiti, Dessalines had called for national unity. He understood that the ideals of freedom, liberty, and equality could not be viable in the long term without fraternity. For Dessalines, blacks and mulattoes (brown-skin people) should be in constant symbiosis. In his fundamental ideals, Dessalines believed that the defense of national sovereignty required solidarity among members of society. He called for a ban on color prejudice and colonial society divisiveness. He perceived every Haitian as generically black. To him, what would prevent the revolution from being successful was division, lack of participation, and inequality or inequity. He understood that everyone had carried their load of the sacrifice and played their role in the fights for independence. Therefore, everyone should have fairly shared the wealth of the nation.

What Dessalines feared the most was exactly what happened soon after his assassination: A divided nation where its independence (politically and economically) had been baffled. That still remains the same today. Almost 220 years later, Haitians continue to have difficulty organizing their own elections fairly and freely without interference of external powers. They cannot afford their national budget without bilateral and/or multilateral financial support in the form of donations or loans.

While the country's political independence has remained partially unachieved, social and economic inequalities have been more than cruel.

Today, the gap is so dismal and unacceptable that a very small minority of the Haitians monopolize the wealth of the nation for themselves. From one government to another, whether military or civilian leaders, every leader seems to be incapable of changing the system.

Of course, inequalities exist everywhere in this world. As an integral part of the social, economic, and political systems that shape the world, this is not new. That is the very fabric of the world we live in. The idea that the world is filled with inequalities is how we have lower, middle, and upper classes. But in Haiti, the system has produced almost no middle, but instead the two extremes: *the haves and the have-nots*. According to Michel-Ange Cadet in *Dessalines' Ideals of Equality for Haiti*, "It is not the inequalities that pose the greatest problem in a society, it is the gaps; when they become too large, they require patches".[5] This is exactly the situation for the large majority of people in Haiti.

Looking at what has become the soul, mind, and body of Haiti over the years, it is sad to say that the Dessalinian ideals collapsed long ago. And the consequences on the Haitian society are almost beyond repair. After the plot that caused Dessalines's death, the plot against the great majority—the blacks and newly freed—began. For years, his successors could not elevate themselves to make the Dessalinian ideals rise again.

Dessalines' ideals were not only for Haiti. He was determined to help free black people from slavery wherever they might be. He genuinely spoke of the social ideals of justice and fairness for all

---

5 Michel-Ange Cadet, "Dessalines' Ideals of Equality for Haiti", Dadychery.org, Haiti Chery, August 9, 2015. https://www.dadychery.org/2015/08/09/dessalines-ideal-of-equality-for-haiti/

oppressed people in the Atlantic world. He felt a sense of duty to assist and share his experience so that freedom would reign wherever blacks were oppressed and wherever freedom was threatened. He saw Haiti as the gold standard for black power and freedom. If anything, this was one of the ideas pursued by both Alexandre Pétion and Henri Christophe, who divided the country into two states after the assassination of Dessalines. Even though they were political enemies and were fundamentally different, they provided support to antislavery struggles in the hemisphere.

By 1816, under the presidency of General Pétion, Haiti revised its constitution to make the country's abolitionist promise more concrete. In article 44 of the amended version of the 1806 Constitution, Haiti offered freedom and citizenship to those born outside of its borders. Anyone who was looking for freedom from slavery and oppression. It clearly stated that all Africans and Indians, and the descendants of their blood, born in the colonies or in foreign countries, who came to reside in the Republic of Haiti would be recognized as Haitians and would enjoy the right of citizenship after one year of residence. Pétion's policies at the time in light of Haiti's promise of freedom made it a safe haven for those fleeing racial slavery and social inequality.

Former U.S. immigration asylum officer Jesus G. Ruiz recently wrote in the *Washington Post* column "Perspective," "In the 1820s, as many as 13,000 African Americans from the United States sought refuge in Haiti." He continued to explain that in 1826, for instance, a "colored emigrant" named Archibald Johnson wrote to a friend in Washington from Haiti, expressing: "I bid an eternal farewell to America. . . . I feel determined to live and die under the safeguard of [Haiti's] constitution, with the hope of aiding to open the door for the relief of my distressed brethren." Haiti's free soil continued to be a haven for black people well into the 1860s. Black migration to Haiti from the United States meant that African Americans could witness firsthand the true promises of liberty.[6]

Above all, Dessalines wanted Haiti to stand with dignity among the community of nations, economically and politically. With that being said, two of his chief concerns as the leading founder of the new black nation were the integrity of the national territory (the freedom of self-determination in Haiti's present and future) and its economic prosperity. Soon after the declaration of independence, he ordered the rehabilitation of the farms that had been devastated by the war, in order to enhance the national economy. He gave formal orders to different generals to revive the plantations regarded during that period as the main source of wealth for the nation. The ideals of national integrity, control of the Haitian territory by its citizens, and freedom and self-determination pushed Dessalines, even amid all the threats, to refuse an offer of protectorate from England.

Today, many advised observers and supporters of Haiti's cause call for the rebirth of Dessalines's revolutionary ideals that died with the assassination of the emperor on October 17, 1806. The revolution was interrupted in its progress because those who plotted against Jean-Jacques Dessalines had a different agenda. They wanted to replace the European settlers in a sort of extension of the colonial system. They saw themselves as directly entitled to the benefits of the revolution. Once they tasted the "Kool-Aid" of power, they had become insatiable and numb to the core of their souls. At the first sip, they wanted more and more

6 Jesus G. Ruiz, "Haiti is a source of refugees today: but it was once a haven for them", WashingtonPost.com, The Washington Post, October 6, 2021. https://www.washingtonpost.com/outlook/2021/10/06/haiti-refugee-haven/

power, not to advance the cause of the majority of Haiti's population—a majority composed of blacks and former slaves; a majority that revolted against the system of slavery and extreme exploitation. But, instead, those leaders wanted to elevate themselves as neocolonialists. A pattern that has continued with the contemporary generations. Many observers often ask themselves how Haiti's elites are so narrow-minded! They do not think in terms of the country or the public good. They have increasingly lost all senses of collectivity.

The reason is simple. The elites have a solution that benefits themselves alone for every problem in the country. So, why would they worry about the underprivileged majority? While the latter are trying to flee misery and insecurity in the country by any means, the former cling to Haiti as their diamond. For instance, the country has no sustainable electrical power system. This is not a problem for the Haitian elites. They can afford their own energy network consisting of solar power, batteries, inverters, and super-silent electric generators and fuel delivered directly to their homes. The public education system is not up to standards and often becomes dysfunctional. That does not bother them either because they have their private schools instituted to run in parallel to the country's official education system. These schools are designed for the privileged few well-to-do who can afford to pay thousands of U.S. dollars in tuition annually. They also have the luxury of sending their children to school in foreign countries such as the D.R. or Cuba, but primarily in the U.S., Canada, France, Belgium, England, and Italy.

What about hospitals? They do not care either because they can be chartered rapidly and urgently to Jackson Memorial Hospital in Miami or other medical centers in Florida, Cuba, or the Dominican Republic. The lack of adequate infrastructure is even used as a way to expose their extravagant lifestyle and make the underprivileged majority feel less human, more envious, and humiliated.

The reactionary and opportunistic ambition imposed from the very beginning by the minority (largely mulattoes) has given rise to all kinds of bad policies and mediocre politicians for the country. It has created a middle class that is not progressive and is detached from its roots—a leadership that works more like a broker of international imperialism and accepts all kinds of multinational economic policies that are against the national production and the welfare of the Haitian people. It has led to a business sector that is against competition and economic development. Social, economic, and political events as they have been happening in Haiti have led to the belief that the country, as we know it today, is merely a result of unachieved dreams and projects. Most of the principal actors of those events have not shown enough interest in making the country a better place for its majority citizens. Instead, all great dreams, ideals, and projects envisioned since the dawn of independence have been interrupted, and therefore they have remained unachieved.

Today's Haiti is a country that is neither politically free from foreign influence, nor independent economically. This is a tragedy for a nation whose glorious history illuminated not just the Americas but also the rest of the world. Haiti's historical experience inspired and encouraged many in their own quests for liberation and progress. But surprisingly, the country's leadership in this stage of history has yet to be translated into further progression. Every other country in the Western Hemisphere has surpassed the Republic of Haiti in terms of socioeconomic development. This is a merely failed state. It is not a surprise that we know how we got into that mess. But the important question is how can we get out of there?

1.2: United We Conquered, but Divided We Stand

In Haiti, there is a proverb for every aspect of life. Politics is no exception. It's the first thing most foreign diplomats learn before entering the country. *Men anpil chay pa lou* is one proverb generally used in calls for unity. Embedded into the Haitian native language, this expression literally means many hands make the load lighter. This old adage comes from a belief deeply rooted into our history, in all of our struggles, in our quest for unity to survive politically, socially, and economically. It is even encapsulated under the coat of arms of the Republic of Haiti in the middle of the blue and red flag as *l'Union Fait la Force* in French, which means strength through unity. This idea has become a popular wisdom of capital importance to the Haitian people over the years. Today, it is so popular that most Haitians confound it with the national motto, which is *Liberty, Equality, and Fraternity*. It is genuinely in the Haitian's belief that no obstacle is too big to overcome through unity, even though it is not practiced often.

Politically speaking, *men anpil chay pa lou* started early on as a motivating tool in support of the slogan *Freedom or Death* (*Libète ou Lanmò* in Haitian) propelled by the revolutionary army leaders during the massive mobilization for the independence of Haiti. After the kidnapping of Toussaint Louverture by France in order to extinguish the fire of freedom, the braves quickly realized that they needed to be united to defeat the common enemy (the colonial powers) to black slaves and mulattoes. That union effectively propelled them to victory over Napoleon's army, one of the most powerful armies at the time, and over England and Spain to a certain degree. Supported by that result, the unifier proverb, profoundly instilled in Haitians' minds, has continued up to the present to produce synergy for different political and social movements in the country.

Even when Haitians appear to be extremely divided, one political leader or a political or social group can quickly rally them behind a cause by playing with Haitians' emotions, using the saying *men anpil chay pa lou* as cataclysm. This ideal has been mastered so well by politicians of all generations for better or for worse. Haiti's political history is almost a mere fabrication of movements resulting from that effort. But for the purpose of this book, we have focused our attention on the most recent and particularly consequential events created in the country that have used the proverb as vehicle.

Three of these consequential political events supported by the belief in unity have been the downfall of the former dictator Jean-Claude Duvalier (known as Baby Doc) in 1986, the election of former Catholic Priest Jean-Bertrand Aristide in 1990, and the ouster of the latter in 2004 toward the end of his second presidential term.

The defeat of the Duvalier regime of dictatorship, after almost three decades (father and son) of reign over the Haitian people, was worthy of praise for unity among the different sectors of the population. The Duvalier regime started with the election of François Duvalier (Papa Doc) in 1957 after a long succession of provisional military governments resulting from the country's consistent power struggles. Prior to the infamous 1957 election, the country had experienced a great deal of political instability with coup after coup. With profound paranoia of political threats over his presidency in mind, Duvalier created the most brutal paramilitary force in the Caribbean.

A warlord goon squad that was nicknamed the *Tonton Macoutes* (Uncle Gunnysack) by the Haitians. The *Tonton Macoutes* formally named the Volunteers for National Security (VSN) gave the Duvalier regime the needed repressive tool to control all aspects of the society and consolidate the regime's harsh rule through terror. Everyone feared tortures, kidnappings, extortions, random executions, etc. To describe the atmosphere in that period, the authors of a report produced by the Council on Hemispheric Affairs (COHA) stated, "The militia consisted of mostly illiterate fanatics that were converted into ruthless zombie-like gunmen. Their straw hats, blue denim shirts, dark glasses and machetes remain indelibly etched in the minds of millions of Haitians."[7] That sums up the challenges faced by the Haitian people when they battled to overcome nearly thirty years of Duvalier. However, Haitians of all creeds with different interests, of course, found the strongest coalition possible among themselves to put an end to one of the most feared regimes in the hemisphere.

Fast forward to 1990, the transition from a series of authoritarian governments to democracy was not an easy task. After the departure of Jean-Claude Duvalier on February 7, 1986, the VSN lost power and was dismantled, while the army regained control quickly with notable support from the population. Although the society as a whole claimed democracy as a new political system in Haiti, the military leaders hungry for power had a different idea of what that democracy would look like in the midst of a new horizon.

First, they began with a provisional government spearheaded by Lieutenant General Henri Namphy as president. General Namphy was assisted by a council of five members - three military leaders and two civilians. The military leaders were colonels Williams Régala, Prosper Avril, and Max Vallès; the civilians were Gérard Gourgue, a

7 Council on Hemispheric Affairs (COHA), "The Tonton Macoutes: The Central Nervous System of Haiti's Reign of Terror", coha.org, COHA, March 11, 2020. https://www.coha.org/tonton-macoutes/

prominent lawyer, human rights activist and critique of the Duvalier regime, and Alix Cinéas a former Duvalier's collaborator . That interim entity, named National Council of Government (Conseil National de Gouvernement in French -CNG), was dissolved less than two months later, on March 20, 1986. A second council of three members would be created with Namphy and Régala keeping their position from the original provisional government. Jacques A. François, a civilian joined them until his death in April 1987. The latter would be then replaced by former Supreme Court President, Luc D. Héctor.

Reducing the influence of civilians to almost nothing, the military leaders did not have a harmonious cohabitation either. They would create chaos to facilitate their personal aspirations: Power control at any cost. From one army general to another, there was a spate of coups followed by several back-and-forth successions of military leaders. They baffled all prospects of democratically elected civilian presidents. We were unfortunately dealing with the continuity of Duvalierism without a person named Duvalier in charge.

Despite the successful adoption of a new constitution at the end of March 1987, excluding those with ties to the dictatorial regime for a period of ten years, Duvalierism was too big to disappear altogether that quickly. Most of the military leaders who nabbed control of the political system were trained under the influence of the Duvalier regime. Their political influence was limited and contained a great deal by the regime. Nevertheless, they were waiting for their opportunity to regain control of power.

If the VSN was formally dismantled, the different military governments used informal paramilitary groups to exacerbate violence, exercise psychological pressure, and carry out murders, kidnappings, extortions, and political tortures on the population. Some of the groups were publicly identified as neo-duvalierist or "attachés," while others operated in the dark under the label "zenglendos." The word zenglendo was regularly used by the Haitian people from the mid-1980s to late 1990s. Depending on who you talk to, the perception of the term zenglendo varies among the Haitian public. But the most common interpretation is the one that defines a zenglendo as a heavily armed and masked young man that executes holdups, individually or as part of a gang, particularly in densely populated areas, in defiance to all established judicial and police orders. They robbed, killed, kidnapped, abused sexually, and tortured under the protection of the army.

Among notorious paramilitary groups that were terrorizing Haitians under the complicit eyes of the former Haitian army leaders, we recall the death squad named FRAPH (Front Révolutionnaire pour l'Avancement et le Progrès d'Haïti). FRAPH, translated into English as Revolutionary Front for the Advancement and Progress of Haiti, was founded by Emmanuel "Toto" Constant. He is the son of the former army general Gerard Constant, who commanded the Haitian military under the François Duvalier regime from 1961 to 1971. Most people believed at the time that death squad leaders like Emmanuel "Toto" Constant were regularly employed to do the dirty work. One of the reasons for this belief was because no formal member of the national forces (police officers and soldiers alike) would ever want to do this kind of work—work that had become more difficult for someone in uniform, especially after the high-intensity movement that provoked the downfall of Jean-Claude Duvalier.

It was in the midst of such circumstances, with the support of human rights organizations—and in part with pressures from the international community—that the civil society called for unity. Unity that could bring about change and democracy. After a number of unsuccessful attempts, Haiti was finally able to elect a president on December 16, 1990, without major influence from the army leaders this time. Jean-Bertrand Aristide, a former Catholic priest who converted to politics, became the first democratically elected president of Haiti in post-Duvalier elections. Alongside Aristide were also the elected legislators of the first parliament—composed of the Senate and the Chamber of Deputies—under the new Constitution adopted on March 29, 1987.

Together, under the Constitution, the president and the parliament were charged to reform the Haitian government and its structures in order to strengthen the institutions of the republic. These democratic institutions, as recognized by Haitian laws, could provide the citizens with adequate protection and services such as electricity, clean water, health care, and reliable infrastructure to facilitate economic and social development in the country. And this continues today to be the hope of Haiti's future goals.

For an overwhelmingly spontaneous and ill-prepared government, the word unity was extremely important. In the absence of a coherent and well-thought-out plan, *men anpil, chay pa lou* became the engine that moved an anarcho-populist train—movement spearheaded by the former priest, confounding the role of the government and that of the citizens. In Aristide's mind, at least in his approach, the government and the people were the inside and outside of the same cloth. During his multiple public appearances, he would often say in Haitian: "Nou se leta, leta se nou" (translation: We the people are the government, and the government is the people). Being the most charismatic manipulator of words in Haitian modern politics, he even translated the proverb *men anpil, chay pa lou* into the following metaphors: "Yon sèl nou fèb, ansanm nou fò, ansanm ansam, nou se lavalas;" "yon sèl dwèt pa manje kalalou," etc. In English he would say, *divided we are weak, together we are strong, together we form an avalanche; one finger alone cannot be used to eat okra sauce.* All might sound very confusing to a foreigner, but very explicit to native Haitians. His approach was full of demagoguery to those who expected concrete plans and good governance.

Fanmi Lavalas (avalanche family) is the name of Aristide's political party today. In most minds, an avalanche contains so much in terms of water and debris of all kinds. It is synonymous with an extreme and unstoppable force that kills and destroys on its passage. So, Aristide's entire political strategy was inspired by words capable of mobilizing the impoverished and oppressed people. More often, the mobilization of these vulnerable people is conducted in a way to turn them into actors of violence and agents of more divisions. This approach has not helped advance their causes. It has only continued to benefit the political interest of a few, as it has in the past. In sum, it is a kind of unity for the purpose of more divisions in the country at the expense of the suffering and damned majority.

In that context, the slogan *men anpil chay pa lou* was on the lips of everyone during that period as a unity motto. From politicians, activists, and grassroots and religious leaders, to diplomats, the proverb went viral. But it was still difficult to know who really wanted unity in Haiti. *Actions speak louder than words*, some would say. Some foreign diplomats would even repeat the proverb, ironically at times, to express their skepticism in a strong and durable unity among Haitians. We vividly remember the statement of the late former U.S. Ambassador to Haiti, Alvin P. Adams, in response to the election of the former leftist priest Aristide as president. To contrast with Aristide's slogan *men anpil, chay pa lou*, Ambassador Adams broke out another Haitian proverb: *Apre bal, tanbou lou*, which literally translated as *after the ball, the drums are heavy*. He wanted to counter the narrative at the time that the country's political, social, and economic landscapes had changed in the right direction with Aristide as president.

Unfortunately, history gave him reason. Not only was Aristide ill-prepared to govern, but he also thought he could solve Haiti's problems simply by using his popularity to wage violence against the elites (he divided them into two camps: patriots and *patri-pockets*[8]), and his political opponents were labeled fake patriots. He was toppled in a violent coup on September 30, 1991, just a little over seven months after his inauguration. Things rolled back. And that was the deep sense of the reality in a country where people are very reluctant to change and the peaceful transfer of power has always been problematic.

The senior military leaders returned to power. But the resistance among the Haitian population continued amid brutality, persecution, and repression. Again, they called for unity under the *men anpil, chay pa lou* slogan in order to impose the respect for the will of the people on the military leaders. They wanted the return of the deposed president from exile. Aided by former president Bill Clinton, unity once again triumphed with Jean-Bertrand Aristide's return to power in 1994, after three years of exile in Venezuela and the United States.

The continuity of Aristide's presidency gave rise to another democratic and civilian government in René Garcia Préval as president.

---

8 Patri-pocket is a made-up word to translate Aristide's word *boujwa-patripòch* from the Haitian vernacular. It defines people who place money over country. Because some of the oligarchs allied with him, and occupied cabinet positions or played important roles in his government, he divided the economic elite class into two categories. *Boujwa-patripòch* were those whom he thought did not want to pay taxes. He called his allied oligarchs who were thought to be paying taxes *boujwa-patriyòt*.

From 1996 to 2001, late president Préval, a former prime minister under Aristide, ran the most stable government in Haiti since 1986. He even served another full term from 2006 to 2011. Aristide, in contrast, Préval's predecessor (1991-1996) and successor (2001-2004), could not complete any of his two terms without interruptions.

Depiction of Unity: 2001-2004

In 2001, Aristide returned for a second term. This time, his election was contested as fraudulent and undemocratic. Nonetheless, with sort of limited influence and less popularity this time, the controversial and combative leader attempted one more time to run the country with the same failed strategy. There was no known concrete plan, but some kind of political poetry inspired by Haitian wisdom. *Men anpil, chay pa lou*; *yon sel nou fèb, ansanm nou fò, ansanm ansanm nou se lavalas*, and *yon sèl dwèt pa manje kalalou* were among dozens of other excessively repeated shenanigans with mostly the same meaning. When he failed to gain enough popular support like before, he returned to the old practices and methods historically used by his anti-democratic and authoritarian predecessors. He became complicit in a government supported by armed gangs.

These gangs were, for the most part, organized into small groups of young men and women called 'popular organizations' as part of a strategy so that people would confuse them with genuine social grassroots and community organizations. They were scattered around main cities and towns. Most Haitians, under the oppression of these armed groups, called them "the chimères." They were simply hooligans often behaving like paramilitary forces of tyranny and repression in favor of Aristide. This was a political strategy engineered by his party to terrorize his opponents and maintain power. During their violent street protests, they would often yell "Aristide ou lanmò" ("Aristide or death") the same way the Tonton Macoutes would scream "Duvalier for life" in the middle of their acts of terror.

Around 2003 to 2004, a coalition of key organized sectors of the civilian society stood together. They used peaceful protests driven by the slogan *nou pa pè, nou pap janm pè* (we are not afraid; we will never be afraid) in response to the intimidation and pressure from the chimères. This was a *men anpil, chay pa lou* sort of slogan. Organized for the most part by university students, musicians, artists, and a sizable coalition of sociopolitical activists and business leaders named Group 184, the movement called GNB (acronym for Haitian expletive *grenn nan bouda*, which expresses bravery, courage, and determination) was inclusive and strong enough to see the premature downfall of Aristide.

The unifier proverb is not only useful to politics. It is also a way of life both socially and economically in Haiti, where basic necessity is a luxury for most people. Haitians use *men anpil, chay pa lou* to encourage a sense of mutual aid in daily struggles to make ends meet, the practice of community farming, community development actions, and the spirit of self-governance to fill the void left by the inadequacy of the central government structures and presence. Beyond a simple proverb or slogan, it is practical in the daily life of the Haitian people.

The earthquake that walloped Haiti in 2010, particularly the capital Port-au-Prince, created a perfect scene of that proverb in practice. With a helpless government, we witnessed how Haitians acted together to pull out people buried under collapsed buildings and save thousands of lives. Everywhere in villages, towns, and cities, people have been trying to stay true to the value of unity. Every time there is a major problem, politically, socially, or economically, Haitians have always known how to mobilize each other in unison in search of a solution. However, most of the time, the unity is based on emotional acts and it is conjunctural. Even if it is unjustifiable, it is understandable that there is a big divide between mulattoes and the descendants of black slaves, between rich and poor, peasants and oligarchs. But it is basically inconceivable that we continue to have so much division in a country populated by a very large majority of people who share the same cultural heritage and social status.

In the Haitian context, the real unity usually takes shape sporadically in dire situations and goes away once the situation seems dissipate, even if the dissipation is temporary. Then the contradictions that have been part of the country's fabrics reappear. Those contradictions tend to dominate our minds more than the values that can keep us united. Among divisive behaviors in Haiti, we can observe jealousy, hatred, discrimination, prejudice, individualism, arrogance, paternalism, irresponsibility, demagoguery, egocentrism, power-mongering, machoism, misogynism, sexism, racism, self-promotion, resignation, and mean-spiritedness. These behaviors have given rise to multiple habits or practices that affect sustainable unity.

In spite of all, the hard and sensible truth is that every single Haitian would genuinely like the country to be united for a better future. But we have been extremely divided on how to do it. Most Haitians criticize divisions every day. But few are able to hold themselves on their own. They cannot escape that old demon and enemy of public good. Keeping unity for long is hard and too difficult for Haitians. Power struggles, corruptions, prejudices, stigmatizations, betrayal, hate, sociopolitical and economic inequalities, injustice, impatience, complacency, scapegoating, and distrust, among other practices and behaviors have lasted far too long within the society. However, looking at the good moments in Haitian history, we cannot resist the hope that change is always a possibility.

1.3: Constant Power Struggles

Haiti has a very long history of power struggles. This piece of land of just over 10,700 square miles as we know it in modern times, one third of the island of Hispaniola, with the other two thirds being the Dominican Republic, is not new to power struggles.[9] This is a troubled land, one would say. Haiti's history with settlement and power struggles may trace back to as early as 4000 BC, when originally inhabited by Arawak migrants from Central America and the other islands in the Greater Antilles. By 1200 AD, civilizations had mixed and evolved into the large majority of Tainos, whom Christopher Columbus encountered at the end of 1492. Through that encounter, native leaders like Queen Anacaona were executed and subjugated. Unable to fight diseases brought by the European settlers and forced to overwork, the Tainos were practically decimated.

From Tainos to European Colonists

By the 16th century, the colonists had started to import enslaved Africans to serve as workers. That led to the triangular trade best known as the trans-Atlantic slave trade. Battles for power control waged on the island of Hispaniola when French and English pirates (Filibusters and Buccaneers) started to settle there as well. Amidst the power battles, Spain ended up ceding total control of the Western part of the island to France in 1697 as a result of the Treaty of Ryswick. After

---

9 Hispaniola was the name given to the Caribbean Island by European colonists when they arrived there in 1492. That was a claim in the name of Spain.

three months and ten days of negotiations between Spain, England, the Roman Empire, and France, the parties agreed for Spain to control the Eastern part known today as the Dominican Republic (San Domingo back then), and France to assume complete colonization of the Western part to be named Saint-Domingue, which is Haiti today.

With the increasing prosperity of the colony, Spain, France, the Netherlands, Portugal, England, and even Germany to some extent, had always shared power over the land until irreconcilable conflicts and over eleven years of nonstop insurrections gave rise to the Haitian Revolution. The revolutionary leaders then removed the name Saint-Domingue and renamed the country Hayti (Haïti in French or Ayiti in Haitian) on January 1, 1804, in reference to the name phonetically given by the Tainos. The name Hayti (also known to the indigenous as Quisqueya or Bohio), which means high land or land of mountains, was adopted by the revolutionary leaders to honor the indigenous inhabitants. Jean-Jacques Dessalines, the first head of state after the revolution, later called it the Empire of Hayti.

The Haitian Revolution has remained to date the first and only one in modern history where a majority of black slaves allied with a few free colored men (mulattoes) destroyed the foundation of slavery and overthrew the entire system. They were able to liberate themselves, seize control of the land, and become the first and independent black nation outside of the African continent. Slaves were liberated by the warriors of independence on the entire island—not just in Saint-Domingue colonized by France, but also in San Domingo (east) that was settled by Spain up to 1794. To save face from political humiliation and tremendous economic loss, France would not concede. The United States, Britain, Spain, and other Western world powers would not trade with Haiti, at least openly, or assist the newborn nation early on. They were extremely afraid and worried that the case of Haiti would serve as an example to inspire all oppressed people to seek freedom from them. This would eventually happen on January 1, 1804, when Haitians declared independence and definitively overthrew the slavery system.

Jean-Jacques Dessalines and Beyond

Jean-Jacques Dessalines and Jovenel Moise were the first and last heads of state assassinated almost 220 years apart. For that long, Haiti has remained a troubled land where crimes, insecurity, violence, and betrayal are fundamentals of a permanent game among a tiny elite for political and economic control. The majority of the population would continue to be impoverished and doomed. Sometime, the actors behind the politico-economic insecurity and criminality are visible, but more often they are not. Regardless, the outcome remains the same: those actors, visible or invisible, always benefit from impunity and the Haitian people continue to pay the costs. The criminalization of Haiti's politics and economy has done so much damage in terms of the loss of human life, from ordinary citizens, honest public servants, tourists, investors, artists, educators, journalists, writers, actors, professionals of all trades, and politicians. Among those who had the chance to escape torture, death, political violence, economic inequity, and social injustice, many have left the country for anywhere they could find refuge and have never returned.

After the declaration of independence, the new leaders were struggling to set up the foundations of the new state. Internal conflicts and fundamental contradictions that predated the revolution led to the assassination of Jean-Jacques Dessalines on October 17, 1806, less than three years after the Proclamation of Independence. Dessalines was the leading figure and the emperor of the new nation-state under construction. His assassination abruptly divided the country into two different governments and that operated as two separate countries. They were the West-South, or the Republic of Haiti, led by the Army General Alexandre Pétion, and the North, or the Kingdom of Haiti, led by the Army General Henry Christophe. During their reigns, both supported civil disobedience and insurrections in each other's territory. They both had to repair their economy due to the damage caused by the effects of civil war.

After the death ofboth Pétion and Christophe, the North and West-South were reunited under Jean-Pierre Boyer (by 1820). Then in 1822, the whole island formerly known as Hispaniola became one nation. That was indeed the Island of Haiti reunified for 22 years. That reunification between Haiti and the Dominican Republic could not survive longer due in part to cultural differences and to the repressive character and ill-managed state of Boyer's reign (1818–1843). "Dominican separatists organized a secret independence movement" and threatened Haiti with massive fires. By 1844, Eastern Hispaniola declared its independence, and the island split again into two separate nations vying for their own statehood, sovereignty, and self-determination.[10]

Going from one military leader to another, Haiti spent its first five decades struggling to settle in as a country. Between the heavy indemnity payment agreed to be made by Boyer to France in 1825 in exchange for the recognition of independence, the agreement with the Roman Catholic Church to officially name Catholicism Haiti's official religion in 1860, and the positive answer in 1862 to a plea from

---

10 Adam M. Silvia, "Haiti: An Island Luminous", islandluminous.fiu.edu, Florida International University Special Collections & Digital Library of the Caribbean. Retrieved March 12, 2022. http://islandluminous.fiu.edu/learn.html

Senator Charles Sumner by Abraham Lincoln for the United States to formally recognize Haiti's independence, the fight for power control at the expense of progress had never stopped. The country's first 11 governments during that period were fighting for survival against internal and external political forces. Their focus was less on state building than it was on power control. Haiti had 29 insurrections in the first 41 years of independence (1804–1845) and counted about 100 more in the next 70 years, from 1845 to 1915.[11] That was more than one insurrection a year during the country's first 111 years of independence.

After two and a half decades of Jean-Pierre Boyer's reign over Haiti, 6 ephemeral presidents succeeded him in just the next four years' time (1843–1847). This kind of political instability was encouraged and supported by the shadow politics orchestrated by the oligarchs (mulattoes), which consisted of selecting ignorant and alcoholic black generals as presidents to help protect their interests. After Dessalines in 1806, four more heads of state were killed from 1870 to 2021.

History recounts the public execution of President Sylvain Salnave on January 15, 1870, by his successor Nissage Saget. About 42 years later, on August 8, 1912, President Michel Cincinnatus Leconte (great-grandson of Dessalines) was burned alive along with several hundreds of his soldiers in a violent explosion at the national palace. That incident happened less than a year to the day from Leconte's inauguration as president. On July 28, 1915, an angry mob lynched President Jean Vilbrun Guillaume Sam during a coup. That horrible event triggered the pretext for the first U.S. military invasion of Haiti. And very recently, on July 7, 2021, President Jovenel Moise was assassinated at his private

---

11 Sauveur Pierre Etienne, *La Drôle de guerre électorale:1987-2017* (Paris: L'Harmattan, 2019), p. 18.

residence in a massive plot involving his opponents and people from his own inner circle as suspects.

Yet in the 1860s, Haiti started to experience some level of economic prosperity. This was due in part to the civil war in the United States, when slave-owning states seceded. The Union blockade on the confederacy made cotton a scarce commodity, which enriched Haiti's cultivators. Under Fabre Géffrard, Haiti built new schools and invited African Americans to move to Haiti in their quest for freedom. Haiti also profited a great deal from the investments made by the Catholic Church in the education system after the 1860 agreement, even though that would renew hostility toward the vodou practitioners (Vodouists).

However, as it had been the case in the country's abundant history, for any step forward, Haiti would go many more steps backward. By 1865, a series of altercations and back and forth opposition fights put Haiti in a dire situation again. The country had become more and more politically unstable. The generals and military commanders who were ruling over Haiti could not hold onto power for as long as they used to. During the first 61 years of independence, Haiti had only 10 changes of regime, compared to 9 in the spate of the next 29 years (1867–1896). In Haiti's modern history, it is even worse. Apart from the time of the U.S. occupation (1915–1934) and the 16 years that followed, the political instability did not end until the Duvalier regime started in 1957. Duvalier, father and son, would rule over Haiti during the next 29 years. Afterward, from 1986 to 2021, we were more or less back to what we were accustomed to in terms of abrupt government interruptions.

In fact, from February 7, 1986, to July 20, 2021, we had 22 different presidents and a football field of prime ministers who quarterbacked team Haiti. Of the 22 presidents, only seven were elected through general elections. Just three out of those seven elections outcomes were not largely contested: Aristide in 1991, Preval in 1996, and Preval again in 2006.

Leslie S. François Manigat was elected in 1988 amid repression and suspicion of political corruption. Jean-Bertrand Aristide returned to the presidency in 2001 as a result of elections boycotted by the vast majority of political parties. Joseph Michel Martelly in 2011 was in fact elected in a run-off in which he did not qualify to participate. And last but not least, Jovenel Moise was elected in special elections in 2016 after results from the previous two rounds were nullified due to alleged massive frauds and irregularities.

Let's backtrack to the end of the 19th century. After a hard-fought war in 1883 between the two major political parties at the time (the National and the Liberal), Florvil Hyppolite, backed by the liberals, seized power with the goal of creating the political stability so vital for the advancement of the country. Aided by his brilliant Minister of Finance and Foreign Affairs, Anténor Firmin, Hyppolite was able to renovate urban spaces, rewrite Haiti's constitution, make peace with the Dominican Republic, and uphold sovereignty over Mole Saint-Nicolas, a port in Haiti's Northwestern Peninsula that the United States wanted to lease. As Haiti's Minister of Foreign Affairs, Firmin worked diligently to demonstrate the country's potential to the world. However, the issue of inequality within Haiti was never resolved—a problem that was considerably accentuated with the arrival of German merchants and Lebanese Christian merchants, particularly encouraged by the United States to fill the void in the economy left by local merchants killed during the 1883 war.

These German and Lebanese Christian merchants settled permanently in Haiti. As the first century of independence was approaching, Haiti was a very unequal place. The merchant houses in the country's port cities continued to amass their fortunes from the very low-cost purchase of coffee, cotton, and cacao cultivated by Haitian farmers and sold to Europe. These farmers whose works sustained the nation had no real defender. The sociopolitical and economic elites were less likely to identify with or understand their struggles to survive.

In 1904, Haiti celebrated 100 years of independence under Nord Alexis in the middle of a weakened economy caused in particular by low coffee prices and political infighting. The economic crisis worsened when the Alexis government could not convince the European overseers at the National Bank to lend money to develop other industries. Desperate for work, Haitians started to migrate to Cuba. The Lebanese Christians who were already disliked for being the importers and sellers of American goods became the easy scapegoats. Alexis was overthrown in 1908 by one of his military commanders in the South, Antoine Simon.

As President, Simon looked overseas to obtain the funds necessary to improve the economy. Haiti's bank reopened with European and American capital amid concessions to the Americans and Germans to build railroads and open businesses. Those concessions provoked nationalist ire from the political opposition. Led by Michel Cincinnatus Leconte, a revolt of provincial leaders overthrew Simon in 1911. With Leconte in power, technicians from the U.S. were appointed to improve schools and install telegraphs. Cars were imported and technology was extolled.

Leconte saw vodou as primitive and reinforced the support for the Roman Catholic Church, which condemned the former's practitioners. When Leconte was killed in 1912 in an explosion at the National Palace, his successors continued the work to improve education in spite of extensive debate over it. In 1914, rival provincial leaders battled over the presidency and brought about a number of ephemeral presidents. About a year later, an angry mob killed President Jean Vilbrun Guillaume Sam. The mob directed their furor at Sam for the extrajudicial killing of political prisoners.

In the middle of all this political chaos, socioeconomic instability, and continued civil unrest, France and Germany sent warships to protect their investments in Haiti. This move worried U.S. President Woodrow Wilson. He thought that Europe could seize the opportunity to breach American security in waters near the Panama Canal. Additionally, like France and Germany, the U.S. had its economic and financial interests to protect in Haiti. Haiti's large debt, 80 percent of its annual revenue at the time, was owed to the U.S., France, and Germany. But the U.S. had become Haiti's largest trade partner, replacing France, with American businesses expanding greatly in the country.[12] With those businesses advocating policies of invading Haiti, President Wilson sent the US military to occupy Dessalines's nation. By that time, the United States had already occupied Cuba, Puerto Rico, Nicaragua, the Philippines, and by 1916, the Dominican Republic.

During the 19 years of occupation, Haiti had three presidents in succession, though the U.S. ruled as a military regime, which took over all major institutions. The first Haitian president under occupation was Senator Sud Dartiguenave, chosen by the U.S. military without the consent of Haitians over fiery politician and medical doctor Rosalvo Bobo. Dartiguenave was one of the first few nonmilitary leaders to preside over Haiti during the first century of independence. He endorsed a treaty

---

12 Wikipedia, "United States Occupation of Haiti", wikipedia.org, Wikipedia, retrieved March 12, 2022. https:// en.wikipedia.org/wiki/United_States_occupation_of_Haiti#American_financial_interests

that allowed the U.S. to dismantle the Haitian indigenous army and build a new Gendarmerie to police the nation. He also dictated and imposed on Haiti a new constitution that allowed non-Haitian citizens to own land for the first time since the declaration of independence in 1804.

Under the new regime dictated by the U.S. occupation forces, Haitians were also forced to labor on the corvee, which built new roads. Opposition against the occupation was mounted vehemently, and provincial leader Charlemagne Péralte mobilized a peasant army, which the Americans tried to suppress. By 1922, a new president, Louis Borno, and an American High Commissioner were installed. They oversaw investments in vocational education and public health, but not without fierce debates.

The occupation weakened Haitian nationalism considerably. However, several intellectuals like Jean-Price Mars denounced American imperialism and looked to ordinary citizens in rural Haiti particularly and the vodou religion to build a new national identity. There was a movement to incorporate peasant culture into music, poetry, and novels. The rebellion initiated against the U.S. occupation of Haiti started immediately in 1915 and is best known as the Caco movement. The name "Caco" was in reference to a local bird. At least 20 percent of the Haitian population took part in the guerilla rebellion, according to Patrick Bellegarde-Smith, a professor of African Studies at the University of Wisconsin, Milwaukee.[13] The U.S. and Haitian governments exerted a vigorous campaign to destroy the Caco rebels. But many intellectuals and politicians united to create the patriotic union (*L'Union Patriotique* in French), which opposed the occupation with support from sympathetic African Americans.

---

13 Westenly Alcenat, "The Case for Haitians Reparations", jacobinmag.com, Jacobin Magazine, January 14, 2017. https://www.jacobinmag.com/2017/01/haiti-reparations-france-slavery-colonialism-debt/

L'Union Patriotique established ties with opponents of the occupation of Haiti in the United States. They found allies in the National Association for the Advancement of Colored People (NAACP), including both white and black leaders. Concretely, the NAACP sent civil rights activist James Seldon Johnson, and its field secretary to investigate the situation in Haiti. In his account published in 1920, Johnson decried "economic corruption, forced labor, press censorship, racial segregation, and cruel violence" that the American occupation introduced in Haiti. He encouraged African Americans to flood Washington officials with letters calling for an end to abuses, and to remove U.S. troops from Haiti. The NAACP's call garnered attention and gave hope to Haitians.

After many protests and strikes involving students, intellectuals, grassroots organizations in urban and rural Haiti, and united sociopolitical leaders, the U.S. decided that it would leave Haiti. In 1930, Haiti's National Assembly selected a new president, Sténio Vincent, with a mandate to oversee the transition that would end the occupation of the country. Vincent appointed only Haitians to take over public works and run the new vocational education system. Vincent wanted to modernize the education system and make it more effective, professional, and democratic. Additionally, he continued the reorganization of the Gendarmerie that was renamed the Guard of Haiti (*La Garde d'Haiti* in French) in 1928. In 1934, the Americans left, and Vincent proclaimed Haiti's second independence.

From American Occupation's Legacy to Duvalier

Inheriting the structure built by the Americans, Vincent continued to invest in public works and education. However, seven years later, in 1941, he stepped down from the presidency owing to the political backlash generated at home after the 1937 massacre of thousands of Haitians in the Dominican Republic by then-President Rafael Trujillo. If the end of the American occupation saw his popularity soar, Vincent had become very unpopular due to his response to Trujillo's reparation. His ambassador to the U.S., Antoine Louis Léocardie Elie Lescot became president. Lescot's presidency would last about 5 years amid widespread and consistent protests.

Lescot's main political dilemma was that his post-occupation policies were judged too friendly to the United States in the context of radical and new political movements. Lescot denied the aspirations and interests of the majority black population in favor of the country's minority mulatto elite. In an effort for recognition as a strong ally to the U.S. government, Lescot took the initiative to be the first leader in the world who declared war on Nazi Germany. Lescot introduced an initiative to produce latex (rubber and sisal) that was needed by the U.S. in WWII for naval cordage. In 1943, he traveled to Washington, DC, to meet with President Franklin D. Roosevelt. During his visit, the two leaders reaffirmed the World War II alliance between Haiti and the United States. Of course, these actions helped Lescot strengthen Haiti's relationship with the U.S. as Pan-Americanism spread in elite circles. But he faced political backlash at home.

In addition to criticism for his alliance with the U.S. government, Lescot received strong rebukes for the permission he gave to the Catholic Church to persecute and label vodou as a superstition. The *noiristes*, who advocated black power, also denounced Lescot's leadership and policies. Feminists wanted to have a say in politics, and even amid openness to compromise, many Marxists, like the influential Jacques Roumain, believed that Haiti needed a new social order that would favor the popular classes as well, not just the bourgeoisie. When Lescot stepped down in 1946, the National Assembly selected Dumarsais Estimé as president. He was a teacher and legislator.

Estimé was more liberal than his predecessors. He allowed workers to unionize and invited *noiristes* to serve as members of his cabinet. Overall, he stood up to American corporations. He even nationalized some U.S. companies like Standard Fruit. But this move ended up being harmful to the banana industry due to ban on exports to the United States; and the government company eventually folded. The military overthrew Estimé in 1950, as he was trying to extend his presidency term. And the unique candidate Army Colonel Paul Eugene Magloire became Estimé's successor in an electoral plebiscite.

Under the presidency of Lieut. Colonel Magloire, Haiti regained some economic successes and therefore prospered. This was thanks to the increase of coffee and sisal prices, as well as a boost in tourism revenue. Magloire hired American company Brown and Root of Texas as contractors to oversee the construction of a huge dam in central Haiti (Péligre) to strengthen the production and supply of electricity, and to control the irrigation within the massive Artibonite downriver that was vital for agricultural production.[14] Politically, Magloire allowed women to vote. He socially instituted structures to take in displaced children who worked as servants with a minimum hope of obtaining an education. The devastation caused by hurricane Hazel in 1954, however, made it difficult for him to recover. Then about 2 years later, in 1956, he stepped down.

After the fall of Magloire, new elections were run to contest the presidency. And a *noiriste* doctor who integrated Estimé's cabinet,

---

14 Jennifer Wells, "A Dam for the People, and a People Damned", *The Toronto Star*, Nov. 21, 2010.

Francois Duvalier, was selected. Along with the presidency of Jean-Pierre Boyer (25 years), the Duvalier regime, including the father Francois (1957–1971) and the son Jean-Claude (1971–1986), was one of the two longest regimes in Haiti's political history. To enhance his power, stoke fear among the people, and terrorize his opponents and critics, Duvalier instituted a militia, the *Tonton Macoutes*.

Except for vodou, all social, political, and religious groups, such as labor unions, the women's movement, and churches, were persecuted. He restructured Haiti's National Assembly to silence protestors and used public works to extort money. In 1961, while he still had two years left on his presidential term, he profited from an election to renew the parliament to make an arbitrary plebiscite for his own reelection by unconstitutionally adding his name on the ballot. He was the only presidential candidate on the ballot. His name was arranged on the ballot in such a way that people were forced to vote for his premature re-election, as they were voting to elect their representatives to the Chamber of Deputies. He used that electoral parody to declare himself president for life against the will of the Haitian people.

However, we must recognize that Duvalier by himself alone could not have pulled that act together. He had his accomplices in government circles and followers who were willing to do anything to keep him in power. Some would support Duvalier because the system benefited them, others because of fanaticism or fear of persecution.

Aided by the assassination of U.S. President John F. Kennedy and the overthrow of Dominican President Juan Bosh, who were working together to overthrow him, Duvalier stayed in power as tensions eased and even received economic and political support from the U.S. government. At this point in time, the United States government wanted to make sure Duvalier would not turn to Communism. And when he died in 1971 of a heart attack, his 19-year-old son, Jean-Claude Duvalier, replaced him at the helm. Jean-Claude Duvalier, nicknamed Baby Doc, showed little interest in his father's *noiriste* ideology. He instead promised to improve the economy, although he and his family misappropriated millions of dollars in public funds.

As Haiti's tourism flourished in 1981, the American medical community dealt it a huge blow when they mistakenly identified Haitians as one of the four groups most responsible for the spread of AIDS. On top of that severe blow, which had a negative effect on the Haitian economy, in 1982, the U.S. government asked Duvalier to kill Haiti's native pigs to eradicate swine flu. Peasants, who were already threatened by soil erosion, were now without livestock and forced to abandon the land and moved to Port-au-Prince, which expanded in size to accommodate the demographic explosion.

Haiti's economy was in shambles, and Duvalier turned to the World Bank (WB) for help. The WB recommended that Haiti put its new urban population to work in assembly industries. Between political repression by the *Tonton Macoutes* of Duvalier and economic calamity, many Haitians braved the ocean in rickety wooden boats in hope of making it to the U.S. They often drowned by the thousands, while many who survived were deported back despite protests from sympathetic Americans. Those who were not sent back to Haiti had to overcome countless daily hostilities, although they persevered until they could settle, particularly in South Florida.

From Duvalier's Fall to Haiti's Struggles for Democracy

By the mid-1980s, discontent with the Duvalier dictatorship had spread nationwide, but more importantly in the Haitian army, the business community, the peasantry, in schools, and in grassroots organizations and local churches. As conspirators in the army were ready to overthrow Duvalier, he resigned and fled to exile in France on February 7, 1986. Presided by Lieutenant General Henri Namphy, a provisional government composed of a 5-member council took over and promised a transition from the brutal dictatorship regime to democracy. The army leadership was acclaimed and dubbed the hero by the majority of people in the country for getting rid of Duvalier and promoting civil liberty. That mixed Council of civil-military leadership did not survive long due to unconscionable frictions and irreconcilable differences among its members.

Once the Council of government was dismantled, Lieutenant General Henri Namphy, who was involved in three coups d'état from 1986 to 1988, assumed autocratically the presidency. But Haitians were quickly dissatisfied with the army's actions. Many people turned to violence to punish the *Tonton Macoutes* and their associates, and prevent those with ties to the Duvalier regime from getting back into power. They also protested new liberal trade deals and policies, and supported the referendum to allow a new Constitution that would limit the army's authority. Four years passed before largely acceptable and democratic elections could take place. It seemed like an eternity because of daily repressions and all forms of persecution used by the military leaders to suppress the opposition and stay in power.

The first attempt at organizing general elections under the new Constitution was made on November 29, 1987. The military leaders, foreseeing a real possibility of their political demise, turned those elections into a blood bath (the infamous *Ruelle Vaillant Massacre*). They panicked and stopped the population from eagerly electing their leaders amid carnage. A prominent lawyer and university professor in Gérard

Gourgue was positioned popularly to become the first democratically elected president of post-Duvalier Haiti. But the military generals had a different idea. After the *Ruelle Vaillant Massacre*, they reran those elections under fear and extreme repression, forcing the large majority of the population and most political leaders to boycott the vote. The civil society and international community called that second attempt by the army a "pseudo election" for its lack of transparency and participation.

From the tainted process of that electoral parody, Leslie F. Manigat, a well-known professor and political specialist, was selected and sworn in on February 7, 1988. Many have said that the army leaders handpicked Manigat as president. Rumors were even swirled that he paid a large sum of money to military leaders in order to get elected. His tenure in power lasted fewer than five months (February 7–June 20, 1988) because General Namphy, who facilitated his selection, ousted him in a coup d'état and regained power. "Due to the grave situation that the country had faced during the last four months, I am obliged to seize for a second time the reins of power," declared the former general to justify his coup.

In reality, if anything, the country was going through a moment of apparent peace and calm, a period of hope among the population, in particular among the youth and the intellectual class. In the end, after a time of contestation and denunciation of the elections, everyone pretty much accepted the fact that Manigat was assuming the presidency in spite of the dubious elections. The problem was that four months were too long for General Namphy to submit to the power of a civilian at the presidential palace. The timing of the coup could not be more notable, as the new government was trying to investigate, for purging and punishment, the role of high-ranking army officers in money laundering and drug trafficking.

From Lieut. General Henri Namphy, who once said unequivocally, "Haiti only has one voter—the army," to the fearsome army general Mathieu Prosper Avril, who grabbed power from the former in a coup in September 1988, the autocratic and antidemocratic nature of the army's administrations inspired more and more protests from Haitians and considerable pressures from the international community, in particular the U.N., O.A.S, U.S., France, and Canada.[15] Their reign was dubbed by many as "the Duvalierism without Duvalier."

By March 1989, the army leaders were forced to step aside and allow Haiti's first woman, a judge from the country's High Court Ertha Pascal-Trouillot, to swear in as president. She was also the first woman to sit on Haiti's supreme court bench. Despite being the sixth in line according to article 149 of the 1987 Constitution, she was the ideal choice of the civil society and political leaders who wanted, after the resignation of Avril, a more distant personality from the military leaders and their allies in the courtroom. The inauguration of Ertha Pascal-Trouillot was the beginning of a tradition instituted by the newly adopted Constitution, which consisted of repeatedly using judges from the supreme court as short-term solutions to fill the power vacuum in the absence of democratically elected presidents.

On December 16, 1990, provisional President Pascal-Trouillot presided over the organization of general elections. Those elections were overseen by a provisional council that represented Haiti's democratic sectors at the time. Jean-Bertrand Aristide, from the Lavalas political movement, handily won those elections considered as the first democratically and uncontested elections held in the

15 Phil Davidson, "Henri Namphy: Coup Leader and Former President", *The Independent*, UK, July 12, 2018.

country in the post-Duvalier era. Aristide, a former Roman Catholic priest repudiated by the Vatican for embracing the leftist theology of liberation, and his highly charged political views behind the pulpit, symbolized hope, change, and progress to many, particularly to the most vulnerable and impoverished Haitians. They affectionately called him *Pè Titid* (Father Titid).

Yet his overwhelming victory and massive support from the Haitian diaspora were not enough to make the transfer of power peaceful. Roger Lafontant, the former chief of the *Tonton Macoutes* and the minister of the interior under Duvalier whose candidacy was rejected in accordance with the 1987 Constitution, attempted a coup on the night of January 6–7, 1991, to overthrow the interim government and therefore prevent Aristide from swearing in. Back in July 1990, Lafontant vowed to stop Aristide from gaining access to power by any means necessary. But his coup lasted only a few hours.

Despite claiming to have the support of the army, the Commander-in-Chief of the military General Hérard Abraham immediately rebuked Lafontant. General Abraham condemned the coup d'état in a statement to the media that Monday morning following Lafontant's unconstitutional move. Urging the population to stay calm, General Abraham explained that the army as an institution was not involved in the coup. He vowed to return power to the Haitian people. Roger Lafontant acted with the support of some military members and militia gangs in his pay, according to Abraham. The former *Tonton Macoutes* chief was nostalgic of his time as a very powerful man prior to 1986. He wanted to stop the democratic process and restore the Duvalierism.

Accompanied by a dozen heavily armed accomplices, including rank-and-file (ordinary soldiers from the army) and militia members,

Lafontant forced his way into the presidential palace; he took provisional President Pascal-Trouillot hostage and forced her to resign. As Lafontant was giving a speech to inform the nation that he was the new president, the army leaders intervened and arrested him along with his accomplices. Although 75 people died and 150 others were injured in the violence that erupted during the failed coup, the military high command for once assumed its responsibilities and calmed the situation down in preparation for Aristide's swearing-in ceremony on February 7, 1991. General Abraham, proving another moment of good leadership, showed abnegation toward politics once again. He opted for the continuity of the democratic process for the common good. Like in March 1989, this was his second opportunity to seize power and become president himself. Instead, he reinstated the provisional presidency of Ertha Pascal-Trouillot, who would then transfer the power peacefully to the newly-elected president.

But the attempted coup was certainly the sign of the political difficulties ahead of the new government. It was a period where every Saturday night, Haitians would go to bed bracing for the eventual news of a coup before dawn on Monday. This was a permanent fever that kept the majority of the population on alert.

News of a coup d'état was slowly but surely arriving. Just over 8 months later, on the night of September 29–30, 1991, Aristide was overthrown by the army in a bloody coup responsible for at least 26 deaths and 200 injuries that day alone. According to numerous reports at the time, thousands more deaths and disappearances would follow. General Joseph Raoul Cédras became president briefly from September 30 to October 8, 1991. General Cédras was born in 1949 to a mulatto family in Jérémie, the main city of Haiti's southwestern peninsula. He became the commander-in-chief of the army just over two months earlier.

President Aristide named General Cédras to replace Lieut. General Hérard Abraham, whom Mr. Aristide pushed into premature retirement. The move by Mr. Aristide on his inaugural day to decree early retirement for Abraham and other high command members of the army was described by advised observers as bolstering his control over the military. Abraham was viewed as one of the few experienced army officers with respectable integrity and a sense of patriotic duty for the common good. Many people saw in Aristide's preference to rely on Cédras—a younger and more manageable soft-spoken military officer in command—a strategy to weaken the armed forces. A novice in real Haitian politics and government affairs, Aristide was perhaps too naive in that regard.

Cédras, who was trained in the United States and Spain would have shocked Aristide, when the first democratically elected president since the downfall of the Duvalier regime was arrested on his way to the presidential palace that Monday morning of September 30 in a desperate attempt to derail the coup against him. He was then brought to the army's high command headquarters to face his fate. Aristide, lucky to escape death on his way to the national palace thanks in part to the help of French Ambassador Jean-Raphael Dufour, who used his diplomatic cover to shield the president, ended up being captive for a moment at the military high command headquarters. Fearing for his life, Aristide was received by a dour General Cédras, who was looking at him in disdain, smiling capriciously and declaring, "I am the president, now."

The aloof Cédras, operating as a CIA informant reporting critical information on the Aristide government to the U.S., asked his soldiers, "What do you want me to do with the priest?" "Kill him," replied the rebel soldiers, who had just killed Fritz Pierre-Louis, the military officer who'd expressed his loyalty to Aristide and was charged to protect the former president as his bodyguard. This was just a gesture to further humiliate Aristide. Cédras, who was in the good graces of the U.S. Embassy in Port-au-Prince to assume power in the middle of that chaos, which confused most foreign diplomats, was ordered to protect the former priest of Saint-Jean Bosco. No one seemed to have a clear understanding of who was behind it all. Yet, Cédras was just an opportunist general emboldened by the secret support of the U.S. ambassador in Haiti, Alvin P. Adams.

The bloody coup was in fact masterminded by Lieut. Colonel Joseph Michel Francois, who was operating in the dark as a drug lord. Supported by a few oligarch families who had their own grievances and resentments toward Aristide, Joseph Michel Francois viewed the efforts by the democratic government to fight drug trafficking as a real threat. After the success of the coup, he was rewarded with the police chief position. Francois was blamed for building shadowy and violent police auxiliaries known as *attachés,* and sponsoring paramilitary organizations like FRAPH. Well informed about the dangerous man, Ambassador Adams instructed General Cédras to do all he could to spare the country from falling into hands of Lieut. Colonel Francois.

During all this, the coup d'état was immediately and unanimously condemned by U.N. and A.O.S officials, who demanded the reestablishment of constitutional and democratic order in Haiti. To compel the army leaders to step down and allow democracy to proceed, the international community (O.A.S.) implemented an embargo that further throttled Haiti's already vulnerable economy. Many Haitians, once more, fled into exile for both political and economic reasons. And their relatives who stayed behind became largely dependent on remittances—a situation that Aristide and others exploited politically.

They recognized the importance of Haitians living abroad for Haiti's economic development. Aristide wanted to capitalize on the support of the diaspora by incorporating it back into the country's affairs. He helped spread the phrase "Tenth Department" in reference to the thousands of Haitian migrants abroad, particularly in the United States, Canada, and France.

A department is the highest level of political and administrative subdivision of Haiti's territorial structure. Back then, the country's territory comprised nine administrative departments. In 2003, Haitian authorities created a tenth department called the Nippes, splitting the department of Grand'Anse into two separate territorial and administrative entities. With an area of 1,268 square kilometers, the Nippes (capital city Miragoâne) is the small department of Haiti. Soon after the establishment of Nippes as a department, some activists adopted the phrase "Eleventh Department" to now describe the Haitian diaspora.[16]

However, except for a few loyalists and those with ties to government officials and the elites, the majority of Haitians living abroad have always been excluded in the country's political affairs. That reality remained largely the same under Aristide as well. Their participation has been almost essentially, until now, limited to what they bring about back into the country financially and economically. Allowing the Haitian diaspora to fully participate in Haiti's affairs has remained just rhetoric and dupery. But that hopeful participation is necessary for a better future in Haiti. To do so, we need to deal with the

16 Since then, however, Haitian leaders have mostly used the designation of "Haitians Living Abroad" to describe the diaspora instead of the term tenth department. A Ministry of Haitians Living Abroad was established in 1991. But that ministry has not achieved much. Its role is more symbolic and ceremonial.

challenges sincerely, and implement effective reforms both legally and logistically.[17]

While Haitians in Haiti and abroad were demanding the return of Aristide to power, which symbolized the country's return to democracy, the international community made a number of forlorn attempts, only to fall short at every turn due to the resistance of the military leaders and Aristide's lack of taste for compromise. Each side was strategically playing their game to doom the other. There was no middle ground for almost 3 years.

In the aftermath of the coup, and in a move to satisfy the international community and send a signal that he did not want power for himself, Cédras stepped down in less than two weeks. He left the presidential palace to Judge Joseph C. Nérette, who became the provisional president until 1992. That gesture from the military leaders, who wanted to convince people with their argument that they only intervened supposedly to save the country from the threat of a populist dictatorship regime about to be installed by Aristide, did not appease the population. Most people familiar with political struggles in Haiti did not buy into that argument. It did not hold any water. The military high command, under General Raoul Cédras, continued to impede the democratic process and impose their rule behind the scenes. They were forced to accept the fact that Aristide was still the president of Haiti, even though he was outside of the country.

---

17 The actual constitution is ambiguous when it comes to people of Haitian heritage with multiple nationalities. The debate is ongoing about different interpretations of articles 11 and 12 on rights and Haitian nationality. Another challenge for integrating the Haitian diaspora in Haiti's affairs is the logistics. Haitian authorities need to establish various and practical structures to facilitate the participation of Haitians in Haiti's political, social, and economic life wherever they may be around the world.

To facilitate the deposed president's return in Port-au-Prince, the army leaders also accepted the designation of Rene Theodore, a political party leader from the left and Aristide's enemy, as prime minister in February 1992. But a divided parliament meant Theodore did not get confirmed to be installed as a condition for Aristide's return. The agreement negotiated by the O.A.S between the parties and signed in Washington, DC failed, and therefore so did the first tentative attempt to restore Aristide's presidency. Then came Marc L. Bazin, Aristide's direct political rival in the 1990 elections and a U.S. government favorite.

Supported by the U.S. Embassy in Port-au-Prince, Bazin, nicknamed Mr. Clean for his experience as a World Bank officer, was appointed and took office as interim prime minister in 1992. He was tasked to negotiate new conditions for Aristide's return on behalf of the military leaders. Unsuccessful, he was forced to step down in 1993. His experience at the World Bank, United Nations, and as a former minister of finance and economy under Jean-Claude Duvalier (Baby Doc) was not enough to help him avoid failure at Haiti's helm.

After that second failed attempt, the military commanders wanted to definitively put an end to the Aristide chapter. In May 1994, they appointed as provisional president Emile Jonassaint from the High Court of Justice. Judge Jonassaint was Haiti's president of the Constituent Assembly during the 1987 constitutional referendum. The military leaders and their allies in the parliament wanted someone in charge of doing their bidding of organizing new presidential elections in an effort to eclipse Aristide completely and definitively. The O.A.S./U.N. emissaries did not back that move. Jonassaint would also fail under pressure from Aristide's allies and the international community led by the U.S., France, and Canada in particular. These three countries, along with Venezuela, were nicknamed "Friends of Haiti" at the time.

Pressured, Jonassaint stepped down in September 1994. After several rounds of negotiations, the military leaders agreed to allow Robert Malval, a businessman from the economic elite and of Lebanese descent appointed by Aristide in August 1993, to become prime minister with the task of reconciling the feuding parties. He then paved the way for Aristide to return and finish his term as president.

Aristide's Return

At the end of October 1994, U.S. forces with the backing of a U.N. military coalition finally intervened to restore Aristide to power after three years in exile in Venezuela and the United States. Aristide, this time, reluctantly promised to work with the U.S. and the International Monetary Fund (IMF) to reform government institutions and enterprises, most notably the telecommunication company (Teleco), the electrical company (EDH), and the sugar (ASCO) and cement (Ciment d'Haiti) producing companies. Mr. Aristide agreed to lower taxes on trade as well. Of course, lower taxes helped Haiti's assembly industries and the American corporations they dealt with. However, they increasingly hurt national production. Peasants, who already had to cope with soil erosion and the extermination of the nation's pigs, could not compete with cheaper imports and the flooding of food aid.

Despite tensions, shivving, and distrust, and notably, divisions among Aristide's allies and foes, new elections were held once again under a new provisional council. Overcoming a barrage of candidates and riding on Aristide's inescapable popularity, René Garcia Préval, Aristide's former prime minister, was elected and sworn in 1996 as president. Aristide then stepped aside and spent 5 years working with his new political party Fanmi Lavalas and operating from his residence in Tabarre as shadow-president to Preval. President Preval would eventually oversee a very contentious presidential election sulked at by the large majority of political parties and the population.

From those elections, the inevitable Fanmi Lavalas candidate Jean-Bertrand Aristide, who had no real challenger, was elected and sworn in for a second term as president in 2001. And this was amid cries of massive voter fraud allegations and a very low turnout. The large majority of prominent opposition parties regrouped into a coalition named Democratic Convergence (CD), hiding behind their own political miscalculations, vulnerabilities, and internal disagreements. The group boycotted the ballot and parallelly named Gérard Gourgue, former leading presidential candidate in the failed election of 1987, as their provisional president. This was a desperate move to prevent or at least to distract Préval from peacefully transferring the power to Aristide (called his political twin brother at the time).

The electoral boycott did not work for the CD leaders. The installation of a parallel president did not either. Préval was able to transfer power to his elected successor on the constitutional date of February 7, 2001. Powerless, without a presidential office or constitutional legitimacy, Mr. Gourgue would shortly abandon the fight for that presidential adventure. Gourgue had dreamed of this adventure since 1986.

But the movement to remove Aristide from power would continue. Mr. Aristide had faced a growing opposition that included almost every sector in Haiti. Among the opposition, we found most notably diverse political groups, popular and grassroots organizations, human rights activists, artists and musicians, religious groups, professional associations and trade unions, and students. Some of the most disturbing elements for the former Saint-Jean Bosco's priest [Aristide] were his former allies and fervent supporters who had turned against him in protests and insurrections. They were frustrated and fed up with sociopolitical and economic conflicts and contradictions within the Lavalas circle.

This time, the opposition to Aristide was a multisectoral movement on the ground where people had been voicing their discontent for a long stretch, non-stop. Protesters would go massively to the streets chanting "Down with Aristide" in one voice. They denounced corruption, political malfeasance, human rights abuse, persecution against the government's opponents, brutal repression against journalists, and the use of street thugs and armed gangs to conduct political violence and killings. In the face of popular revolts and insurrections, Aristide resigned on February 29, 2004. On that day, the California-based Steele Foundation private security company, which he entrusted his personal security, escorted Former President Aristide into exile all the way to South Africa, where he lived for 7 years.[18]

Then another caretaker government supported by the U.S. and U.N., and led by Prime Minister Gérard Latortue, was installed to work with provisional President Boniface Alexandre. Alexandre, once again a judge from the High Court of Justice, was sworn in immediately after Aristide resigned in February 2004. He was the last judge from the High Court to run the country under the 1987 constitution before its amendment around 2011–2013.

---

18 David C. Adams, et al., "The Depiction of the Second Presidency of Jean-Bertrand Aristide", Alterpresse.org, June 8, 2022. https://www.alterpresse.org/spip.php?article28370&utm_source=dlvr.it&utm_medium=twitter

Préval's Return

The Alexandre/Latortue government oversaw elections that elected Préval for a second term in 2006. In a field crowded with candidates as usual, Préval benefited from his own political residuals as both former prime minister and president. He also acquired the support of Aristide's followers, who believed at the time that Préval was the one president to bring Aristide back from exile—a promise he did not make. He did not even try to fulfill that dream for Aristide's supporters either. Préval did not want to upset the international community, particularly the U.S.; and very importantly, he did not want to return to governing in Aristide's shadow like during his first term in 1996–2001. As a result, Aristide supporters and political allies were furious with Préval and looked for any reason to blame him in protests.

Aristide, on his part, held an unforgivable grudge against Mr. Préval for being left in political desperation and solitude. Aristide's discontent followed Préval all the way to the latter's grave. Like Haitians usually say to express the level of their unforgivable grudge held against someone, *Toutotan 10 mil liv tè pa tonbe sou lestomak Aristide, li pap janm padone Preval.*[19] When former President Préval—who became Aristide's friend in the 1980s—died on March 3, 2017, Aristide did not publicly reach out to his former prime minister's family; he did not officially express any sympathy, nor did he even attend the funeral, to the stupefaction of many observers.

When you commit a political sin in the eyes of former President Jean-Bertrand Aristide, you are forever condemned. There is no

19 This Haitian metaphoric expression can be translated as "Aristide would not forgive Preval until the former's death."

forgiveness. Besides, people familiar with Aristide's thinking speak of him becoming jealous of Préval. René Garcia Préval was the pioneer on top of a list of the very few elected presidents who were able to finish a full term in modern Haiti. He did not once, but twice (1996–2001 and 2006–2011).

Even in the midst of political turmoil and different crises, Préval managed to finish two presidential terms and transfer the power to an elected successor each time. Far from Aristide's shadow during his second term, Préval was able to restore relative peace and political stability in the country. In contrast to Aristide, Préval was an introvert leader and less controversial. He was more open to dialogue and was receptive and attentive to his political opponents. Préval listened more than he talked. Some people considered this as a strength. Others, particularly Préval's political critics, considered his deliberate mutism as a weakness, a sign of his incompetence or carelessness. His second term was marked primarily by restoring law and order in the country after a period of violence and destabilization related to the political climate both under and after Aristide.

Préval also continued the economic and institutional reforms started during his first term (1996–2001). He reestablished some rigor and efficiency in the public sector. This enabled his government to increase revenue for socioeconomic programs beneficial to the country, particularly the most vulnerable citizens.

Under Préval's presidency, the government built more schools than all the presidents before him combined. Préval gave the highest raise to teachers. All these factors, among others, contributed to making Préval a more successful president than any other in post-Duvalier Haiti, in spite of his many sociopolitical and economic challenges.

From 2007 to 2010, President Préval faced a growing food crisis, a spreading cholera epidemic, and then a devastating earthquake. Those three major calamities that lamentably exacerbated Haiti's ever-present dependence on the international community and nongovernmental organizations (NGOs) hit the country like a giant category-5 hurricane. Despite all, Haiti persevered resiliently. The country had started to rebuild until efforts were hampered by political and social tensions once again: tensions orchestrated by factions within the political arena and political leaders fighting for power during electoral processes. Different interest groups engaged in multiple violent protests and unrest to impose their will on the system. Many people were also impatient and desperate in their demands for better socioeconomic conditions. Nonetheless, Préval managed to create positive conditions for the election of his successor under intense national and international pressures pushing for several turns of events.

Martelly and Moise: The Surprised Package

On May 14, 2011, Joseph Michel Martelly, a prominent musician and singer best known by his stage name Sweet Micky, became president against all odds. Not many people took Martelly's candidature too seriously. They joked about him as being the *compas* president instead. This was in reference to the style of dance music sung predominantly in the Haitian language. Martelly popularized a new generation of smaller bands relying on synthesizers and electronic instruments. Joseph Michel Martelly was also known for his connection with the former military leaders of the 1990s, in particular former police chief and putschist Joseph Michel Francois.

Martelly had no previous political experience and no background in government or public affairs. Elected after a hotly contested presidential election in two rounds, he promised continuity in rebuilding efforts after the 2010 earthquake. He proposed to open the country for business to improve the economy, education, and the energy sector. Within the first three years of his presidency, Haiti registered a 26 percent increase in per capita gross domestic product (GDP). He instituted a tax on money transfers and telecommunication services to finance his education programs.[20] Backed by the United States and its allies, Martelly also promised institutional reforms, respect for human rights, and political fairness. However, hundreds of millions of dollars were spent during the 5 years of his administration for dismal results.

Martelly's first political act was to open the door for all former presidents in exile to return to Haiti and participate in the country's reconstruction—a public commitment that comforted and reassured both former President Jean-Bertrand Aristide and Jean-Claude Duvalier (Baby Doc). Aristide had already returned to the country on March 18, 2011, right before the presidential runoff, after seeing the return of his eternal archenemy, former dictator Jean-Claude Duvalier, in the middle of political chaos on January 16, 2011. Baby Doc, before his death in 2014, tried to reinsert himself into the political game after 25 years of political exile. But a lot had changed in the country politically from 1986 to 2011. He could only appreciate the opportunity to get out of solitude in

20 This tax has since sparked outrage from families and relatives in both Haiti and abroad. Despite their will to contribute to rebulding Haiti and funding education for Haitian children, many people felt that Martelly's plans were too vague and would lead to more corruptions. In fact, there has been no real report and accountability for the money collected. The tax consists of $1.50 on money transfers and a five-cent surcharge on international phone calls. Martely's successors have continued to collect the taxes and fees for a non-existent education progam. In 2018, a group of plaintiffs in the United States filed a lawsuit against Haitian government officials and corporations such as Western Union, Caribbean Air Mail mostly known as CAM, and Digicel Haiti and USA. Despite early challenges, a U.S. Federal Court ruled on March 31, 2022 that this law suit may move forward.

Europe and die gracefully in his homeland. The attempted probe against him for embezzlement, corruption, abuses, atrocities, and other crimes committed under his presidency did not bring justice for his victims. In 2012, an appellate judge dismissed the charges against Duvalier because he found them being run out of Haiti's statute of limitations.

Aristide, for his part, has continued to exercise greater influence on the political scene since his return to Haiti. Although he has not been as vocal as he was before his seven years on the African continent, he has nonetheless continued to inspire and lead his considerably weakened party, Organization Fanmi Lavalas (OFL). He perhaps has learned from past political gaffes and naivety. Operating in complete silence seems to keep him out of exile. He has maintained his former president status in the comfort of his home surrounded with high walls, in Tabarre; a fashionable exurban district located about 5 miles east of the center of Port-au-Prince. People often refer to him as the "baron of Tabarre". The reason for that nickname is understandable.

A fusion of populist politics and liberation theology had brought Aristide to power. But many Haitians have, since the late 1990s, seemed to see in Aristide someone who had long departed from his populist and theological principles. He had left the priesthood to marry a light-skinned, upper-class woman (mulattoe). Mr. Aristide had built a multimillion-dollar mansion for himself, while not much has changed for the millions of impoverished Haitians who had voted for him both in 1990 and 2001. But his party has been fractured and divided into a number of small units that have the same approach to power.

Despite all this, Aristide has still remained a major player in Haitian politics. Under his influence, political resistance and turmoil were often raised against the government and against the Electoral Council (CEP) to prevent the peaceful transfer of power from Martelly to a new elected president in 2016, who was suspected of not being from Fanmi Lavalas. The first presidential candidate directly from Aristide's party after his downfall in 2004 was medical doctor Maryse Narcisse. She did not even come close to winning on the list of candidates that looked like a crowded flea market. Dr. Narcisse finished fourth in both the 2015 quashed elections and the 2016 re-run, with respectively 7.01% and 9.01% of the votes. The 2015 elections, which took place according to the constitution to replace Martelly (whose term was going to end on February 7, 2016), were hotly contested, debated, protested, and voided. Martelly was forced to leave office on the constitutional date of his term with no elected successor.

Then the Haitian parliament selected Jocelerme Privert. A compromise facilitated by the amended constitution allowed him to run the country as caretaker president. Mr. Privert, then president of the Senate and ally to Aristide, was charged to oversee the rerun of the 2015 quashed elections.

Those elections were finally rerun in 2016. And once again, as he did in 2015 without any surprise, Jovenel Moise won. An ally to Martelly and a banana exporter-turned-politician, Mr. Moise was elected from a runoff to become the 58th president of Haiti. He was sworn in on February 7, 2017. Those elections, yet again, were tainted with a process that was marred by delays, allegations of voter fraud, and an abysmal voter turnout.

As soon as Moise took office, he encountered all kinds of oppositions and protestations from political groups, particularly those with ties to Aristide's movement. Ranging from violent street protests, looting, fire barricades and roadblocks, vandalizing and kidnappings, the strategy of the opposition was aimed at stoking fear and creating so much chaos that rendered the country ungovernable.

The leaders behind that rising opposition movement were almost rewarded with the overthrow of Moise, when between July 2018 and September 2019, Haitians experienced probably one of the worst series of violence and economic stagnation they had ever seen. The scenes of violence, which were sometimes very sporadic and improvised, stemmed from clashes between law enforcement authorities under President Moise and the protesters.

By September 2019, the violent protests lasted for a long stretch (operasyon peyi lòk, meaning country lock operation), bringing Port-au-Prince and other major cities and towns around the country to a standstill. Local human rights organizations like CE-JILAP dubbed 2019 the deadly year. In Port-au-Prince alone, according to these human rights organizations, 500 people were killed due to violence related to political unrest.[21]

The opposition movement called for Moise's resignation and the formation of a transitional government. They alleged that the Haitian government had misappropriated billions of dollars meant for social development projects. Outrage over those allegations served as the initial impetus for the protests. But frankly, the opposition sought to harness the anger that was in part due to the political acrimony that had seized Haiti since the results of the 2015 elections.

The intention was to force President Moise's ouster anyway. It is hard to imagine or concede that in just 2 years in office, Jovenel Moise had been the main culprit for the misappropriation of public funds and the lack of socioeconomic development in the country. In all fairness, he inherited what happened during the previous 20 to 30 years under military leaders—Aristide, Préval, Martelly, and all the provisional

---

21 Jocelye Colas Noel, *Conference Episcopale Justice et Paix* (CE-JILAP), reported at a press conference, Port-au-Prince, December 23, 2019.

presidents combined. Most of the accusations and allegations (from petrochallengers)[22] have to do with funds generated by the sales of oil products from Petrocaribe, an oil alliance founded in 2005 involving Venezuela and Caribbean member states wherein Venezuela offers other members oil supplies based on a concessionary agreement.

Haiti officially became a member state of the Petrocaribe's alliance under President Préval on August 29, 2006, with the approval of the parliament. Oil purchased on credit at a preferential price (40–70% of actual value) and a 1% annual interest rate was supposed to return millions of dollars to the country for investment in sustainable infrastructure, education, sanitation, and other socioeconomic and development projects. Instead, Haiti had accumulated debt up to almost $4 billion dollars in the oil-purchasing program; almost $2 billion out of $3.8 billion of that total debt occurred between 2008 and 2016. [23] And remember, Haiti started receiving funds from the Petrocaribe deal in August 2006. But major investments in socioeconomic and development programs had been nowhere visible. By the time Jovenel Moise was sworn in, the money was already all but gone, and Venezuela in a deep sociopolitical and economic crisis discontinued the sweet oil deal that left a legacy of debt and corruption.

Moise, on his arrival in February 2017, promised to improve the economy, develop the national agriculture, vamp up the energy sector, and build adequate infrastructure—promises that he could not materialize. His administration, like many other governments before, faced not only allegations of corruption but also was plagued

---

22 Petrochallengers referred to a group of activists of all backgrounds, particularly a blended younger generation of Haitians, who were demanding accountability for billions of dollars embezzled by Haitian leaders from the Petrocaribe contract.

23 Edwige Dandicat, "Haitians want to know what the government has done with missing oil money", *The New Yorker*, October 19, 2018.

with incompetence, inexperience, and a lack of good leadership. Meanwhile, important elections to renew the parliament and municipal representatives could not be run.

The opposition continued unequivocally to demand Moise's resignation at any cost and without condition. But he continued against all odds and pressures to pursue his term. His power was kind of consolidated by mid-January 2020 when he became, with the exception of 10 senators out of a total of 30 seats in the Senate, the only elected official in government whose term was not ended.

Political move by President Moise or misinterpretation of the constitution? How come two-thirds of the Senate was gone at the same time? The answer is marred by ambiguity. As for the constitution, each of Haiti's 10 departments is represented by three senators elected in the following order: a 6-year term goes to the candidate with the most votes, a 4-year term to the one in second position, and a 2-year term to the 3rd placed one. That means, elections to renew a third of the Senate should technically be run every 2 years. However, the government had missed two important electoral dates at that point in 2020. No local and legislative elections took place as prescribed by the Constitution.

Anyway, Mr. Moise showed the door to the legislators without compromise. The bicameral National Assembly (149 members) was tacitly dissolved because 100% of the lower chamber (the Chamber of Deputies) and 75% of the Senate did not get renewed due to elections not taking place on constitutional schedules. Mayors throughout the country were replaced by interims. And Moise started to rule by decree in absence of the legislative branch to provide checks and balances. He made a number of controversial and some unconstitutional decisions, such as the publication of a decree reforming Haiti's penal code, the installation of a new provisional electoral council without consensus or agreement among key sectors, bypassing even the Supreme Court, and the project for the adoption of a new constitution via referendum.

Moise also decreed that acts such as robbery, arson, and even blocking public roads—a common ploy during protests—would be classed as terrorism and subject to heavy penalties. He also created an intelligence agency that answered only to the president. Opposition leaders grew worried that he had amassed too much power. Officials from the Core Group, an international entity formed in support of democratic reinforcement, including representatives of the United Nations, the European Union, O.A.S., and ambassadors of the United States, Canada, France, Germany, Brazil, and Spain also questioned those moves. In a joint statement issued after the publication of the decrees, the officials said: "The decree creating the National Intelligence Agency (ANI) gives the agents of this institution quasi-immunity, thus opening up the possibility of abuse. These two presidential decrees, issued in areas that fall within the competence of a parliament, do not seem to conform to certain fundamental principles of democracy, the rule of law, and the civil and political rights of citizens."[24]

In addition to the political advantage offered to Moise by the absence of the legislative branch, the COVID-19 pandemic, which limited people's ability to gather, and the mechanical fix made to the devaluation of the national currency (gourde) against the US dollar seemed to help him score some points on the opposition. His political machine, which looked broken beyond repair for most of his time in office so far, seemed to be reinvigorated and found the necessary

---

24 Evens Sanon and Danica Cotto, "Haiti braces for unrest as opposition demands new president", The Associated Press, January 15, 2021.

fuel to deliver some of his signature promises. By the end of 2020, the government was able to artificially force the reduction in prices for most consumer goods and regain focus on building more power plants to improve the distribution of electricity in the country. The government had contracted General Electric to help repair and revamp the country's electrical grid. Works on some projects to facilitate transports through reliable roads were resuscitated.

Seizing the opportunity given by the New Year for good luck and wishes, Moise declared 2021 as a very important year for the future of the country. He put out a calendar, according to which a constitutional referendum would take place in April; local, legislative, and presidential elections would be scheduled for the month of September; and possible runoffs would be held in November to elect his successor, who would take office on February 7, 2022. But the opposition strongly believed that Moise's term should end on February 7, 2021, instead.

According to their position, Moise's five-year term started in 2016, not 2017 when he was officially sworn into office. They argued that article 134-2 of the constitution, amended on May 9, 2011, supported their argument that Moise won the 2016 presidential election, which was the continuity of the process started in 2015. Therefore, a delay for his official installation meant that he simply lost a year of his term. They accused Moise of violating the constitution by not organizing elections in 2019 and ruling by decree. They reiterated their demand for his resignation and called for a transitional-interim government with the primary task of organizing new elections.

But President Jovenel Moise and those who supported him argued that the constitution does not support the opposition argument because the 2015 elections were totally quashed; a provisional president,

Jocelerme Privert, was installed by the parliament to oversee new elections a year later. Moise held firm on his power for one more year. Sadly, for Haiti, article 134-2 of the amended constitution can validate both arguments, for it is very ambiguous in both syntax and semantics. On top of that, there is no available institution (judiciary or legislative) with the authority to impose an interpretation and definitive decision on constitutional conflicts or constitutional misinterpretations. Everyone obsessed with that ambiguous article 134-2 makes their own interpretation according to their personal view or agenda. In this context, only a political compromise, as has usually been the case in Haiti's chaotic climate, could at least temporarily appease minds.

President Moise based his position essentially on the letter of the constitution, which establishes a five-year term for the president. But despite ambiguities, the opposition—which included political leaders, religious leaders, university students, human rights organizations, judiciary authorities, and what was left of the parliament—found the loophole to base their argument on the spirit of the constitutional calendar to declare Moise's term as being over as of February 7, 2021. The constitutional calendar was established by the constitution in 1987 and started effectively with the first of Haiti's widely recognized democratic elections in December 1990. From there, the calendar goes like this with potential presidential inaugurations:

February 7, 1991 (Aristide)
February 7, 1996 (Préval)
February 7, 2001 (Aristide)
February 7, 2006 (Préval, sworn in on May 14, 2006)
February 7, 2011 (Martelly, sworn in on May 14, 2011)
February 7, 2016 (Privert instead of Moise, one year of provisional presidency)
February 7, 2021 (Moise hung on to compensate for his lost year)

Paradoxically, the opposition counterpart could also argue that the constitutional calendar began on February 7, 1988, instead, when the first elected civilian leader, Leslie Francois Manigat, was sworn in and received the presidential sash under the constitution. That would even push us up to February 7, 2023, as the next presidential inauguration date. That argument made plenty of sense at the time, when a sector of the opposition proposed to replace president Moise with a provisional president for two years. That was in fact a tacit acknowledgement that the constitutional calendar began on February 7, 1988, instead 1991.

On each of these dates, there should have been a new president installed. But as you can see, there have been several instances where no new elected president was inaugurated on the constitutional date of February 7. Presidents had also seen their terms shortened due to chaotic situations or coups. However, the legislative authorities and the Préval administration that amended the Constitution in 2011, tried to deal with that issue by making provisions saying that when the inauguration happens late, the presidents lose time off their terms.

But what happens when the inauguration happens early? Would the presidents gain more time on their terms, or would we consider a presidential vacuum? Nothing is said in that sense. Their efforts, instead of fixing the problem, have made it more complicated for politicians to handle. Article 134-2 says that if the election is held late, the new president would be inaugurated right after the election. The Provisional Electoral Council (Conseil Electoral Provisore - CEP, in French) declared Moise president-elect on January 3, 2017. Amid a constitutional crisis, no one could fully break the deadlock. That left the leaders with only a political consensus as a possible solution. But each side of the political spectrum wanted no less than a win; and each one thought they had the upper hand to do so.

Even though the opposition seemed to be considerably weakened in comparison with their stances during the 2018 and 2019 general protests, they nonetheless had the support of some national institutions and notable voices in their battle against Moise. Among those agreed with the assumption that Moise's term ended included the head of the Catholic church via the Conseils of Haitian Bishops (Conférence Episcopale d'Haiti, or the CEH), the Superior Council of Haiti's Judiciary (CSPJ), the Young Bar Association of Port-au-Prince, Bars Federation of Haiti, different Haitian diaspora organizations, and some lawmakers from the U.S. Congress. But Moise managed to secure the support of the international community through the U.N. and O.A.S., and the backing of the U.S. government particularly.

On February 5, 2021, the Biden administration, through the State Department spokesperson Ned Price, indicated that President Jovenel Moise's term would end on February 7, 2022, weighing in on a contentious question that had roiled Haiti for months. "In accordance with the [Organization of American States'] position on the need to proceed with the democratic transfer of executive power, a new elected president should succeed President Moise when his term ends on February 7, 2022," declared the State Department spokesman Ned Price.[25] This came as a signal to the opposition leaders that the newly installed Biden administration, as it was the U.S. policy posture during the Trump administration, would not recognize nor support any opposition transitional president resulting from an eventual premature departure of Jovenel Moise.

---

25 Sandra Lemaire, "Haiti President's Term Will End in 2022", VOANEWS.com, Voice of America, February 5, 2021. https://www.voanews.com/a/americas_haiti-presidents-term-will-end-2022-biden-administration-says/6201681.html

That signal from the Biden administration was not to be taken lightly when you know that Haitians had long been incapable of running anything without foreign influence. They cannot organize their own elections without the financial and logistic support of the US. for the most part. Meanwhile, the majority of Haitians, suffering under abject poverty and daily violence imposed by gangsters, had continued to quietly but defiantly observe the political theatre displayed by both camps.

The opposition and its allies have persisted in their grind to force Moise out. They are divided on a viable alternative to the president in case of his eventual downfall. Yet, they called for the creation of a fifteen-member committee commissioned to plan the transition and pick a provisional president with a two-year term. The initiators called that committee the National Commission for the Transition (CNT). That proposition for a long political transition was in complete violation of the same constitution that they used to accuse Jovenel Moise of grave violations. None of the antagonists here is exempt from political malfeasance or malpractice. And the mess is everywhere.

Failing to rally a large consensus among the multitude of opposition groups, and support among the country's key sectors and the representatives of the international community in particular, the CNT was no more than a joke and an announced chronicle of political debacle. It was dead before its arrival. All attempts to get rid of President Moise on the D-day have been unfruitful.

First, there were supposedly the opposition's failed coup attempt and the plot of Moise's assassination on Sunday, February 7, 2021, according to a statement from the president himself before departing for the southern coastal town of Jacmel to participate in the opening ceremony of its yearly carnival, which was being held amid the COVID-19 pandemic. And secondly, there were twenty-three arrests made, followed by the firing and replacing of three Supreme Court judges whose names were circulating earlier as possible candidates proposed by opposition leaders to replace Mr. Moise on an interim basis. The political inability and mediocrity of the opposition leaders had meant that the Moise/Jouthe government was running roughshod over anyone who tried to get in its way.

Moise announced on that Sunday afternoon that the National Police arrested more than twenty people in a meeting staging his assassination and the overthrow of the government in a coup d'état without providing further details or any specific evidence. Confusion . . . but smoke never arises without a fire started somewhere, Haitians often say. You just need to find the fire and who started it.

One of the problems with Haiti's justice system is that most of the time, authorities get the wrong people or the less important accomplices in trouble and make them suffer, while the real masterminds and executors of a crime walk around freely. Also, a traditional lack of transparency often makes people doubt justice and law enforcement decisions.

Among those arrested were Judge Yvickel Dabrézil from the Supreme Court, who was allegedly preparing to become provisional president, and Police Inspector General Marie-Louise Gauthier. The police inspector—arrested along with her sister Marie-Antoinette Gauthier, a former presidential candidate—was allegedly coordinating with high-ranking security officials at the National Palace to arrest President Moise. Prime Minister Joseph Joute said later in the day that authorities found several weapons and a speech that Supreme Court

Judge Yvickel Dabrézil had allegedly prepared to give if he were to become provisional president. The other two judges on the opposition's radar for a potential transitional president were Joseph Mecene Jean-Louis and Wendelle Coq Thelot.

In the middle of the confusion and fresh lurch of political theatre, Judge Jean-Louis had also prepared and even delivered a speech on a video circulating on social media accepting the choice of the opposition to become provisional president. Meanwhile, in Cap-Haitian, the main city of northern Haiti, another political theatre was playing; a separate ceremony took place to install a lawyer, Carl-Heins Charles, as president. His supporters claimed to make the new seat of the Haitian government the old revolutionary Palace of Sans-Souci, built by King Henri Christophe, also in the north, thus resurrecting one of the oldest enmities in Haiti—the competition for preeminence between Cap-Haitian and Port-au-Prince, North and South. No word of interim was mentioned in the Charles announcement. It had a secessionist flavor. But his ridiculous effort did not go anywhere.

In truth, and in the view of most observers at the time, this whole back-and-forth over Moise's constitutional term was far from being a dispute over democracy and progress for all. It was a kind of paper cover for the real need just to get rid of the president; it was a fight aiming to defang and disempower former President Martelly, who was the real muscle behind President Moise, according to some opposition leaders. This has been a common denominator in Haitian politics. The curse of being an outgoing president and leader of an incumbent party at the same time.

We had observed the same situation at the end of Martelly's term in 2015, and with most of the opposition protests against former

President Aristide and late President Préval. The rallying cry just switched camp every political cycle. Haitian political leaders do not believe in impartiality and political fairness. To them, going to elections with an incumbent party is just political suicide. The electoral council is not that independent and usually heeds pressures from the political and diplomatic actors. The opposition parties always feel more comfortable with a provisional president that is "less partisan" while in charge of the executive branch during an election year.

It was in that context that they had created or provoked political instability, insecurity, and chaos to prevent President Moise from being able to oversee time-sensitive local and legislative elections in 2019. And above all, they did not want to see Moise organize presidential elections for his successor. In the end, and in the middle of an institutional vacuum, they would get what they had wished for: a transitional government born suddenly from a conjunctural compromise. They had, rightly or wrongly, cultivated the fear of Martelly's return to compete for a second term.

Each president's term in Haiti is a constitutionally dictated five years, and he or she may serve two terms, but not consecutively. After more than five years out of office, Martelly could constitutionally run for a second presidential bid as an official candidate of the incumbent party. And each leader of the divided and diverse opposition knew their chance of defeating him through elections was extremely slim. Despite the blah blah blah, as we usually say it in Haiti, Martelly had remained somewhat popular among key demographics that were more inclined to vote on election day. As meager as his popularity could look to many, it had still been seen as a considerable advantage for an incumbent leader facing multiple candidates from a very divided opposition. Most of those omnipresent opposition leaders had never amassed more than 1% of the votes in any past elections.

Since the 1990 elections that elected Aristide, no one had ever been elected in Haiti from an opposition party. Michel Martelly broke the trend in 2011. He was elected as an outsider under the banner of *Repons Peyizan*, an organization that was spearheaded by groups or political platforms formerly associated with the Aristide movement. Mr. Martelly took over by creating his own political cycle with Jovenel Moise. They allegedly had a twenty-year plan to pass the presidency back and forth between them, according to the opposition and some civil-society groups—a plan that neither Martelly nor Moise had denied. During an interview with Jon Lee Anderson of *The New Yorker Magazine* on January 25, 2016, as he was preparing to leave office that year, Martelly replied to a question regarding his intention to return to power in a spin of five years by saying, "If there is continuity, I can come back." And Moise himself also confirmed the twenty-year plan to trade places with Martelly. Cited later by another *New Yorker* writer, Edwidge Dandicat, he was quoted saying to Anderson of their plan, "It's a good plan. We need stability; we need it."[26]

Looking at the political landscape in Haiti, we see division in its entirety. The political tendencies, which were leading the fight against Moise, were divided between the moderates, who would have liked a negotiated and orderly departure and had the support of certain foreign governments, and the radicals who hoped for a process of refoundation—a "tabula rasa," a sort of deconstruction of the government into a ground zero. Both were divided into sub-factions that were often imposed by the system of clientelism. However, various processes were underway to reunite the galaxy of the opposition at a time when power was literally in the hand of President Moise.

---

26 Edwige Dandicat, *Haitians Are at an Impasse Over the Country's Future*, The New Yorker, February 19, 2021.

Mr. Moise, in his orbit, could not avoid erring at his own political detriment in making overtly a series of decisions and adopting behaviors judged inadmissible in the eyes of both his detractors and allies, in Haiti and within the international community. Among those decisions and behaviors considered as political suicide, we can recount:

1. Organizing the yearly carnival in the middle of COVID-19 as a super-spreader event.
2. Arresting and firing judges in violation of the constitution.
3. Creating a National Intelligence Agency (ANI) seen as an authoritarian tool to neutralize his opponents.
4. Excessive ruling by decree after the nonrenewal of the parliament.
5. Installing a new electoral council without consensus or legal legitimacy.
6. Pushing to unilaterally and unconstitutionally change the constitution by referendum.
7. Inaction against violence, chaos, and rampant insecurity that provoked all sorts of peculations over his allegiance to certain armed gangs (an exacerbated version of the *Tonton Macoutes*) involved in terror, kidnapping for ransom, and other criminal activities.

Under Moise's presidency, while the extraordinary accumulation of wealth continued for the political and economic elites, the majority of Haitians continued to live an economic nightmare that forced a lot of them to seek refuge elsewhere, notably in the Dominican Republic, Brazil, Chile, Mexico, the U.S., and Canada. Luxury villas, cars, and other expensive possessions had long become an emblem of the gap between Haiti's impoverished people and the political and economic elites.

The COVID-19 pandemic accentuated the already dire situation of Haiti's economy. It worsened and shrunk a further 3.8% in 2020, according to the World Bank; humanitarian needs were exacerbated, with acute childhood malnutrition among children under five. The rate of malnutrition had increased by 61%, and the admission of severely malnourished children in health facilities across Haiti jumped by 26% during the first 3 months of 2021, according to a UNICEF report. On top of that, the country's political and social woes had deepened; gang violence spiked heavily in Port-au-Prince and across major cities, inflation spiraled, and food and fuel had become scarcer in a country where 60% of the population made less than US$2 dollars a day. These troubles came as Haiti was still trying to recover from the devastating 2010 earthquake and Hurricane Matthew that struck in 2016, amid rampant corruption, the mismanagement of resources, and a lack of proper planning at all levels of government.

Despite all this, Moise, who strongly relied on the support of the international community, particularly the U.S., O.A.S., and the U.N., seemed to be winning the political war against his opposition. It appeared as if he had more than enough wind beneath his sails. He seemed to be comfortable in his position not to leave office before holding general elections at the end of 2021. He reiterated his desire of transferring the power to a duly elected successor on February 7, 2022. And he wanted to fill all the institutional vacancies that had occurred under his watch instead of stepping down, as demanded by opposition leaders.

However, the psychosis of power and the contradictions within appeared to wallop Mr. Moise. O.A.S. emissaries helped broker a proposal after a number of meetings and negotiations between Moise and opposition leaders. In agreement with a proposal concluded at the end of June 2021, President Moise accepted to let his prime minister, Claude Joseph, clear the way for a government of consensus that would include representatives of Haiti's key sectors and the opposition. He agreed to appoint a new prime minister and reconfigure the government cabinet in a compromise with the opposition.

For the prime minister job, Moise appointed Ariel Henry on July 5, 2021. Mr. Henry is a neurosurgeon and member of the opposition. The new government would oversee the organization of democratic, peaceful, and fair elections between September 2021 and January 2022. With that compromise, President Moise hoped to find peace and enable Haitians to see better days ahead.

Assassination, Intervention, and Impunity

Criminal violence had escalated in Port-au-Prince, which had been reeling from insecurity for months because of rival groups battling one another or the police for control of the streets, arsonists burning business buildings and ransacking civilian homes, and armed gangs displacing thousands of people and worsening the country's humanitarian crisis. In the morning of July 7, 2021, Haiti and Haitians living abroad woke up in shock, consternation, and soul-searching. There was no earthquake, coup d'état, or major hurricane as we have been accustomed to in terms of media attention to Haiti.

The intrigue this time for the big screen was that President Jovenel Moise had been assassinated in the middle of the night. A group of about 30 heavily armed men—a number that kept changing while investigators put together a complicated international puzzle to find the masterminds and their motives—gunned him down in solitude and abandonment. As a result of a massive manhunt orchestrated by the Haitian police immediately after the assassination, around 50 suspects, including 18 specialized Colombian killers (mercenaries), 3 Haitian Americans from South Florida, and 20 Haitian police officers, were arrested. There were 3 suspects associated with a security service company in Port-au-Prince and 3 presumed assassins killed in fights with Haitian security forces.

The assassins stormed Moise's private residence in Pelerin 5, a leafy Port-au-Prince district of Pétion-Ville (a Northeastern suburb of the capital). The assailants, posing as Drug Enforcement Administration agents, fatally wounded the head of state around 2 a.m. The Haitian president's body was found in his bedroom filled with bullet holes. The government official tasked with documenting the crime scene said that Moise had suffered a broken leg and serious facial injuries. The injuries were described as signs of torture. He was riddled with a dozen bullets. First Lady Martine Moise was also shot in the attack, but she survived after receiving emergency treatment in Haiti and then being transported to Miami, Florida for further treatment at Jackson Memorial Hospital.

Despite the abundance of bullets documented inside the president's home, not a single member of the president's security detail or residential staff was hurt. How could the mercenaries get access so easily to the president's bedroom in a multimillion-dollar mansion, escaping four different specialized security units? The crime had the smell of an inside job with the help of foreign mercenaries.

Exactly what happened inside the president's home and who masterminded the attack remained at the heart of multiple investigations involving senior agents from the United States and Colombia, in addition to local authorities. Top foreign officials, including members of the U.S. National Security Council and Colombia's chief of national intelligence, visited Haiti several times in the wake of Moise's death.

One of the 26 Colombian men allegedly involved in the assassination, Mario Antonio Palacios Palacios was arrested by U.S. authorities (6 months later) in Miami and charged in the Southern District of Florida after managing to flee Haiti. A criminal complaint, drafted by the FBI, charged Palacios with conspiracy to commit murder or kidnapping outside the United States and providing material support resulting in death, knowing that such support would be used to carry out a plot to kill the Haitian president.

According to a CNN report, Palacios previously placed himself in the president's bedroom on the morning of his death, telling Colombian weekly *Semana* in August 2021, "I don't know who killed him (Moise) because when I arrived, commanders Yepes and Romero were already there." Palacios told *Semana* that the president was already dead when he arrived at the scene. "I don't know who killed him. I'm telling you from the bottom of my heart, on my family and on my kids," he said.[27]

How Palacios managed to flee Haiti, leaving his other compatriot mercenaries behind, remained unclear. He was first captured by Jamaican authorities for entering the country illegally. He was then deported and arrested during a layover in Panama in early January 2022 instead of being extradited to Haiti. Jamaica and Haiti have no convention of extradition between them. He was subsequently extradited from Panama to Miami. The U.S. Department of Justice

---

27 Matt Rivers et al, "U.S. Charges Colombian man with conspiracy to kill Haiti's president", cnn.com, CNN, January 5, 2022. https://www.cnn.com/2022/01/05/americas/haiti-president-assassination-suspect-charged-intl/index.html

confirmed that the three countries (Panama, Columbia, and the United States) were in constant communication coordinating the suspected assassin's deportation and extradition to the U.S.

Many people, especially Haitians, expected at the time that the arrest could prove to be critical to U.S. authorities who were investigating several South Florida individuals and businesses in connection with the crime, and more importantly bring some clarity as to finding the masterminds and their motives. We may never know exactly what happened. Most of the investigation process has been concealed. Information about possible suspects has been circulated in the news outlets, leading to a lot of people raising concerns over the suspicion that the U.S. government was trying to control the narrative about the assassination. Acting Prime Minister Ariel Henry fueled that suspicion further when, in an interview to the *Miami Herald* on February 11, 2022, he disclosed his willingness to turn over key suspects held in detention in Haiti to U.S. authorities.[28] The U.S. Department of Justice has continued to argue that it has jurisdiction in the case because it says some of the alleged co-conspirators met in Miami to plot the murder.

Soon after the arrest of Mario Antonio Palacios Palacios, a series of high-profile fugitive suspects, who had been wanted in connection with the crime, were also arrested in neighboring Caribbean countries. Former Haitian Senator John Joel Joseph, who appeared on the political scene in 2004 and was elected under the late President Preval's political party banner, was apprehended in St. Elizabeth, Jamaica along with his wife and two children on January 6, 2022. To escape from arrest and prosecution in Haiti, Former Oppostion Senator John Joel Joseph

---

28 Jacqueline Charles and Jay Weaver, "Haiti prime minister says he'd hand assassination suspects to U.S.", *The Miami Herald*, Feb. 13, 2022.

was said by investigators to have paid US$12,000.00 to flee to Jamaica by boat in December 2021. Jamaican autorities extradited him to the U.S. on May 6, 2022. During his initial court apprearance in Miami on May 9, 2022, a federal judge charged Mr Joseph with conspiracy in connection with President Moise's assassination. Haitian investigators had identified Joseph as a prime suspect just days after Moise's murder. The Haitian police investigative report said he "was instrumental in his fierce will to kill the president".

One day after the arrest of Former Senator Joseph in Jamaica, Rodolphe Jaar, another high profile fugitive wanted by the prosecutors, was arrested in the Dominican Republic at the request of the FBI. He was later extradited to the U.S. where he was charged in connection to the crime. A fourth fugitive, Haitian businessman Samir Handal, who was suspected of complicity in the crime, was also arrested in Turkey on November 14, 2021.

The answers to the questions surrounding the crime are not just about justice for Moise, his family, and allies. It is mostly about Haiti. It is precisely about Haiti's continuity as a nation; the story needs to be told in a compelling way so that people truly understand who we are and what steps need to be taken so that terrible events like this one are not repeated. Moise's assassination, as terrible as it looks and as shown in this chapter, is not the worst thing that has happened in the long history of political and social struggles in Haiti. All the bad events that happened before happened because people like the ones who killed Moise continue to exist. But they do not represent the majority of Haitians. What the vast majority of Haitians wants is the projection of a better image of the country. To do that, the majority needs to come out together as better angels to foster changes and take measures preventing the minority from executing what is conceptualized in their minds.

Habitually, Port-au-Prince has never been short of all sorts of rumors. In the wake of a crime of that magnitude, hearsay news usually intensifies. Early in the aftermath of his assassination, it was rumored that the crime was directly connected to President Moise's efforts to rein in and dismantle an important narcotics and arms trafficking network in the country. This was alleged to be part of a series of broader clashes Moise had with powerful politicians and business leaders since his arrival at the helm of Haiti's supreme office. The rumor was later consolidated further by the *New York Times* in a report produced by Maria Abi-Habib citing a number of national and international sources.[29]

According to those sources familiar with the information, in the month leading to his assassination, President Moise had been working on a dossier consisting of a list of politicians and business people suspected of involvement in narcotics and illicit arms trafficking. His intention was to hand the dossier over to the government of the United States once completed. He had ordered the officials tasked to work on the dossier to spare no one, not even those who had helped propel him to power. Some of the Haitian officials who were interviewed by the *New York Times* admitted that Moise had known several powerful people for years who were supposedly on the list. They were motivated to assassinate him because they felt betrayed by him.

A few months prior to his death, Moise took some important steps to clean up Haiti's customs department, nationalize a seaport with a history of smuggling, destroy an airstrip used by drug traffickers,

---

29 Maria Abi-Habib, "Haiti's Leader Kept a List of Drug Traffickers: His Assassins Came for It", nytimes.com, The New York Times, December 12, 2021. https://www.nytimes.com/2021/12/12/world/americas/jovenel-moise-haiti-president-drug-traffickers.html/

and investigate the lucrative trade, which had long been identified as a conduit for money laundering in Haiti.

His assassination is symbolic of a failed state where the leaders continue to manufacture crises that they are unable to resolve, and disasters that they are incapable of handling, let alone natural disasters. As of February 7, 2022, Haiti had no elected leaders apart from 10 senators who have been completely out of sight since mid-January 2020, and whose term continuity has been in question. As it stands today, it is not a surprise that the country has no rule of law except the rules of scattered individuals in a chaotic society.

Moise's death created a huge distraction in regard to Haiti's fundamental issues and came against a backdrop of political instability. There is a vacuum in many key roles in the country's system of government, including the High Court of Justice, which is without a president (Judge René Sylvestre was next in line of presidential succession but died a week earlier due to COVID-19 and has not yet been replaced), and the parliament, which was effectively defunct 18 months prior. In the aftermath of Moise's death, Interim Prime Minister Claude Joseph immediately became the de facto president amid a constitutional crisis.

There was no president at Haiti's Supreme Court to take over in conformity with the constitution. According to the constitution, parliament approval is needed for the prime minister to be able to fill the vacancy. But there was no functional parliament either. Muddying the waters further, as previously indicated, Moise had just designated another prime minister in Dr. Ariel Henry, who was preparing to form his cabinet and take over from Prime Minister Joseph, who had already resigned. Dr. Henry was Moise's seventh prime minister appointment in his four years in office.

The big political dilemma was that we had two prime ministers and neither had constitutional legitimacy—one interim prime minister whose term legally expired after 30 days of his official resignation, and another one legally appointed by the President of the Republic but did not have the time to select his cabinet and be installed, and who also claimed the presidency. Addressing the nation after the assassination, Acting Prime Minister Joseph, supported by the police and the army forces, declared a state of siege, decreed 15 days of national mourning for President Moise's death, and pleaded with citizens to remain calm. He said he would stay in charge until elections could be held. But Henry, whom the president appointed (but was not installed yet) shortly before his death, told Haitian newspaper *Le Nouvelliste* on the same afternoon of July 7 that "Claude Joseph is not prime minister, he is part of my government."[30]

Another possible line of succession scenario is the precedent created in 2016 where the president of the National Assembly filled the presidential vacancy after the country failed to have an elected president to replace Joseph Michel Martelly at the end of his term. But again, the National Assembly was disbanded in mid-January 2020 after the country failed to hold legislative elections in October 2019 due to political turmoil and division among the political actors. Only a third of the Senate, practically dysfunctional, was still active and presided over by then-Senator Joseph Lambert. In a move to add more fuel to the fire, some of Mr. Lambert's fellow lawmakers nominated him on July 9, 2021, to assume the presidency ad interim without a legal quorum, making him a third figure claiming the presidential sash.

---

30 Robenson Geffrard, "Claude Joseph n'est pas premier minister: Il fait partie de mon gouvernement", lenouvelliste.com, *Le Nouvelliste*, July 9, 2021. https://lenouvelliste.com/article/230284/claude-joseph-nest-pas-premier-ministre-il-fait-partie-de-mon-gouvernement-affirme-ariel-henry

At least 2 out of the 10 active senators opposed the decision publicly. One of them, Senator Patrice Dumont, said he stood firmly against an interim government led by Claude. But he also did not sign the resolution to name a new president because he understood that such a decision could not be taken in a small room behind closed doors. He asked for a special public hearing so they could explain their rationale. In the absence of a constitutional solution to the power vacuum, political party leaders and some private-sector figures called for a political consensus among Haitians.

But Senator Lambert, infamously nicknamed "Animal Lambert" for his involvement in Haitian political theatre and tricks, as one of the kingmakers over the last two decades, wasted no time. He multiplied meetings trying to convince a small group of leaders from opposition parties, platforms, and civil organizations, including the assassinated President Moise's own party (PHTK). Some diametrically opposed parties such as RDNP, AAA, and Fusion also took part in conversations with Senator Lambert. He wanted to rally enough support behind him. Those leaders from the opposition and PHTK agreed to make Mr. Lambert provisional president and Moise's appointee Ariel Henry prime minister for a one-year term. Despite that agreement among those national leaders who said they prioritized a solution without foreign influence, all eyes were directed at the Core Group to find out whether the international community would agree and support the installation of a government led by Lambert-Henry.

Amid uncertainty and looming chaos, the U.S. was quick to say that it believed elections should go ahead as planned to bring about a peaceful transfer of power. They seemed to back continuity in any way possible, irrespective of any particular individual. The triumvirate

Joseph-Lambert-Henry had to deal with it. Meanwhile, Lambert's swearing-in ceremony that was supposed to take place in the parliament on the afternoon of Sunday July 11, 2021 was postponed sine die without much explanation to the pool of reporters waiting in the Senate.

As questions swirled about the main reason for the delay, news broke that a delegation of American officials composed of representatives from the National Security Council (NSC), the State Department, and the Department of Homeland Security had arrived in Port-au-Prince. As has been the case since the downfall of the Duvalier regime in 1986, no one would take any decision or declaration made by Haitian politicians seriously unless it was in direct line with Washington, DC. The American interagency delegation met with all three players, including Interim Prime Minister Claude Joseph as well as his challengers Appointed Prime Minister Ariel Henry and Senate President Joseph Lambert, in an open and power-sharing dialogue for a political agreement. After the meeting, the American government, through the words of Emily Horne from the NSC, reiterated that the goal of all meetings with Haitian officials was to help find a political solution that allows for the organization of free and fair elections in the country. But that did not happen. Crises kept piling on top of each other, as 2021 was a year for Haitians to forget.

Meanwhile, a platform of Haitian civil-society groups that was formed many months prior to the assassination of Moise brought together more than 300 organizations representing unions, farmers, churches, anticorruption activists, feminists, human rights organizations, and many others. These groups had met several times with the aim of releasing a plan to create a transitional governmental council to lead the country temporarily. The meetings resulted in the formation of the

Commission for a Haitian-Led Solution.[31] The commission planned to convene a political conference in Port-au-Prince on the weekend preceding Henry's inauguration announcement. The conference would have begun earlier, but hotels refused to provide space. Many participants received pushback from political leaders across the arena. The commission's work was seen as a threat to the political class. It was also considered as a threat to the holding of rushed elections. In fact, the decision to choose a leader for the country had long been a foregone conclusion.

A statement published on Saturday July 17, 2021 by the Core Group did all but confirm that assertion. In their statement, the Core Group called for Prime Minister Ariel Henry to form a new government and organize presidential elections "as quickly as possible."[32] Many observers saw in the Core Group's statement a snub to parts of the opposition, which openly opposed Henry, and to the civil society commission, which had advocated a transitional government that could oversee needed reforms, restore some semblance of faith in the government, and oversee truly free and fair elections. Wishful thinking!

As early as Monday morning July 19, 2021, news broke that Acting Prime Minister Claude Joseph would step down and hand power over to Henry. Joseph, who initially vowed, and appeared to be backed by foreign actors, to lead the country until presidential and legislative elections take place, accepted, begrudgingly perhaps, to retain the

---

31 Jake Johnston, "Haitians don't need another President chosen behind closed doors", prospect.org, The American Prospect, July 19, 2021. https://prospect.org/world/haitians-dont-need-another-president-chosen-behind-closed-doors/

32 Haiti Libre, "Turnaround of Core Group in Favor of PM named Ariel Henry", haitilibre.com, Haiti Libre. https://www.haitilibre.com/en/news-34260-haiti-flash-turnaround-of-core-group-in-favor-of-the-pm-named-ariel-henry.html

previously held position of foreign minister in Henry's government. And to justify his big and quick U-turn, Joseph said, "I just decided to transfer power to him because he was the last wish of the president, even though the process was not completed."[33] Henry, with the blessing of the international community, was sworn in on July 20, 2021, without a president but with a new cabinet negotiated behind closed doors. To those who were asking, Henry responded, "We do not need a president until the elections take place."[34]

However, Prime Minister Henry became logically the de facto president of Haiti. In his inaugural speech, Henry promised (with the exception of late-President Moise's controversial constitutional referendum project thrown into the oubliette) to maintain the former government priorities, including restoring a climate of security, pursuing the organization of general elections, and relaunching the economy wrecked by violent crimes and the COVID-19 pandemic.

Whether or not the compromise between Claude Joseph and Ariel Henry, and particularly the spectacular disappearance of Senator Joseph Lambert from the political equation, was done under the influence of the Core Group is of minimal importance at best in the Haitian context. The fact that these leaders were quickly able to avoid a deeper crisis even with the perception that international actors were once again putting their fingers on the political scale was huge for the country. By accepting

---

33 Anthony Faiola, "Haiti's acting prime minister Claude Joseph says he will step down amid leadership dispute", washingtonpost.com, The Washington Post, July 19, 2021. https://www.washingtonpost.com/world/2021/07/19/haiti-claude-joseph-ariel-henry/

34 Robenson Geffrard, "Pour Ariel Henry, il n'y aura pas de President au Palais national avant les elections", lenouvelliste.com, *Lenouvelliste,* January 17, 2022. https://lenouvelliste.com/article/233696/pour-ariel-henry-il-ny-aura-pas-de-president-au-palais-national-avant-les-elections

a political solution, even without the participation of the majority of Haitians, to a multifaceted crisis without further complicating things, they demonstrated for once a little more of the courage, abnegation, unselfishness, clairvoyance, patriotism, and statesmanship so needed on the land of Dessalines. Usually, in a situation like that, Haitians would take months arguing childishly without an outcome in sight.

The fragile compromise seemed to be a response to some of the short-term questions about the continuity of President Moise's assassination investigation, executive authority, electoral process, safety, security across towns, and more personally for Haitians about their daily struggles to make ends meet; but a more long-term question remained. And that was, even before the assassination of Jovenel Moise, how does Haiti get rebuilt democratically, socially, and economically?

The answer to that question will never be easy. But one thing remains for certain. No serious rebuilding effort should start with more closed-door meetings among national elites and representatives of foreign powers with the influence of expensive Washington, DC lobbyists. The vast majority of the Haitian people deserve to have a say in their own destiny. That has always been the sense of their fight.

Agreements reached or decisions made behind a closed door, like the one that led to the inauguration of Ariel Henry as new head of state with two hats (de facto prime minister and chief executive) at the expense of legality, legitimacy, and representativity for durable peace and public good, are not always the subject of sensational reporting in mainstream international media—just an announcement in a few media outlets and all went on quietly. Most international news media are often waiting for more drama, violence, tragedy, death, and chaos to reappear suddenly, and start reporting about Haiti. And their reporting is often in relation to politics. This partly explains why most reports on Haiti's issues in Western media are barely deep, without clichés and prejudices. Their pursuit of incentives to stay on the ground is in contrast with the interest of Haitians, and their picture of Haiti is conjectural. We have seen that movie so many times that many people watching from outside of Haiti have become numb to it by thinking that Haiti mostly produces chaos, tragedies, and disasters.

On the afternoon following the assassination of President Moise, the *Washington Post* editorial board published an opinion piece pushing for an international military intervention in Haiti. The idea was met with disdain among most Haitians and immediately rebuked by a number of Haiti's foreign sympathizers and scholars, notably on social media, pointing out how the country had been burdened with the legacy and painful memories of different international military interventions. Apart from sexual abuse and the exploitation of women, which increases the number of single mothers and fatherless children in the society, exacerbates corruptions, teaches all sorts of vices to young people, divides families, spreads disease like cholera, leads to the uncontrolled exploitation of natural and environmental resources, and contributes to a lot of money being spent in operations and lifestyles, the different military interventions did very little for Haiti.

Usually, at their arrival, the foreign forces provide a false sense of security and social stability with sporadic calm in the country. Once they leave, things become worse than they were before their interventions. One of the main problems is that the approach of the international community has not sufficiently taken into account the weakness of Haiti's institutions for their necessary and useful reform and reinforcement.

Three major U.S. military occupations in less than 89 years and different U.N. peacekeeping missions between 1993 and 2019 did not mean any significant form of progress for Haiti. But the *Washington Post* editorial board argued, "The country needs elections to produce a government that would be seen as legitimate in the eyes of most Haitians. The hard truth, at this point, is that organizing them and ensuring security through a campaign and polling, with no one in charge, may be all but impossible. To prevent a meltdown that could have dire consequences, the United States and other influential parties—including France, Canada and the Organization of American States—should push for an international peacekeeping force, probably organized by the United Nations, that could provide the security necessary for presidential and parliamentary elections to go forward this year, as planned."[35]

The mere idea of foreign military assistance to Haiti makes most people who are concerned about the country's welfare feel aghast. Haitians have mixed views about foreign military intervention. On the one hand, they see it as a way to shore up security and stability in times of unrest and standstill. On the other hand, most Haitians view foreign forces on home soil as an insult to the warriors of independence. They also consider it as a sign of being incapable of self-governing; they need some sort of guardianship from time to time. Another reason for fuss about foreign military interventions in Haiti is that past interventions had left a legacy of human rights and sexual abuses, exploitation of national resources, increased debt for Haiti, and a weaker state, among other consequences. But the truth is most Haitian leaders always work

35 Editorial Board, "Haiti needs swift and muscular international intervention", washingtonpost.com, The Washington Post, July 7, 2021. https://www.washingtonpost.com/opinions/2021/07/07/assassination-its-president-puts-haiti-risk-anarchy-un-must-intervene/

hard to create messes that they are unable to fix themselves—messes that often put them in hot water and leave them begging for foreign help.

While some human rights activists were furious about the suggestion of military intervention in Haiti on social media networks, Acting Prime Minister Claude Joseph confirmed in an interview with CNN's Eleni Giokos that he had spoken to the U.S. Secretary of State Antony Blinken about the United States' support for Haiti. Joseph said that he had asked for technical assistance for the Haitian National Police (PNH) so that they could secure the population, help track down some gangs, and also help the country hold elections.

U.S. State Department spokesperson Ned Price also confirmed that the Haitian National Police requested investigative assistance. And at the U.N. Security Council in New York, Special Representative of the Secretary-General for Haiti Helen La Lime confirmed to reporters that Mr. Joseph made a request for additional security assistance to the council in a closed briefing. And on July 9, during a press briefing, the White House Press Secretary Jen Psaki confirmed to reporters that FBI and U.S. Homeland Security officials would travel to Haiti "as soon as possible," where they would assess the situation and provide assistance on security and the investigation.

Jen Psaki took the time to outline existing U.S. assistance to Haiti, including the State Department Bureau of International Narcotics and Law Enforcement's direct assistance to the PNH on gang violence and community intervention, the Department of Homeland Security's extension of the Temporary Protected Status (TPS) to Haitians (an estimated 100,000 to 150,000) for 18 months, and the donation of vaccines against COVID-19. Even though the Biden administration fell short of confirming the deployment of U.S. forces in Haiti at the time, some American media networks were parading with the cause supported by France and other foreign powers. Various media outlets were reporting words from Haiti's government officials requesting that the U.S. send troops to help stabilize the country and secure critical infrastructure like oil reserves and its ports and airports.

The Biden administration went from "we have no plan to provide military assistance at this time," to "as for their requests, we are aware of it at the Pentagon, we are reviewing it" (Pentagon Spokesman John F. Kirby told reporters).[36] It only took them about three days to shift their position from the initial rebuff of the Haitian government's request for U.S. troops. As time went by, the Biden administration, which announced the end of U.S. military engagement in Afghanistan by August 31, 2021, did not show any real appetite for another intervention in Haiti. Instead, all signals from senior State Department officials pointed toward more diplomatic, logistical, financial, and technical assistance.

By July 22, 2021, the State Department had appointed Daniel L. Foote, a career member of the Senior Foreign Service, as its Special Envoy for Haiti. In a press statement made public by Spokesperson Ned Price, the U.S. government indicated in full detail Ambassador Foote's mission. The U.S. Department of State's website said, "The Special Envoy will engage with Haitian and international partners to facilitate long-term peace and stability and support efforts to hold free and fair presidential and legislative elections. He will also work with partners to coordinate assistance efforts in several areas, including humanitarian, security, and investigative assistance."

---

36 Jake Dima, "Pentagon Analyzing Haiti's request for U.S. Troops after Assassination", washingtonexaminer.com, Washington Examiner, July 11, 2021. https://www.washingtonexaminer.com/news/pentagon-analyzing-haiti-request-us-troops

"Additionally, the Special Envoy will engage stakeholders in civil society and the private sector as we pursue Haitian-led solutions to the many pressing challenges facing Haiti. The Special Envoy will, along with the U.S. Ambassador to Haiti, lead U.S. diplomatic efforts and coordinate the effort of U.S. federal agencies in Haiti from Washington, advise the Secretary and Acting Assistant Secretary for the Bureau of Western Hemisphere Affairs, and coordinate closely with the National Security Council staff on the administration's efforts to support the Haitian people and Haiti's democratic institutions in the aftermath of the tragic assassination of Jovenel Moise."[37] But the *Washington Post* would continue to persist in their view that a new military invasion was the necessary means to solve the country's problems. "Haiti needs elections—and outside forces to make them safe," pushed by the *Washington Post* in another opinion piece published later on.[38]

But the appointment of Daniel L. Foote as the U.S. Special Envoy to Haiti backfired as a result of the U.S. policy of hubris toward the country. Ambassador Foote occupied the position for only two months. He resigned on September 22, 2021, citing political intervention to undercut his works and the inhumane deportation of Haitian migrants from the U.S.-Mexico border. In his resignation letter addressed to the Secretary of State Antony Blinken and published all over social media on the morning of Thursday September 23, 2021, Mr. Foote plainly

---

37 Ned Price, "Announcement of Daniel Foote as Special Envoy for Haiti", state.gov, U.S. Department of State, July 22, 2021. https://www.state.gov/announcement-of-daniel-foote-as-special-envoy-for-haiti/

38 Editorial Board, "Haiti needs elections and outside forces to make them safe", washingtonpost.com, The Washington Post, July 27, 2021. https://www.washingtonpost.com/opinions/2021/07/27/haiti-needs-elections-outside-forces-make-them-safe/

expressed his frustration and made sure people got a glance of what had been wrong with the U.S. policy in Haiti.

Former Ambassador Foote started by saying, "With deep disappointment and apologies to those seeking crucial changes, I resign from my position . . . I will not be associated with the United States [the United States'] inhumane, counterproductive decision to deport thousands of Haitian refugees and illegal migrants to Haiti, a country where American officials are confined to secure compounds because of the danger posed by armed gangs in control of daily life. Our policy approach to Haiti remains flawed, and my recommendations have been ignored, dismissed, when not edited to project a narrative different from my own. The people of Haiti mired in poverty, hostage to the terror, kidnappings, robberies and massacre of armed gangs and suffering under a corrupt government with gang alliances, simply cannot support the forced infusion of thousands returned migrants, lacking food, shelter, and money without additional, avoidable human tragedy." In his opinion, Haiti as a collapsed state has been unable to provide security or basic services, and more refugees would fuel further desperation and crime. He saw the U.S. deportation policy as a way of adding to the Haitians' unacceptable misery.

Mr. Foote's reading of Haiti's situation at the time was that the country needed immediate assistance to restore the government's ability to neutralize the gangs and restore order through the national police. They needed a true agreement across society and political actors, with international support, to chart a timely path to the democratic selection of their next president and parliament. He expressed the desire to see the Haitians receive enough humanitarian assistance, money to deliver COVID vaccines, and many other crucial things.

But at the same time, Mr. Foote recognized, what Haitians themselves really wanted, and needed, was the opportunity to chart their own course, without international puppeteering and favored candidates but with genuine support for that course. Ending his letter, he stated the obvious by saying, "The cycle of international political interventions in Haiti has consistently produced catastrophic results. More negative impacts to Haiti will have calamitous consequences not only in Haiti, but in the U.S. and our neighbors in the hemisphere."

In Port-au-Prince, the rumor was swirling around and made people believe that the real friction between Daniel Foote and the Biden administration was the fact that the latter had rejected, at least at the time, the idea of a U.S. military intervention in Haiti. It was an option, according to a number of people familiar with the situation, which former Ambassador Foote would have seen as necessary if the United States truly wanted to help resolve the multifaceted crisis in Haiti. In response and to turn the page on the former Special Envoy, the United States sent a high-level delegation to Haiti.

The delegation included Brian Andrew Nicolls, who was the Assistant Secretary of State for Western Hemisphere Affairs, and Juan Sebastian Gonzalez, the Special Assistant to President Biden and Senior Director of the National Security Council (NSC) for the Western Hemisphere. They were charged to listen to the Haitian people for a better understanding of how to proceed, according to U.S. Deputy Secretary of State Wendy R Sherman during an interview with the *Miami Herald*.[39]

After arriving in Haiti, the U.S. special delegation met with Prime Minister Henry and representatives of political parties and civil-society

39 Kevin McClatchy, "State's Sherman: Envoy wanted to send in U.S. Military", The Miami Herald, September 30, 2021.

organizations on September 30, 2021. According to the U.S. Embassy in Port-au-Prince, the two high-level American diplomats discussed the need for a broadly inclusive political solution, democratic elections, the response to Haitian migration, security, support and rebuilding following the August 14 earthquake, and the COVID-19 pandemic.

Soon after the U.S. Special Envoy left Haiti, the State Department announced Ambassador Kenneth Merten's return to Haiti as Chargé d'Affaires. The official appointment was made public on a Twitter post by Secretary of State Antony Blinken on October 12, 2021. In his note, Secretary Blinken stated, "The United States is a steadfast partner to Haiti, and we remain committed to supporting the Haitian people." The move indicated that the United States did not intend to change the policy in Haiti despite the former Special Envoy's ire and the media campaign of those allied to his position concerning the situation in Haiti, where there had been no shortage of crises. A week prior to Mr. Merten's appointment, Daniel Foote once again criticized the U.S. policy in Haiti during his testimony in front of the U.S. Congress, saying the United States had basically chosen the country's last two presidents. He said it was time for a change.[40]

However, the Biden administration announced the return of a diplomat involved in both those events. Kenneth Merten served as a U.S. ambassador to Haiti from August 2009 to July 2012 and acted as the U.S. special coordinator for Haiti from August 2015 to October 2021 in the Bureau of Western Hemisphere Affairs. In the meantime, Under Secretary of State Uzra Zeya visited Haiti. Her mission seemed to aim at bolstering Ambassador Merten's confidence ahead of his return to the scene.

---

40 Ryan Devereaux, "Haiti Envoy Who Resigned: No Body Asked me about the Deportations", theintercept.com, The Intercept, October 7, 2021. https://theintercept.com/2021/10/07/haiti-migrants-daniel-foote/

During her visit, Under Secretary Zeya met with Prime Minister Henry and all the major national and international players in Haiti. She reiterated the U.S. government's pledge to support inclusive political dialogue among Haitians—actions that allow for the reinforcement of security, fight against corruption, and the reinforcement of democratic governance. The American diplomat also confirmed the engagement of the Biden-Harris administration in providing the Haitian government with an additional $15 million in financial support to their efforts to reduce gang violence and ameliorate the country's penitentiary infrastructures. Following up with Ambassador Zeya's diplomatic tour, the Assistant Secretary of State for International Narcotics and Law Enforcement Affairs Todd Robinson (another high-profile visitor to the Haitian capital) arrived on November 8, 2021. The mantra for the U.S. diplomats was and remained the dismantlement of the armed gangs in Haiti and the eradication of the main causes of their affiliations.

When in mid-October 2021, a group of North American missionaries and their families, including 16 Americans and one Canadian, were abducted by a powerful gang while returning from an orphanage based in Gauthier, an area east of Port-au-Prince, many people believed that the table was turned and a U.S. military intervention in Haiti was imminent. The missionaries, who came from different Amish, Mennonite, and other Anabaptist communities working with Ohio-based agency Christian Aid Ministries (CAM), were held captive for two months by the notorious gang called 400 Mawozo. The hostages spent two months in captivity before they could escape their captors without the appearance of the United States government's direct involvement. A group of 5 were released days ahead before the other 12 made a daring overnight escape by eluding their captors and walking for miles over difficult terrain full of brambles and briars. They navigated by stars and moonlight to reach safety.

Many Haitians believed that the kidnappers let their captives go after receiving a hefty ransom, maybe millions of dollars, as has usually been the case for quite some time now in Haiti. Others thought that the missionaries just found a way to escape from their captors. Whether or not either one of those two assumptions were true is left up for debate in the absence of tangible proof. CAM director general David Troyer confirmed for Associated Press that supporters of the agency did raise money for possible use for a ransom, but he did not say if one was paid for the release of any of the missionaries.[41] However, one obvious thing is that the U.S. government did not intervene to rescue them in spite of pleas coming from everywhere and the fact that the Biden administration had shown no appetite for U.S. military intervention in Haiti.

It all looked suspicious and had the smell of a political theatre. Up to that point, American citizens had always been off-limits to gang members who appeared as the de facto rulers of Haiti since the assassination of President Jovenel Moise. As the gangs were negotiating with the captives' families and demanding millions of dollars in ransom in exchange for their release, the FBI agents, who had been present in Haiti since the abduction of the missionaries and were giving guidance to the Haitian government, seemed surprised by the events surrounding the liberation of the hostages on the weekend of December 18–19, 2021. It appeared that they had no clue about what happened and how it happened.

Calls from the Haitian authorities for a U.S. military intervention or US-UN military assistance had been rejected in Washington, DC,

---

41 Peter Smith, "Agency: Haiti Missionaries Made 'Daring' Escape to Evade Kidnappers", christianitytoday.com, The Associated Press, December 20, 2021. https://www.christianitytoday.com/news/2021/december/haiti-missionaries-escape-kidnap-gang-christian-aid-ministr.html

which was said to be trying to instead convince other countries like France, the United Kingdom, and Canada to help shore up security and resolve the multifaceted crisis in Haiti. Some people saw in the whole kidnapping ordeal as a setup event to create more pretexts for a U.S. military intervention. But in the end, after two months of unsuccessful maneuvering, those begging for U.S. military assistance in Haiti allegedly became hopeless and the gate to let the captives go free was left wide open.

Regardless of opinions and speculations, the political struggles continued amid fights for control between different factions in the country where a multitude of small parties and political groups could not find common ground for a modus operandi. Everyone wanted a solution made in Haiti and by Haitians. But it has always been difficult to conclude on what exactly the solution should look like and on the mechanism of its implementation in a satisfying way to most people. The more closed-door meetings among different actors, the more confused the population was. Propositions of solutions were flying everywhere, from every corner, with no actual materialization of a real national consensus. Moise's assassination seemed to serve as an engine to reunite some politicians and leaders of civil-society organizations who saw in the late president a common ally or foe. At the same time, however, it also created deeper divisions within the political class, as everyone was trying to seize the opportunity to get either a piece of the pie or the whole pie for themselves alone. Diehard Moise allies broke rank with leaders of the assassinated president's party (PHTK), whom they saw as traitors for their presumed involvement in the assassination.

Among the dissidents are Rénald Lubérice, the former secretary general of the Council of Ministries under late President Moise, both Prime Ministers Claude Joseph and Ariel Henry, and the popular singer-turned-politician Jacques Sauveur Jean. Lubérice not only resigned from his position in the government cabinet but also left the Parti Haitien Tèt Kale led by Line Baltazar, whose name was floated among several other political figures listed by investigators as one of the possible intellectual suspects in the killing of Moise. He argued in his resignation letter published in mid-September 2021 that he could not in good conscience serve in a government led by someone who was accused of involvement in the killing of a president who named him prime minister two days before the assassination took place. He was referring to Dr. Ariel Henry, whom Port-au-Prince's chief prosecutor Bed-Ford Claude was seeking to charge in connection with the assassination.

The morning of the assassination, investigators found records of telephone conversations between Henry and Joseph Félix Badio, one of the prime runaway suspects in the hunt by law enforcement authorities to find a mastermind and motive. Henry denied involvement in the plot. But Mr. Luberice announced a new political movement named in French Rassemblement des Jovenelistes pour la Democratie (RJD), which can be translated as Rally of Jovenelists for Democracy. His new party consists of some allies, friends, and close relatives of the late president.

Former Senator Jacques Sauveur Jean, who was another ally, preferred to go a separate way by creating his own political party after announcing that he was leaving PHTK, a party which he had cofounded along with twenty other leaders, including his fellow musician-singer-turned-president, Joseph Michel Martelly. Former Senator Jean's party named Parti des Artistes et des Paysans (PAP)—Party of Artists and Peasants—was added as one more to the list of hundreds of political parties and organizations already existing at least by name in the country, like Lubérice's RJD. The PAP's mission statement or motto could not be more unequivocal and less xenophobic. It is read in French as *Prospérité dans un pays nègre, par les nègres et pour le nègres*, which can be literally translated into English as prosperity in a negro country by and for the negroes.[42]

With that mission statement, and using controversial word "negro," Jean seems to reignite the debate on the question of color in Haiti, where more than 95% of people are blacks, the vast majority of which are impoverished. The former senator, who is from northeastern Haiti like late president Jovenel Moise, vowed to continue the fight orchestrated by the assassinated president to, according to him, restructure Haiti in line with its African roots and make prosperity accessible to the large majority through an equitable distribution system. The former senator, born in 1967 to a former military serviceman and a peasant mother, was raised by his maternal grandparents, who were peasants, during the Duvalier regime. He has been devoted to defending the peasants and the underprivileged majority as an artist, entrepreneur, businessman, and politician. He is proud to be called a *noiriste* in reference to his fight for a new system that favors black people.

Amid criticism from left to right, confusion, divisions, and the creation of more political parties, the majority of leaders opposed to late President Moise found a political agreement with de facto Prime Minister Henry on September 11, 2021. The terms of that consensus required notably the replacement of the Provisional Electoral Council (CEP) installed by Moise before pursuing the electoral process and the reshuffling of the government to make it more representative of the parties involved in the negotiations.

---

42 In Haiti, the connotation of the word negro changes depending on who uses it and the context where it is used. For instance, a Haitian activist may self-identify as negro to exhibit pride of their African roots. In contrast, another person may derogatively use the same word to insult someone else.

With Henry, those who fought hard against Jovenel Moise and his allies for control found the political opening. In fact, first there was the decree published by Henry to dismiss the CEP, and then by the end of November there was the recomposition of the ministerial cabinet led by Henry. The new cabinet installed on November 24, 2021, consisted of 18 ministers, of whom only 2 members, including Henry himself, were chosen by assassinated President Moise. For the remaining 16 members, they were all handpicked by leaders representing interest groups and parties vehemently opposed to Jovenel Moise.[43]

The constant fight among elites and political leaders for positions in government, to share the cake as Haitians often put it, instead of seeking real consensus for durable solutions is precisely Haiti's dilemma. Groups of every stripe have been calling for compromise among Haitians to change the country's fate. But we have yet to find a genuine agreement on our own that aims to profoundly address Haiti's complex and overlapping issues. Monique Clesca, a member of a society-civil commission to search for a Haitian solution, stated in a piece published by the *New York Times* on December 1, 2021, "Perhaps the Biden administration and other foreign leaders feel they are doing what's best for Haiti by standing behind Mr. Henry. They are actually standing in the way of what's right: letting Haitians save our own country."[44]

On the one hand, Ms. Clesca is right that it is indeed in Haitians' best interest to be the ones saving Haiti. That is exactly what Haiti

43 Robenson Geffrard, "La Composition du Cabinet Ministériel d'Ariel Henry après Remaniement", Le Nouvelliste, November 26, 2021. https://lenouvelliste.com/article/232847/la-composition-du-cabinet-ministeriel-dariel-henry-apres-le-remaniement

44 Monique Clesca, "My Group Can Save Haiti. [:] Biden Standing in Our Way", nytimes.com, The New York Times, December 1, 2021. https://www.nytimes.com/2021/12/01/opinion/haiti-commission-government.html?partner=IFTTT

needs in order to emerge from the state of perpetual transition, massive corruption, impunity, violence, human rights abuse, unequal social justice, irresponsibility, and unaccountability. It is up to Haitians to complete these tasks. No foreign leader would do them for Haiti. Why would they, anyway?

On the other hand, by saying "My group can save Haiti. Biden is standing in our way," Ms. Clesca, who is a long-time human rights activist and former U.N. official, is particularly daring and pretentious at best. For as inclusive in appearance her commission to find a Haitian-led solution to Haiti's crisis looks on paper, it is functionally not different from pretty much all other failed post-Duvalier and Aristide coalitions. To repeat the words attributed to the highly decorated U.S. Army General Norman Schwarzkopf, "The truth of the matter is that you always know the right thing to do. The hard part is doing it."[45]

Firstly, no particular one group can pretend to have the definite solution for Haiti's problems. Clesca's group is not that perfect. Like a myriad of other groups and coalitions in both the past and present, her commission suffers from the deficit of a deeper soul-searching and broader representativity necessary to gain the national permission for its leadership authority. Secondly, her view of Haiti's conundrum is too simplistic. She plays directly into the hands of people who think that everything starts and ends with the government of the United States. It is a blame game that continues to hide more complex issues among Haitians themselves and their inability to find a tenable breakthrough.

Blaming Washington for everything that is wrong with Haitian politics may give interest groups and some individuals a podium, both

45 This quote is written on the wall dedicated to the U.S. Army General at the Liberty International Airport in Newark, New Jersey.

nationally and internationally, but it does not yet help advance Haiti's cause. This excuse has continuously contributed to give Washington more power and control over Haiti's political psychology. The fact that the Biden administration shows support for the actual de facto prime minister does not preclude Haitians sitting together and seeking a more viable and durable solution to their country's problems. If Biden is effectively standing in the way of Haiti's well-being, he can be pushed away by Haitians with great leadership and real solidarity among them. No force is stronger than sincere unity behind a common purpose.

From Trump to Biden, Washington vowed its support to Jovenel Moise, but it could not or did not help him implement his different controversial plans, let alone help stop his assassination. The Biden administration also showed support for Claude Joseph, who became the de facto chief executive minutes after the breaking news of Moise's death. But days later that support was not only eroded; Joseph, who got the consolation prize by retaining the minister of foreign affairs position in Henry's cabinet, was also dismissed from the government altogether a few months later when the cabinet was once again shuffled. Naturally, most relations in politics are temporary and are functions of the balance of power. Haitian leaders tend to forget about that factor very quickly.

Chapter Two

The Power of Betrayal and Hate

Betrayal and hate have always been part of politics and social discourse in the world. Haitians certainly did not create these old demons. They are politico-social viruses that no specific country or society is immune to. Frankly, no system can boast having the means to completely root out betrayal and hate within. There will always be fringe elements and extremism everywhere because of the imperfect nature of human beings. Imperfection, whenever it is not minimized, is deemed to be detrimental to mankind. But human nature is not just a sum of imperfections.

The better angels in us make us equally capable of good, and this happens more often than not. The only difference in the Haitian context is that, for the most part of our history, we have seemed to be incapable of finding a durable breakthrough. The bad side of human nature seems to have run its course for far too long without a reprieve. In Haiti, betrayal and hate tend to be the norm in politics, and have their effects on all aspects of the society as a whole. Political allies turn against each other more quickly than they change their shirts. Their constant quarrels and infighting, not their ideological contradictions, have given rise to a multitude of small parties and political factions. More often, the vast majority of those political organizations have no difference in ideologies or principles.

Since everyone is protecting themselves against betrayal, it looks easier for each individual to run their own party, even with very few or no affiliate members at all. Why not? But everyone pretends to be the leader who talks on behalf of the Haitian people. Everyone claims to have received legitimacy and a mandate from the people naturally. They want to be trusted but they do not trust anyone other than themselves, not even the people in their own circles. They cannot wait for anyone to govern because they do not want to be governed.

They want to be governors even if they do not know how to govern. Socially, the different groups, like in all sides of the political spectrum, seem to equally live in a permanent state of distrust among themselves, which is a social context favorable to the practice of hatred toward one another.

In this chapter, we look to underline the root cause of that problem, and how different efforts and initiatives to create a more coherent and united nation to date have always been short-lived.

Not discounting external factors, behaviors and attitudes within the Haitian society deeply rooted in betrayal and hate have also contributed, in no small part, to impede the democratic progress and socioeconomic development in Haiti. Yet, unity and love, when given the slimmest chance and possibility, have always proved to be very important in our quest for quality changes.

2.1: A Nation Built on Distrust

Haitians have been carrying bitterness and resentment inside of them, and mainly against each other, for so long. Most people recognize that we will not be able to build the dream nation-state with that current state of being. The consensus among Haitians of all backgrounds is that we must deal with one another more positively. But it is easier said than done. There is a saying in Haiti that echoes the sentiment of distrust felt by Haitians toward one another in general.

In the Haitian language, you often hear people say *depi nan ginen nèg rayi nèg* ("negroes hated each other all the way back from Guinea, Africa) to explain the reason behind acts of hatred or betrayal. It is another way of saying that hatred and betrayal in Haiti originated all the way back from African tribal societies, from which the large majority of Haitians are directly descended. To the adepts of this theory, slavery was possible greatly because Africans of different tribes turned against each other in favor of European slave traders, in exchange for a little something or nothing. According to them, the very construction of the Haitian society would be based on the scars of betrayal from tribal struggles.

In other words, according to that theory, betrayal and hate are fundamental to the basis of the Haitian society, and things are predestined to stay the way they are. While there may be some, perhaps very little, historical elements of truth in that idea, it is too dubiously simplistic to consider those elements as permanently unshakable. That idea is suspiciously crafted and wrapped into the old racist theory that black people are incapable of maintaining harmony among themselves and are therefore incapable of governing. The same reasoning made us believe that the leadership of white people was needed to prevent blacks from killing each other. This too, from the Willie Lynch's playbook, has contributed to exacerbating distrust and divisions among people and creating conditions for imperialist dependence and domination. That simplistic view of the root cause of discords among Haitians deserves to be forcefully rebuked and revolutionized.

To break with that theory, which has held black people hostage for so long, we should reverse it by saying Haiti is made of Haitians who must love each other. Otherwise, we will all suffer the consequences. The January 2010 earthquake reminded us of this reality. The quake did not choose who to strike in Port-au-Prince. The losses were collective. Haitian comedian Jesifra illustrates that viewpoint well in his theatrical satire entitled *Pourquoi pas l'Union des Noires et des Mulâtres avant la Fin.*[46]

Love is the only force capable of trumping hate and its corollaries. Furthermore, hate is not genetic. It is a venom acquired within societies. It is important for any people-group to understand that love and education can set the pace for eradicating hate among them. If it is true that most Haitians' ancestors were from Guinea (Africa) as suggested in the above theory, that was over 500 hundred years ago. The more than 11 million Haitians living in Haiti in addition to another 3.5 million living abroad have never lived in Africa.

Things are more complex in Haiti than just what the above theory suggests. This complexity that can be understood by comprehending the country's long and rich history of social and economic contradictions. First, there were the transatlantic slaves trade and the conditions of slavery itself. Then, there were the slave fights to free themselves and overturn the whole slavery system. And lastly, there came the independence and the struggles to maintain it, and above all, to create a just and equitable society in its political, economic, and social structures.

Stakeholders of diverse interests have everlastingly been clashing over the process, generating deep divides that have not been reconciled to date. The agreement necessary among the population as a whole to favor the establishment of sound institutions capable of guaranteeing progressive continuity has never been realized. Every attempted solution has been and remains today temporary and shallow. The very

---

46 Jesifra, whose real name is Fernel Valcourt, is a contemporary Haitian comedian who uses theater scenes to depict the harsh and vivid reality of the Haitian society. In *Pourquoi pas l'Union des Noirs et des Mulâtres avant la Fin*, he preconizes unity and love among the two major race groups in Haiti: blacks and mulattoes.

construction of the nation has been based not on collective forces, but on providentialism, individual charisma, and heroism. It seems like Haitians have always been looking or waiting for that next leader who alone could bring about change—someone who would be capable of resolving all problems in record time. That is how we have created an environment favorable to a legacy of authoritarians and despots with little to no belief in democratic institutions. The same leaders who promote democracy in words are, in their actions, the very enemy of such a system.

Additionally, the slavery system, for its long and brutal reign, dehumanized people and forced them to treat each other as enemies even though they were facing the same harsh treatments from slave owners. The masters would strategically make one slave turn against another in exchange for favor or good grace. In addition to putting slaves in charge as supervisors of others to give them a false sense of leadership and superiority over their peers, the planters would encourage slaves to be obedient, to tell on each other. Anyone who was accused of anything was punished harsher than the accuser. That was textbook intimidation and division, enough to create fear and orchestrate grudges among them.

The division sowed by slave owners got the better of the enslaved blacks and held the system together for longer. The revolutionary battles could have been shorter if it were not for a number of betrayals among the slaves, who were always in rebellion to get rid of the slavery system. The first important slave uprising against the system took place in 1679 when the Padrejean insurrection burst in the Northwestern part of the colony.[47] And several outbreaks periodically and unsuccessfully took place through 1789. A real breakthrough did not happen until black leaders, who were from runaway families often referred to as maroon

47 Rhodner Orisma, From Revolution to Chaos in Haiti (Columbia, SC: Xlibris, 2020), p. 38.

negroes—some of whom had never known slavery—got into the mix to forge unity and provide the slaves with the necessary psychosociological strength through all sorts of fights against the colonists.

By 1791, the Mackandal's prophecy of black slaves overthrowing the system and becoming free was on its way to being accomplished. Several historians revealed that François Mackandal, famously known as the foreleader of the "marronage movement," had organized a meeting to mobilize and raise awareness for the revolution. At some point during the meeting, he grabbed three scarves: one yellow, one white, and the other black. He plunged them into a vase and pulled them out one by one in the order of yellow, white, and black to express what was going to happen in the hierarchy of the socio-politico-economic structure in the colony in the near future. When he pulled the yellow out, he said it represented the former inhabitants of the land, the Tainos. Then, he pulled out the white scarf and indicated that it was representing the white masters of Saint-Domingue who were considered as the aristocracy above the mulattoes (*affranchis* or free colored people), who were the second class. And finally, he pulled out the black scarf and implied that it was the symbol of the bottom class made up of the black slaves, who consisted of the majority of the population.

Mackandal pointed out that these enslaved people would be soon liberated. They would sweep away the entire system and gain control of the lands, the properties, and the colony, and reorganize the production system for their benefits equally.

In making its way to fulfillment, Mackendal's prediction of revolution was achieved in 1804. But his vision of the new order to come was artificially modified by the course of history and the forces engaged in making that history.

First of all, there was the French Revolution of 1789, which guaranteed human rights and equality for all. Then, the 1791 general slave revolt conditioned the climax of the slave liberation movement. These two events contributed to convince the free colored people (the second class of citizens) to claim equality with the white masters and to ally with the black slaves, whom they had no profound empathy for, in order to fulfill their ambitions.

Even though the mulattoes were half black, half white, they tended to identify themselves more with the white Europeans than with the black African descents. Even if it was at a lesser degree, they owned properties and slaves like the whites and received their education in Europe. What the mulattoes missed in privilege was abysmal in comparison to the demands of the poor black slaves. But together with the black people, they had one common enemy in the white colonists, who also wanted autonomy from France in light of the French Revolution.

While black people demanded liberation from the slavery system installed by white people, mulattoes demanded equality with whites socially, economically, and politically. The alliance between blacks and mulattoes would be later revealed as suicidal for the majority of blacks. But black leaders could not, it seemed, see it coming. They probably thought that, rightfully so, the 50% of black blood flowing in the mulattoes' veins would be enough to make them feel the necessity to fight for both common cause and common good. Yet, behind one mountain there are plenty of other mountains, which is often said in Haiti.

François-Dominique Toussaint Louverture, the clever strategist and the leading precursor of the Haitian Revolution for many, understood the different conflicts of interest, and how like the white planters, most mulattoes did not want to give up their status on the land. They all rebelled against France, Britain, and Spain. They wanted a new order under their own rules apart from the European powers by any means, even if it meant to abolish slavery. But in the end, at least in their mind, they would still be the rulers and the overwhelming majority of the population, which is black, would still be their subjects, under their feet. That was the real plot that Louverture was strategically dealing with during the outbreaks leading to independence.

But Toussaint Louverture's own camp misunderstood him at times. Some of his fellow black allies and own rank-and-file fighters aligned themselves naively on the side of their enemies in the name of freedom. They were made to believe that Toussaint Louverture was in it for himself, and he did not want the abolition of slavery—a conspiracy that played an important role in his kidnapping and deportation to France in 1802.

> *Brothers and friends,*
> *I am Toussaint Louverture. My name has perhaps become known to you. I am bent on vengeance. I desire the establishment of liberty and equality in St. Domingue. I strive to bring them into being. Unite with us, brothers, and fight with us in the common cause.*
> *Your most obedient and humble servant,*
> *Toussaint Louverture.*[48]

These words, attributed to Toussaint Louverture inviting his fellow black fighters to unite under his leadership for liberation and equality, sum up what was going through their minds at the time.

Even Jean-Jacques Dessalines had played into the hands of the enemy. After a great number of losses in the battlefield, he surrendered

---

48 Rhodner Orisma, From Revolution to Chaos in Haiti (1804-2019) (Columbia, SC: Xlibris, 2020), p. 53.

to French forces thinking that Louverture and Christophe had betrayed him by submitting themselves to the French army general in Saint-Domingue, Charles Victor-Emmanuel Leclerc. He too did not understand Louverture's tactic of surrender. In fact, the revolutionary leader agreed to surrender in return for several conditions: Freedom would be respected for all on the island; all officers of his army would be integrated into the French army and be allowed to maintain their rank; and Louverture himself could retire to a location of his choice in the colony, retaining his staff. He refused Leclerc's overtures, including the offer of the position of lieutenant-general, and he also rejected offers to dine.

After his surrender, Dessalines was ordered by General Leclerc, Napoleon Bonaparte's brother-in-law, to arrest Louverture, but he nonetheless declined despite his disappointment. But aided by opportunist fighters within Louverture's camp, another French army general, Jean-Baptiste Brunet, facilitated the capture of the Haitian revolutionary leader on June 7, 1802, when he invited him to a meeting to supposedly discuss troop movements.

Toussaint Louverture, fully aware of who the real enemies of emancipation were, way ahead of his arrest, wrote a letter to the Republican mulatto fighters in 1793, a day after the French Republican government recognized, through Sonthonax, the de facto reality of the abolition of slavery in the hands of black insurgents. In his letter, the revolutionary leader detailed the opportunistic and tricked character of the so-called emancipation proclamation under the order of French Republicans. He wrote:

Brothers and Friends,
I can only groan at the state in which you have been plunged
for so long and at the misfortune that might occur after you

> *have persisted with such unity in defending laws that can offer no more than an apparent happiness, but which you believe to be very real. You do not know the person who is addressing you. Be assured that he is a true brother who thinks and can see that you are among enemies without realizing it. Goodness, integrity, and humanity are the foundation of our characters. I want freedom and equality to reign in Saint Domingue. I have been working since the beginning to bring it into existence to establish the happiness of all of us. But alas! You unfortunately cannot see it. Equality cannot exist without liberty, and for liberty to exist we need unity.*[49]

A number of free colored and black fighters, including Henry Christophe and Jean-Jacques Dessalines, would eventually unite behind Louverture. But some leaders like mulattoes Andre Rigaud, Alexandre Pétion, and black General Moise (a district inspector trained and mentored by Louverture) betrayed him for one reason or the other. Toussaint Louverture suffered terribly to oversee the death of Moise after the latter refused to execute his orders for "public good."

Louverture expressed his frustrations with the fact that he was not understood by so many mulattoes and black leaders alike. According to Forsdick and Hogsbjerg, recalling how he had had in-depth conversations with Moise for ten years, Louverture lamented how "in a thousand of my letters . . . at every opportunity, I sought to explain to him the holy maxims of our faith . . . instead of listening to the advice of a father, and obeying the orders of a leader devoted to the well-being

---

49 Charles Forsdick and Christian Hogsbjerg, Toussaint Louverture: A Black Jacobin in the Age of Revolutions (London: Pluto Press, 2017), p. 50-51.

of the colony, he wanted only to be ruled by his passions and follow his fatal inclinations: he has met with a wretched end."[50]

At this stage, Louverture's future as a revolutionary leader and newly self-declared "Governor for Life" was doomed. He was forced to embark on a French warship to Europe for a hard 26-day journey of no return across the Atlantic. As described in most accounts, Louverture was incarcerated without access to a trial in a damp cell partly submerged in the rock of the Jura mountains in Eastern France; the window was almost entirely bricked up, meaning that he was completely deprived of light. He could not survive the harsh reality of ill-treatment in the dark prison, the cold in the glacial mountains of Jura, particularly starvation and yellow fever. He died agonizingly before mid-year 1803. He meant to pay the price and go with certainty that his dream of liberation for all was not going to die, even though he did not live to see the full fruit borne by the giant tree he had planted.

Toussaint Louverture alluded to this hope in a statement after his arrest while getting onboard of the French warship when he declared famously, "In overthrowing me, you have cut down in Saint-Domingue only the trunk of the tree of liberty. It will spring up again by the roots because they are numerous and deep." That was his hope after defeat. And that hope materialized on the battlefield from 1803 to 1804.

On the one hand, Louverture's downfall was inevitable because he had enemies everywhere, including in his own camp. He seemed to understand why and how the real enemy played in the mind of his people against him. But on the other hand, Louverture believed enough important works had already been done as an impetus to provide

---

50 Charles Forsdick and Christian Hogsbjerg, Toussaint Louverture: A Black Jacobin in the Age of Revolutions (London: Pluto Press, 2017), p. 98.

continuity to the revolutionary movement. In fact, after his capture, most of the mulatto and black leaders, who were left running the show behind, managed to build a coalition that would fortify the end of slavery for good and consolidate the Haitian Revolution.

However, that fragile coalition would soon be exposed by personal ambitions, class warfare, prejudices, extrapolation, excessive zeal, passions, and naivety. Dessalines became the first major casualty of post-independence betrayal when the mulatto General Pétion conspired with his allies to overthrow him through assassination in 1806. The plot that dealt a blow to Dessalines signaled the tragedy of a nation whose very foundation was built on shaky ground, on a high level of distrust among its citizens. By leaving its fingerprints all over the society, that reality persists today and has continued to daunt Haiti in a way that makes it almost impossible to trust anyone, regardless of environment.

Most Haitian leaders have always lamented the negative effects of distrust within the society, particularly among the country's political, social, economic, and religious elites. But not enough effort has ever been put forward to change course. Before his assassination, President Jovenel Moise, during his address on the 218th anniversary of the Haitian flag (May 18, 2021), complained that division and self-driven interests had made any possibility of conscious dialogue among vital sectors of the society wishful thinking. Mr. Moise asserted that it was difficult to govern Haiti because the president would not find sincere interlocutors; they would have one position in front of you at night and another one in complete opposition the next morning, he explained. Additionally, late President Moise said:

"I am actually living a unique experience with the political, economic and cultural elites. You could have the best conversation with someone the night before, the next day that person would show up first thing in the morning news with a totally different face, with a position in complete contrast to the one agreed upon the day before. And when I asked them for explanations, they would pretend it was the rule in politics."[51]

Nothing new here when it comes to the Haitian leaders and Haitian politics. If anything, President Moise was just adding himself to the long list of complainers-in-chief of a problem he became another victim of when he was assassinated less than two months later. Almost every president before him cried out in vain against division and distrust.[52] Aristide, Preval, and Martelly, who were also elected in the midst of turbulent and steep infighting between 1991 and 2011, all denounced the accelerating level of selfishness, mistrust, and hypocrisy in Haitian society. However, no one seemed to be willing to exercise the necessary leadership needed to change the pretexts giving rise to the problem. Here we are talking about the will of leadership, but in some instances, the continuity of the state of Haiti just underscores the incompetence and ignorance of most leaders.

2.2: A Lasting Political and Social Culture

Haitians have had a hard time getting over the negative effects of the old vices and customs from their past. Yet, it has not always been difficult for the majority of people to forge unity or share their daily lives

---

51 Jean Daniel Sénat, "Jovenel appelle au dialogue et a l'organization des elections", lenouvelliste.com, Le Nouvelliste, May 19, 2021. https:// lenououvelliste.com/18-mai-2021-Jovenel-Moïse-appelle-au-dialogue-et-à-l'organisation-des-élections.html

52 Before late-President Moise, other presidents, notably Préval and Martelly, made the same remarks about most Haitian leaders.

and struggles in their communities, because what helps create bonds with each other is far more important than what divides them. But that positive element has been overshadowed by the negative behaviors of politicians, religious leaders, and others with great influence on the sociopolitical, economic, and cultural structures.

Another problem is that poverty, the lack of socioeconomic development, and a relatively low social education level tend to make people use each other as a target. And very often, people cast the blame upon the wrong object or subject for their issues, either because of mere ignorance or hatred cultivated from their struggles with reality. A vicious circle that continues to produce and reproduce actions of betrayal and hate. These actions have contributed to the shortfall of democracy and progress in the nation. With that being said, politically and socially, Haiti seems to be in a permanent state of transition; economically, the fundamentals seem to consistently lack coherent and efficient managerial structures.

Politicizing Life and Disliking Politics

Everything is politics in Haiti, and every Haitian is political. It is not an exaggeration to say that Haitians breathe politics, and they live for and by it. But as paradoxical as it seems, people hate politicians. In the eyes of most Haitians, politicians are not trustworthy for they are full of dupery—all of them. No parent wants a career in politics for any of their children. They are afraid of the danger and uncomfortable with the labels that come with being a politician in the context of Haiti. Persecution, exile, deaths, character assassination, and injures. In most people's perception, politicians are too deceptive; they are liars, corrupt, incompetent, and they kill for various reasons or no reason at all. They have no shame, some people would say.

The Haitian people see politics as a game of tricksters. Therefore, it is a dirty game. People often say "politics in Haiti is a cannibal jungle." Professional politicians call each other "politicians" pejoratively when expressing disdain for one another. Most of the time, they baselessly discredit each other in very harmful and hateful ways. These practices, among others, make people see politics as a detestable field. No one likes to be called a politician even if they play politics with each other the very same way. This has long been a sociocultural trend in the country. Most sociocultural life practices in Haiti mirror the general practice of Haitian politics—people have lived through mostly coups d'état, dictatorships, and internal infighting.

With so much opposition to being in politics and yet needing to participate in politics at the same, one question is how can anything get done in the country? What we have seen in Haiti's political culture is that a lot have been done for personal gains, but very little for the advancement of the nation as whole. The way people see politics is one of the reasons why the country's affairs often fall into the hands of incompetent or autocratic politicians who are willing to do anything to hold onto power.

That, in addition to some major structural and organizational deficiencies in Haiti's electoral system, including major obstacles in voter registration and voter ID cards delivery, also causes a decline in voter turnout. Most elections in Haiti are generally contested, tainted with irregularities, disenfranchisements, and exclusions. After the fall of Duvalier's dictatorship, Haitians were more enthusiastically engaged and more hopeful about a positive outcome in the future of Haiti. Voter turnout reached 50% in 1990, and 63% between 1995 and 2000. As conditions worsened, expected reforms and changes have not been achieved to the satisfaction of the majority, people have become more and more passive. Average participation in all elections after 2000 has not exceeded 21% of registered voters, according to a report from the Council on Hemispheric Affairs (COHA).[53] [54] The turnout was just about 17% during the presidential election of November 2016.

Another question is, if people dislike politics so much in Haiti, why are so many in it? The answer is not sophisticated. Many Haitians do not like the way politics is practiced in the country. They do not like the tendencies, behaviors, and attitudes of most politicians. But that does not mean they do not see the value of being in politics for the common good. People often get involved with the primary goal of changing the practices described above. Unfortunately, most of the time, the established status quo obstructs their will for change through divisions, counterproductive actions, and gratuitous quarrels. Many times, in Haiti's history, people have gotten into the political system to change it; but it changes them instead. Generally, individuals who primarily see politics as a shortcut to economic and financial success and social status mobility for themselves tend to be a small minority. However, as it is the case in many other countries with similar challenges, the will of the minority in Haiti has been overshadowing the goals of the majority for too long.

For a long stretch, formal political practice was the affair of the Haitian army. Besides, it was Haiti's longstanding national institution

---

53 Elena Tiralongo, "Haiti's Elections: Low Turnout Reflects Lack of Hope for Change", coha.org, Council on Hemispheric Affairs (COHA), November 12, 2015. https://www.coha.org/haitis-elections-low-turnout-reflects-lack-of-hope-for-change/

54 COHA is an independent nonprofit research and information organization based in Washington, DC. According to information found on its website (www.COHA.org), it was founded in 1975 to promote the common interests of the hemisphere, raise the visibility of regional affairs, and increase the importance of constructive inter-American relationships.

from independence until the mid-1990s, when it was controversially disbanded by former President Aristide. That unconstitutional move from Aristide, despite expert advice to do otherwise, seemed to be a political revenge. Disbanding the military institution instead of reforming it added more security problems to Haiti.

Many national and international advisors on the question encouraged a reform of the Haitian army, which needed to become more professional and apolitical to better serve the country. Traditionally, Haitian leaders have run the army either as a political enterprise or repressive machine against the population. They would use the army to betray one another, the presidents who had promoted them, or to persecute those of whom they do not agree with. Several high-ranking military officials saw the institution as a way to serve their political and economic ambitions through coups d'état and activities of self-enrichment.

The way the army was visibly managed had a negative influence on the society as a whole. While the military leaders were actively doing dirty politics, engaging in repression and human rights abuses, and participating in illegal behaviors and illicit activities, ordinary citizens would replicate the same kind of behaviors and attitudes among themselves. The generals were virulently going after each other in their power struggles. The rest of the society was building on the same political attitude that is still a reflection on today's daily life of survival. Under all appearances of goodwill and a sense of harmonious communities lies the country's fundamental problems in real time: betrayal, hate, racism, fratricide, conspiracy, falsehoods, gratuitous accusations, character assassinations, gossiping, discord, dupery, corruption, patronizing, racketeering, self-promotion, egoism, jealousy, selfishness, pride, hypocrisy, revenge, xenophobia, sorcery, witch hunts, witchcraft, complacency, blind subordination, a cult of personality, and more.

As a society, we can change course together by promoting more civic and social education. And more importantly, we can make sure that people understand the difference between reality and falsehood, constructive perception and misconception. What gives us hope is that the majority of Haitians are conscious of the problem and would like to see changes. They need some transformational leaders within.

Due to the nature of political practice in the country, formal and conventional political parties or organizations did not exist in the early years of independence. From the mid-19th to the mid-20th century, Haiti had two major political parties: the Nationals and the Liberals. The Nationals party was composed mainly of the lower-and middle-class black majority. They were ideologically in favor of a strong executive government. The Liberals, by contrast, were composed mainly of the wealthier and "better-educated" mulatto minority; they preferred a government controlled by legislators. In fact, their political will prevailed for most of Haiti's history. The hegemonic mulattoes inherited their wealth from the French colonists who departed during the war of independence.

In 1950, when President Dumarsais Estimé, a liberal black president, started to promote fellow blacks, the issue of color intervened. The mulatto elite in the army was frightened. They betrayed Estimé and turned to another ambitious black general, Paul Eugene Magloire, whom they felt was more manipulable, to depose the former. After the coup, the first universal presidential election was run and Magloire won 99% of the votes—a true plebiscite. Magloire was already wealthy with the mulattoes' help. They were happy that he was now fronting their shameless privilege and barely concealed racism. His rule marked the apogee of their power—some would say their last stand—and the genial "Iron Pants," as he was known at the time, dovetailed with the mulattoes' lifestyle. With his passion for extravagantly distinguished uniforms, horses, and fine whisky, Magloire staged endless dazzling social events and ceremonies, even reenacting the final battle for Haiti's independence from France on its 150th anniversary in 1954.

But corruption, growing repression, the destruction wrought by Hurricane Hazel in 1954, and the theft of subsequent relief funds turned the tide against Magloire. In 1956, disputes broke out over when his term of office should end. Under pressure from strikes and demonstrations mounted by his rivals, the army abandoned him and he fled abroad. After a year of political chaos, François "Papa Doc" Duvalier won the presidency in a rigged election. And Magloire along with his mulatto allies quickly became the scapegoat for Duvalier's *noiriste* movement designed to fortify his dictatorship reign. As an absent scapegoat, opposition to the new regime was blamed on him, and used by Duvalier to build his reign of terror.

Magloire was even stripped of his Haitian nationality. But after the Duvaliers fell in 1986, he quietly returned to Haiti from exile in New York. Two years later, the army, once more in power, briefly used him as an adviser. Many people saw in the military leaders' reunion with Magloire a token attempt to make it up to the old general they had earlier rejected.

To get back to our subject of political parties, it is worth noting that under Papa Doc's regime of terror from 1957 to 1971, political practices were not allowed. His son and successor, Jean-Claude "Baby Doc" Duvalier, allowed some political activities. That climate gave rise to the opposition party the Haitian Christian Democratic Party (PDCH), founded in 1979. By October 1980, the leader of that opposition party was arrested because Baby Doc had decided to mute most dissidents yet again. Several party members were arrested in 1983 on incitement and national security charges.

After the military ousted Jean-Claude Duvalier in 1986 with the support of popular and widespread protests nationwide, dozens of parties emerged. The most prominent one was the National Front for Change and Democracy (FNCD), a coalition composed of some small parties from the Haitian leftist movement and popular grassroots organizations, which backed Aristide in the December 1990 elections. But Aristide later disassociated himself from FNCD because he could not convince most of the platform leaders to support his populist view of government.

Clashes first erupted over the choice of a prime minister and personal interests. Just a few months in office, Mr. Aristide shamelessly and preemptively claimed that he was never a part of the political organization, that he only borrowed its umbrella as a hat he wore to facilitate his candidacy for president. That statement from Aristide provoked the ire of the FNCD's leaders, in particular Evans Paul, also known as "K-Plim," Jean-Jacques Clark Parent, Turneb Delpé, and Victor Benoit, some of whom were either government officials or were in the Haitian parliament at the time. Weakened and humiliated by Aristide, these leaders would eventually turn against him and against each other before they eventually dismantled FNCD in despair into its original individual pieces, such as the National Congress of Democratic Movements (CONACOM), Movement for the Organization of the Country (MOP), and Committee for Democratic Unity (KID).

Other important political organizations led by a generation of intellectual politicians were the Rally of Progressive National Democrats (RDNP) of former late President Leslie François Manigat, the Revolutionary Progressive Nationalist Party (PANPRA) of former late Senator Serge Gilles, the Movement for the Installation of Democracy in Haiti (MIDH), under former late Prime Minister Marc Bazin, the Movement for National Development (MDN) of late neo-Duvalierist Hubert de Ronceray, the National Agricultural and Industrial Party (PAIN) of late Louis Déjoie II, the Unified Party of Haitian Communists (PUCH) of late Rene Theodore, and the National Party for Work (PNT) of late Thomas Désulmé, among others.

As political vicissitudes and divisions have continued to dominate the national discourse, new leaders have been emerging as well as new parties from both the left and right ideologies. Early on after his swearing-in as president in 1991 and splitting with FNCD, Aristide wanted to create a party viewed in light of his Lavalas movement. By 1995, the foundation of the Lavalas Political Organization (OPL) had become a reality both in concept and structure.

Ingeniously engineered by Gerard Pierre Charles, who was a well-known economist, author, and former leader of the Unified Party of Haitian Communists, OPL was the dominant party until Aristide once again broke rank with the other Lavalas leaders to formally register his own party in 1997 under the official name of Organization Fanmi Lavalas (OFL). At this point, anti-Aristide sentiment led Pierre-Charles and company to consciously redefine the acronym OPL as the Organization of Struggling People (Organisation du Peuple en Lutte).

Then, OPL and OFL had become the two leading political forces in Haiti until the 2015–2016 elections, when Bald Head Haitian Party

(PHTK), (Parti Haitien Tet Kale, in French and Haitian languages combined)—formerly known as Peasant Movement (Mouvman Peyizan)—founded by former President Michel Martelly, became the front runner. Other significant political groups rooted in previous allegiance to both OPL and OFL were the Front for Hope (Lespwa) led by former Aristide ally President René Garcia Préval, and its successor, the Unity party (Inite) from 2005 and 2009, respectively. There was also the center-left Democratic Alliance coalition (Alyans). Today, there are about 300 different political organizations officially registered in Haiti. And this is without exaggeration. Most are led by former political allies who have become rivals or each other's worst enemies. A lot of political parties only exist on paper or by name; some have few affiliations; others have no registered members other than their founders.

While some of these parties and political platforms may have mainly been walloped by betrayal, self-interest, and visceral hatred, at every new dawn of elections, multiple new political organizations tend to emerge one way or the other. Everyone wants to have their own party for themselves. That is how you run for office without challenge within. If anything, you are the one in charge of selecting the candidates for as good it seems to you. Many political leaders look for those who are weaker than them—those they can dominate as they were, at some point of their political career, dominated by others. They are not looking to ally themselves with the most capable and loyal to the country's cause. They look for people who are faithful to them as their leaders. Even that often comes with heavy costs.

A devoted loyalist today is usually a candidate to become an enemy, oftentimes the worst enemy of the individual with or for whom he/she had worked. One error is enough. Very often, the unforgivable sin is the mere fact that someone shows their aspirations for leadership roles. Most Haitians have always found it difficult to forgive others. You would hear people saying things like "I will never forget or forgive what so-and-so did to me; I will take this with me to my grave." It is a way of saying that revenge is on the air. In Haiti's political world, as it is anywhere else in the society, compromise is rare and almost unacceptable; and the sentiment of gratitude is mainly for the cowards. Former dictator Papa Doc perceived gratitude or acknowledgement as cowardice. And that view, which had poisoned the minds of even good people, reflects largely in the way we continue to treat each other today.

The religious institutions, at least by conceptual design, that are supposed to be the barometer and compass of moral values, education, and unity, are unfortunately reflective of the images projected by the society globally. In churches, as it is in vodou temples, the same acts of betrayal, hatred, and other questionable conducts have been observed. Conducts that have contributed to make perdure the negative image of Haiti can be observed among both religious leaders and faithfuls. The behaviors and attitudes manifested by politicians and individuals in other parts of the society are also found inside religious institutions in Haiti. Everyone uses the same playbook. Like political parties, Protestant churches of all denominations multiply every day. Most of those churches present in every corner of urban and rural areas look like small shops.

Although, a better organization of these churches through centralized structures to provide checks and balances and facilitate accountability could have served the country more effectively. We do not intend to fall into the rabbit hole of empty criticism about faith-based organizations. We do not minimize or underestimate their valued works in different communities. We must recognize that without the works of several faith-based organizations throughout Haiti in education, community health, human rights, and social and microeconomic developments, things would have been more precarious, particularly in rural and remote areas. If it were not for the efforts of those organizations, notwithstanding great risks, people's general conditions in these areas would have been worse. Several regions in Haiti lack the presence of basic government services and infrastructure.

Thanks to faith-based organizations and institutions, a lot more Haitians have earned degrees at universities and acquired professions at trade and vocational schools. These organizations have also been one of the major sources of employment in Haiti. They are without doubt an integral part of the country's hope in the future.

However, the problem remains that some leaders have been defeating the purpose by their behaviors and attitudes. Many local churches, Protestant and Catholic included, are not there just because of the need to spread the gospel in the country and enhance people's living conditions. Their presence is mostly justified by the fact that they are part of an old system of exploitation. Their leaders strive against progress by perpetuating lies, disinformation, divisions, betrayal, and the promotion of self-interests stemming from the agenda of oppression, knowingly or not. Like in the government system, a major reform is also needed in the organizational structure and long-term goals of the religious institutions to make them more positively effective in Haiti's socioeconomic development.

Preaching, like doing politics in Haiti, is a lucrative business. It comes with considerable influence and privileges at the expense of the most vulnerable people. It also enhances social status. Coups, intolerance, hate speeches, plots, and witch hunts, among other practices, are regularly used in the religious circle to advance one's own agenda at the expense of others. Some religious leaders, including Christians, Vodouists, and others, do not trust each other. They behave the same way some politicians and business leaders act.[55] They do not see eye to eye. And that kind of leadership sets the tone for ordinary citizens in other sectors of activities. Often, Haitians have a hard time not thinking of each other as eventual traitors and not hindering each other's opportunities. They have difficulties identifying their real enemies because of confusion deriving from falsehoods and propaganda. This situation often causes innocent people to be victimized.

Is there a rainbow in all that? Of course, there is. While these negativities continue to be contributing factors to Haiti's lack of social progress and economic development, they do not define Haitians. Most Haitians are better than that. They want harmony, peace, and progress in Haiti. The majority of Haitians suffer from the weight and effects of these practices in society instead of them [most Haitians] being part of these practices. That is why, a lot of times, Haitians try to leave Haiti in search of better opportunities and places where law and order help curb harmful political, social, and economic practices. Anywhere Haitians find places and opportunities like that, they strive. There are positive and success stories of Haitian immigrants, particularly in North America, South America, and Europe, among other places around the world. Haitians excel in almost everywhere they are involved, including education, research, workplaces, business, arts, music, and sports. What most Haitians need is a chance to maximize their strengths and a leadership that can help turn their weaknesses into positive forces for change in Haiti.

---

55 Vodouists refer to the believers of the vodou religion. The 1987 Constitution guarantees equal rights to the practice of vodou as any other religion in Haiti.

Chapter Three

The Blame Game

Apart from betrayal and hate as discussed in the previous chapter, the culture of scapegoating is another big problem in the Haitian society. Instead of looking at the real authors and coauthors of an act, the root cause of an issue to effectively tackle it, we tend to always shift the blame on someone or something else. Conspiracy is an important part of Haiti's way of life. You find the most bizarre and irrational explanations for anything, from the causes of illness, death, natural disasters, and failure in business or education—like it is virtually in any other type of enterprise—to the reasons for the country's collective failure.

Misfortunes or misdeeds are generally seen through the lens of conspiracy theories, unfounded claims, or accusations that cannot be verified in a million years. It has become very usual for people to charge and condemn others of wrongdoing in the court of public rumors without any element of proof; hearsay is an essential way Haitians spread information or disinformation. That phenomenon does not stop journalists and some segments of the Haitian media from falling into laxity and laziness. The traditional mentality is that if something is said on the radio, it must be true.

Nowadays, it is even worse with uncontrollable access to social media. It has become a custom that anyone can falsely accuse whomever as they please without any consequence. Defamation and libel are concepts that only exist on paper and in the constitution. Scapegoating, rumors, hearsay, and unfounded allegations or false claims have had a heavy cost on human lives and general progress in Haiti. But the fact that the 1987 Constitutional Assembly made sure to address these issues in the main law of the land gives us hope. That legal tool can be served as a reminder, a compass, and an impetus for change.

It is our understanding that if you do not at least try to comprehend a problem and lay the responsibility where it is supposed to be for real accountability, any argument about finding a solution to that problem is just wishful thinking; you risk exacerbating the problem as opposed to resolving it. In the case of Haiti as a country, we have experienced that conundrum for far too long. Most Haitians tend to live in their past. Instead of learning from a past event and moving positively with lessons learned from it onto the present and the future, they keep dwelling under it. A good event in the past is considered as a source of absolute and complacent pride, while a bad event in the past is there to stay as a pretext for holding us back. We do not use good experience to build on, nor do we use bad experience to correct the present for a better future. But one thing is certain, we will never forget either way.

Haitians are continually talking about the extraordinary exploits of the 1804 revolution as if everything had stopped with those exploits; no continuity was needed in terms of hard work and efforts to build on the legacy of Mackendal, Bookman, Toussaint Louverture, François Capois (nicknamed Capois-La-Mort, Capois-Death), Jean-Jacques Dessalines, Henri Christophe, Alexandre Pétion, and other forefathers. By the same token, they continue to use the indemnity paid to France in exchange for the recognition of independence as one of the main reasons for the country's permanent economic trouble and lack of social progress. We are not saying that this act of extortion did not play a certain role in Haiti's economic hardship early on. However, if it is true that the indemnity paid was an important factor in impoverishing Haiti from the beginning, it is also arguably true that with the right leadership and sociopolitical and economic projects, the country could have recovered from it.

The international community, in particular the U.S. and France, have been constantly blamed for their role in Haiti's failure politically and economically. Of course, they are not innocent, as Jakob Johnston of the Center for Economic and Policy Research put it during his recent analysis of Haiti's crisis on Aljazeera TV network. He pointed out how foreign powers, notably the United States, could have been more useful with their intentions in Haiti. Mr. Johnston stated, "It's easy to look at Haiti and say oh, this is a failed state. But we never look in the mirror and look at what our role has been in precipitating that crisis."[56] But we continue to expect the resolution of all our problems to come from them. We despise them or worship them when it is necessary for convenience or expediency.

In sociocultural areas, we tend to look back at some individual and exceptional accomplishments from past generations as a source of pride. But we do not do enough to support and encourage the creativity and ingenuity of new generations to overcome the challenges of their time and reach new heights.

Additionally, we do not continue to build on any good legacy from our past, nor do we appreciate or encourage current generations enough in order to push them to move further. More often, Haitians use someone's past struggles against present success. People can work very hard to become successful economically and socially, but others will still use a person's unfavorable situation in the past as a bumper sticker on their forehead to shame them, to minimize their achievements. If you were better off in the past, but you somehow have lost your status due to some tough times, people will use your previous position to drag you even further down. They do not want to see you rise again once you fall, nor should your efforts bear good fruit in the eyes of your own people.

---

56 Marc Lamont Hill, "Foreign Intervention in Haiti", facebook.com, Aljazeera, November 17, 2021. https://www.facebook.com/watch/?v=314875216853015

It has become a cultural thing that Haitians barely congratulate or recognize others for their efforts. Some parents do not have anything good to say to their children other than negative criticism. This is a culture where people believe applauding their children for their good works may make them feel too important or jinx them. In reality, this comes from the general premonition of jealousy, insatiability in case of the parent-child dynamic, and where celebrating someone else's accomplishment is perceived as flattery by the society. Another factor is the fact that corruption has become normal in Haiti. Nowadays, people do not even think that someone can become successful without wrongdoing. To many Haitians, living a decent life without cheating is something of extraterrestrial dimension. It is always something . . . rather derogatory. Many Haitians believe that if someone else's life is better than theirs, it is because that person has been the beneficiary of some unfair, illicit, or illegal practices, such as favoritism, racketeering, theft, drug trafficking, dupery, or oppression. This is one of the main reasons why it has always been difficult to have any kind of protests in Haiti without the destruction of properties (public and private), vandalism, and human casualties.

Furthermore, some Haitians seem unable to understand the difference between the act and the actor, the product they consume and the manufacturer of that product. They confuse the fridge we import with the brand or the manufacturer, the car we drive with the make. For some Haitians, any fridge is a Frigidaire, and any sport-utility vehicle (SUV) is a Jeep. They define most consumer goods by the first brand they know or come in contact with the most. And that will not change over time. Any SUV, no matter what make and model, is defined as a Jeep by most because that was either the first brand of this type of vehicle introduced to them or the one they mostly see around them. That goes the same for Frigidaire, and other manufactured goods. This total misconception may be confusing to a foreigner, but not to Haitians.

Confusing the function of a material with that of the manufacturer is a big problem. Take for example a bed someone sleeps on. If that particular bed is not good, and hurts that person's back, the maker of the bed is the one responsible. The bed itself is not at fault. Either the consumer changes makers, which causes the maker to lose a customer, or the maker is forced to correct the defects in its product. It is not the bed; it is the manufacturing company. Switching the same products from the same bad manufacturer may not be the best way to resolve the problem. Applying this to politics, voting for the same kind of incompetent, selfish, corrupt, autocratic, greedy, power-mongering, detached, egocentric politicians will not move the country forward. These types of politicians need to be held accountable by getting them out of office and punishing them according to the law.

We blame the constitution for our political and social turmoil, suggesting that it is too complicated in its applicability, but we cling to that same constitution as our God-given instrument when it is convenient. Changing the constitution will not resolve our bad governance issue. Haiti had changed constitutions at least twenty-four times in its history. But the severity of the country's problems had simply worsened over the years. Most observers who have been following Haiti's evolution would agree that the country does not have a problem of constitution, but a problem of governance stemming from the lack of long-term good leadership. We are stuck in a permanent stage of unnecessary ambivalence. Haitians live in a state of eternal conflicts: a sort of futile debate of comparison between the ancient and the new, the past and the present, the beautiful and the ugly, white and black, good taste and bad taste, the beginning and the ending, you and me, them and us, rich and poor, city and countryside, urban and rural, civilized and uncivilized, intellectuals and illiterates, Haitian (Creole) and French, religion and non-religion, God and the devil, etc.

In this chapter, you will find in the context of this book the most common irrationalities that have become central to people's reality in Haiti. For good measure or not, those irrationalities have been developed over the years by politicians, social and religious leaders, and the economic oligarchs. Intentionally or not, scapegoating as a way of thinking and explaining facts distracts, deviates us from reality, and plays an important role in preventing Haiti from overcoming the lack of progress.

From blaming others for our infighting and rivalrous behaviors, to riding essentially on luck, providentialism, secret societies, and religions, among others, for our misfortune, the contagion affects all aspects of the Haitian life. Looking for a scapegoat in every situation in Haiti is like the curse absolutism that most people seem not willing to depart from. Here, we outline the most common expressions of blame used by Haitians, some more irrational than others, from ordinary people in the streets to the highest level of leadership in political, religious, social, and governmental institutions, among others.

3.1: They Are Always Against Us

Yo pa janm vle wè Ayisyen. Tout kote nou pase yo rayi nou (other people never like Haitians). This idea in the Haitian language is nourished by the belief that most other countries/foreigners are always working against Haiti. In most Haitians' minds, it is as if other people hated them everywhere. That belief is an exaggeration at best, and an excuse for Haitian leaders' failures, misdeeds, incompetence, and lack of a coherent vision. The *blan* (white people in Haitian vernacular, which in essence means foreigners regardless of skin color) is often accused of being behind most of our problems. The reason given is simple, and most Haitians are very affirmative about it. They firmly believe that most foreign countries have been jealous of the uniqueness of the Haitian Revolution. They think that some foreign actors have never given up their imperialistic grip on the country, while others might have been just racist and prejudicial toward the black nation.

Haitians are right to some extent in this regard. No one can sincerely deny that reality even in the 21st century. Yet at the end of the 19th century, during his lecture on Haiti in Chicago, Frederick Douglass rationally asserted, "Haiti is black, and we have not yet forgiven Haiti for being black . . . after Haiti had shaken off the fetters of bondage . . . We continue to refuse to acknowledge the fact and treat her as outside the sisterhood of nations."

Regrettably, if he were alive today, Douglas would still have the same view about how some people in some countries see Haiti. Unfortunately, that perception has created a permanent victim mentality in most Haitians. It has had a long negative effect on the Haitian society, often preventing the people from striving. It does not only shape Haiti's interactions with other countries, but also the relations among Haitians themselves as well. The same way Haiti has always been watching its back against its counterparts, seeing their every move as a sort of trick to trap or a plot to take advantage, individuals—regardless of social status or affiliations—also see each other as antagonists.

In the minds of many Haitians, there is always an enemy. To them, other people hate us just because we are Haitians. We achieved the first and biggest black revolution in modern history. We showed everyone in the hemisphere how to defeat slavery and become an independent nation. We helped other nations in the quest for freedom, and we have always received foreigners with great hospitality.

We produce good coffee, cocoa, vetiver for essential oils, citrus, the best mangoes in the Caribbean, among the most important export crops. Haitians often argue about being the producer and exporter of the best rum—Rhum Barbancourt—in the Caribbean, which is one of the finest rums in the world. The Société du Rhum Barbancourt was founded in 1862 and is one of Haiti's oldest and most famous private companies.

In sports, Haitians have never stopped talking about the exploits of the national soccer team at the 1974 FIFA World Cup in Munich, Germany, when Haiti became the first Caribbean team to qualify for the prestigious international tournament. From their very first game in the tournament, they broke the Italians' hearts in the inaugural match by ending 1,143 minutes of Italian goalkeeper's Dino Zoff goalless record. That ended one minute after a scoreless halftime, when the unheralded 22-year-old Emmanuel Sanon scored a memorable goal to put Haiti ahead of Italy. For almost two years prior to playing Haiti, Zoff had frustrated many of the greatest strikers in the world.

"They hate us for our success; they plot our misery and rejoice in our failure," some would emphatically say. Haitians who think like this do not see an accident like everyone else. In their minds, nothing happens by mere accident or rational cause. Causes of events more often are explained by rumored claims in relation to people's customs, tradition, and religion. Someone operating in the dark is supposedly running afoul. Most Haitians do not even believe they can be sick or die naturally. They do not understand the concept of mental health, or they just do not believe in the reality of it. Someone with symptoms of schizophrenia or dementia is generally castigated as being crazy or considered to be possessed by demons at someone else's expediency.

Nothing is natural. No, it must be due to witchcraft. "They cast this sickness on me so that I can die in order for them to steal my lands and all my assets," said Francoise Pascal, a woman from northern Haiti who was celebrating her 127th birthday on January 5, 2021. Yes, you read it right but got it wrong! Exception . . . The birth certificate that she presented to a reporter was later revealed to be fake, not hers. She had falsely claimed to be born on January 5, 1895 in Dafou, a village located in Limonade, Haiti.[57] But research at the National Archives confirmed that *Manmi* Pascal, as everyone in her village calls her, who appeared to be too young for that age was not who she claimed to be.[58] Claims of that sort are very frequent in Haiti.

Many Haitians deeply believe that someone may hate you so much that they employ supernatural forces through some secret society to make you sick, even kill you. While they believe that most families have their protective spirits inherited from their ancestors, they also believe in acts supposedly committed against them from time to time by some malicious spirits served by their elders and ancestors. *Pèsekisyon vye dyab rasyal*, they often say. This is more or less what they

---

57 Le Nouvelliste, "127 ans Pour Francoise Pascal", lenouvelliste.com, Le Nouvelliste, January 5, 2022. https://lenouvelliste.com/article/233509/127-ans-pour-francoise-pascal

58 Le Nouvelliste, "Trop Jeune pour avoir 127 ans", lenouvelliste.com, Le Nouvelliste, January 7, 2022 https://lenouvelliste.com/article/233548/trop-jeune-pour-avoir-127-ans

are accustomed to because doctors and access to quality medical care have not been available to everyone equally.

Instead of seeking the attention of medical professionals when they are available, most Haitians prefer alternative treatments rooted in traditional rituals and beliefs. And most of the time, the finger could be pointed at a family member or a neighbor as the mischievous person, as the culprit. This fundamental belief makes it very difficult for most typical Haitians to agree with any science, period. Witchcraft is the cause of illness and death, and therefore treatments require the same kind of intervention. A lot of people truly believe that natural disasters are either orchestrated by imperial powers, the devil, or God as a form of punishment.

The influence of many religious leaders has not been helpful either. If anything, influential religious leaders, nationally and internationally, have accentuated the issue by spreading these theories and continuing to reinforce them in people's minds. One of the most recent and striking examples is the response to the January 12, 2010 earthquake. One of the most influential American televangelists, Marion Gordon "Pat" Robertson, suggested at the time that the devastating earthquake occurred because Haiti had entered into "a pact to the devil."[59]

Mr. Robertson, a media mogul and amplified voice in the American conservative politics arena, is a former Republican presidential candidate and Southern Baptist minister. Leaders like him

---

59 CNN, "Pat Robertson says Haiti paying for pact to the devil", cnn.com, CNN, January 13, 2010. http://www.cnn.com/2010/US/01/13/haiti.pat.robertson/index.html

did not stand up for Haiti when Haitians were falsely accused of being at the origin of HIV/AIDS in the 1980s, nor did they stand up against the way international institutions and U.S. government convinced the Haitian government to eliminate the indigenous (Creole) pigs in their efforts to supposedly control African swine flu (ASF) while favorizing the increase of American farmers' market share in Haiti. In slaughtering the indigenous pigs, Haiti had lost a staple of the peasant economy. The hardy Creole pigs brought families economic stability, devoured food waste, and occasionally became a religious sacrifice in the vodou rituals. The famous 1791 Bois-Caiman Ceremony led by runaway slaves during the massive revolt for total liberation, where a pig was sacrificed, is widely used as an example of historical importance.

It was not a surprise either that U.S. media reports quoted former President Donald Trump referring to Haiti as a "shithole" country during a meeting with a group of bipartisan senators in 2018. He was trying to explain the reason why he wanted to end the Temporary Protected Status (TPS) program for Haitians. "We don't need more people from 'shithole countries'. Why can't we have more immigrants from Norway?" "Why do we need more Haitians, take them out," he said, according to various media reports.[60]

To Trump's credit, though, he directed the same insult not just toward Haiti but also to other countries in Central America and Africa, which are beneficiaries of the U.S. immigration TPS program. However, a little after he left office, he doubled down on his disgusting rhetoric when he stated in an interview with Sean Hannity on Fox News that

---

60 Eli Watkins and Abby Phillip, "Trump decries immigrants from 'shithole countries' coming to the U.S.", cnn.com, CNN, revised January 12, 2018. https://www.cnn.com/2018/01/11/politics/immigrants-shithole-countries-trump/index.html

Haitian migrants trying to enter the U.S. and seek asylum, after crossing the southern border with Mexico, might even have HIV or AIDS. He argued that the Biden administration should have kept all of them out because they represented a danger for Americans.

"Haiti has tremendous problems, they may have AIDS and represent a danger for the American people," said the former president to explain why Haitians should not be admitted to the United States. Frankly, that is perhaps the view secretly held about Haiti in the 21st century by a certain group of people in the U.S., but most of them do not have the audacity to say it publicly and so loudly like Donald Trump and even Pat Robertson.

Of course, xenophobia, bigotry, racism, and acts of evil exist. But Haitians have given way too much power to it, which is very damning psychologically.

What about God, then? Sure, God exists, and He is the creator of the universe. He is forever on his throne looking at us as fools for making Him the architect of events that actually happen because of our own foolish will. By the same token, it is important to recognize the weight of history on the Haitian people. Our long history as a people has been shaped by existential contradictions stemming from slavery, a system of dehumanization, a culture of hate, prejudices, racism, witch hunts, oppression, and inequity. But we are not the exception.

The modern Atlantic world is built on the foundation of those attributes. Similar to Haiti, other Caribbean and Central American countries experienced the slavery system as well. And today, they too, continue to be schooled by imperial and super powers. The only exception is that Haitians fought and won the war for independence as opposed to autonomy being given to them. And they have been struggling for a lot longer with the effects of slavery.

The wreckage of the old system continues to daunt the country and be the foundation of its present social construction and the political and economic fabrics. Almost everyone recognizes that problem. But there has not been enough collective and continued leadership capable of dealing with it appropriately enough in order to move the country forward. The leadership of the country has consistently failed to seize any opportunity to build a nation-state that could be elevated to rank with most countries in the Western hemisphere with similar experiences, more broadly speaking. Haitian leadership has flatly failed the valiant people of Haiti.

No doubt about that. Our adopted leitmotif remains and is to be maintained that Haiti's leadership over the years has failed the people. That the interference of foreign powers has undermined political stability and socioeconomic development in Haiti cannot be considered as an understatement. But at the same time, foreigners have never acted alone in the past; they cannot act alone in the present and will not be able to do so in the future without Haitian associations. They always have national actors—including government officials and key figures of civil-society sectors—as accomplices and agents to facilitate the implementation of policies that are detrimental to the Haitian people.

Again, the indemnity paid to France and the trade blockade after independence are the two most widely used reasons, among other external factors, for Haiti's past and present economic problems. Of course, as previously conceded, they contributed considerably to slow the process of nation-state building during the early stage of the country's birth. But as things evolved geopolitically, technologically, economically, and socially, our own doings internally seem to have leapfrogged those external factors.

Even if it was an act of extortion from France that paralyzed Haiti economically in the early years, corruption and impunity practiced by Haitian leaders who stole billions of dollars from Haiti's coffers have caused a lot of damage. There is nothing to prove that if France had not made Haiti pay that money, Haiti would have had beneficial social-development projects. This view is not intended to reward foreign nations (Britain, France, Spain, Germany, and the United States in particular) for trying to sabotage the success of the Haitian Revolution from day one by withholding official recognition, restricting trade routes, levying heavier trade duties, and imposing a large indemnity.

In the case of the United States, not counting short-term humanitarian missions, Haiti registered three major military interventions in 89 years (1915, 1994 and 2004). All three of those military interventions led to catastrophic outcomes. And it is a fact that the modern, racist, imperialist, capitalist world driven by the Christian religion could not accept the very idea of a black and independent Haiti in the heart of the Atlantic.

However, what drove and inspired Haiti was far superior than the interests of those foreign powers. It was the ideal of universal freedom, equity, and human dignity. That ideal was short-lived because national leaders failed to place the collective well-being before their personal interests. But that is what all Haitians need to concertedly reclaim with profound and unshakable sincerity. Haitians need to exhibit and reinforce unbreakable love for one another to defeat their real enemies. Haitians—present and future generations—need to truly embrace the idea of a Republic shaped by liberty, equality, and fraternity within.

Of course, the Haitian Revolution was unique for what it did to the slavery system. But the influence of foreign powers, exploitation, colonialism, and imperialism have not been imposed only on Haiti. And it should not be a surprise that the black nation born from such a revolution has paid a punitive price at the hands of colonial powers, European imperialists in particular. But what is simply inconceivable is the lack of cumulative, collective, and convergent efforts to overcome the mischievous actions of foreign powers against national interests and progress. Amid all the deceptions and misdeeds, history always gives you the possibility of redemption and conquest through opportunities. Unfortunately, Haiti has continued to be a no-show when it comes to its dates with history.

Over the years, Haiti had many opportunities for recovery from the perceived failures in the hands of foreign powers and empires. But most of the past leaders had not shown enough statesmanship and had continuously sought to extend the colonial system by becoming neocolonialists themselves over their own people, whom they were supposed to liberate and protect. Although the Haitian people (the "True Haitians," according to Jean Casimir in his book about the Haitian Revolution) resisted the reimposition of the plantation economy and succeeded in reconstructing their sovereignty and institutions to support it outside of the different constitutions and laws instituted by the Haitian leaders with colonialist priorities, they simply became the shadow of that resistance as time evolved with the influence of telecommunications and social mutations.

In his book, Casimir cites the institutions and mechanisms with which the people resisted, such as "gender relations, family, the *lakou* [clusters of homes around a central courtyard], indivisible collective property, Vodou temples, rural markets, garden-towns, leisure, crafts,

[and] the arts." He also notes the important role played by the Haitian *Kreyòl*, a common language that sustained these forms of resistance over time. But, the Haitian leaders, allied with the oligarchy instead of being united with the people to strengthen these forms of resistance and build a state together for common good, disenfranchised them politically, alienated them, and worked in opposition to the very cultural and social landscape of the nation in order to gain recognition and help from foreign empires.[61]

Haitian leaders have made all sorts of compromises that have not translated into progress for the country as a whole, nor have those compromises ever helped them avoid humiliation. They have never acquired from foreign powers the level of prestige they have always been so desperate for. To paraphrase Casimir, the more the Haitian administration and Haitian politicians knocked at the door of the imperial powers and managed to accelerate efforts at rapprochement, the more Haiti found itself subjugated and humiliated. Perhaps Haitian leaders would have been better off siding with the majority of the Haitian people, who have always rejected the state system that sought to reproduce imperial hierarchies and institutionalize social divisions on the basis of racial discriminations.

We continue to insist and maintain that a stronger and more durable union between and among former enslaved blacks and free people of color (mulattoes) could have strengthened Haiti amid concurrences between foreign imperial powers. The Haitian leaders could have navigated the country's diplomatic opportunities and possibilities better in light of openings and weaknesses shown by those

61 Jean Casimir, Jean, *The Haitians: A Decolonial History (Chapel Hill, USA: The* University of North Carolina Press, 2020), p. 22, 452.

foreign powers in search of monopoly. More inclusive sociopolitical and economic development projects would have reinforced Haiti's standing in the aftermath of the revolution. That did not happen. But there is still good news. The hope is that today's generations can look back and learn from the mistakes made in order to lead the country to redemption.

First, let's look at the indemnity paid to France in exchange for the recognition of independence, for example. How had we managed to overthrow the whole French colonial system but could not ignore the pressures from France? As a result, we had to agree to pay millions of francs in gold to them for reparations—money we did not even have but had to borrow from British, German, and American banks at an exorbitant rate of interest. Instead, over two decades deep into our independence, we should have been the one imposing our demand for reparations to France for the atrocities suffered by our people due to slavery.

The same way today's Haitian government, rival politicians, oligarchs, business leaders, and other interest groups are paying millions of dollars to Washington lobbyists in order to win the influence of the United States, it was the Haitian president Jean-Pierre Boyer who agreed in 1825 to pay 150 million gold francs (reduced to 90 million in 1838) to France for the independence that we had already won over two decades earlier. Wait a minute . . . What were Boyer and his government afraid of? Despite the gunboat diplomacy from France to impose the payment, there was no guarantee that Haiti could not have defeated them once again. Boyer and other mulatto leaders were too accommodating to Paris. They were, perhaps, too eager to make themselves look good and obedient in the eyes of imperial powers that they were willing to pay any cost.

We are still experiencing the same kind of attitude from Haitian leaders today. On top of that, they continue to rob Haiti. According to several reports, the Jean-Claude Duvalier regime alone diverted more than $1 billion from the country's teasury. After Duvalier, the different governments that have succeeded continue to siphon off more and more billions from the Haitian people.

The second thing is that the blockade on trade was never total. Foreign nations and imperial powers like Great Britain and the United States saw the defeat of France as a great opportunity to initiate their own trade treaties, even unofficially, with one the most important islands in the Caribbean. Even when negotiations failed, trade still indeed happened between these nations and Haiti. They did not want to show support for Haiti's independence openly—oscillating between implicit and explicit policies—in fear of creating rebellion and disruption in their own slavery system in addition to diplomatic animosity between themselves. Nonetheless, various historians, notably Dr. Julia Gaffield in her book about recognition after the revolution, noted the efforts by the U.S. and British representatives from very early on to concoct trade agreements with Haiti.

Even though the United States, for instance, had a trade interdiction in place, American merchants never stopped finding ways to trade with Haiti. They saw in Haiti a profitable market that the U.S. government should have ushered by establishing contact with Haitian leaders. American merchant Jacob Lewis, cited by Dr. Gaffield, clarified the U.S. perspective and approach in his letter to the Secretary of State James Madison in October 1804 when he wrote, "I cannot help thinking that if the policy of our government is to encourage the trade to this Island, it would be well to communicate with the Emperor [Dessalines], if not directly, let him have the assurances of our friendship and our determination to support our commerce with them while the property and Citizens of the US are respected and favored in this Island." Lewis expressed himself in these terms to the U.S. government from Port-au-Prince with the knowledge that the American merchants were doing business in Haiti without stiff competition. He knew that the British government was trying to sign a formal treaty with the Dessalines regime in early 1804 and therefore feared that the British might succeed ahead of the U.S. in establishing a trade monopoly over Haiti.[62]

Another proof of foreign powers' silent cooperation with Haiti after the revolution was the participation of German and British engineers in the construction of a series of historic buildings in the Northern Kingdom of Haiti ruled by Christophe. If the relations with these international competing forces were well managed diplomatically by Haitian leaders, the country could have been in a better position today. Looking at a number of historical records and the conditions that still exist in Haiti today, it seems like we have been against ourselves a lot more than they have been against us.

Again, we do not intend to give imperialism and neoliberalism a free pass for their roles in Haiti's current legacy. Our point is that it has always been too easy for us to point fingers at foreign powers, particularly the United States, for our problems, a number of which have resulted from our own actions or inactions. The foreign powers do not act alone in undermining Haiti's well-being. They certainly use national accomplices. In this world, people respect or do not respect you just because of your history. But they do or do not respect

62 Julia Gaffield, *Haitian Connections in the Atlantic World* (Chapel Hill, USA: The University of North Carolina Press, 2015), p. 61-82, 124, 126-129.

you because of the kind of legacy you continue to build from one generation to the other.

The world is not static. It is constantly moving as a result of the adventurous and insatiable nature of mankind. Socioeconomic and political contexts keep changing and evolving according to the needs of the time. Countries will always need leaders who can understand and elevate themselves in meeting the challenges of their time. Each era presents its series of challenges and opportunities. A country's success or failure during an era depends largely on the kind of legacy it inherits from its past leaders and how present leaders continue to build on that legacy as a bridge to future generations.

In Haiti, making others the culprit overrides any concerted efforts to resolve our problems. This is a psychological blowback for the nation's mindset. And this tends to give Haitian leaders a way to distract the population and divert people's attention from their incompetence, corruption, malpractice, malfeasance, misfeasance, and nonfeasance for more than two centuries. The blame game touches every aspect of life in Haiti. It crosses paths with every subject and issue, such as politics, religion, education, public health, the environment, national production, livestock, transportation, infrastructure, migration, natural disasters, and more. The blame game has become an escape haven for Haiti's lack of good leadership.

3.2: We Are the Lean Dog

Se sou bannann mi dan pouri gen fòs (bad teeth only have strength to eat banana); *ravèt pa janm gen rezon devan poul* (chickens are always right over cockroaches). The translation: those with might always impose their reason. It is a sort of Jean De La Fontaine's wolf and sheep philosophy.[63]

These two proverbs in the Haitian wisdom sum up a fundamental issue with Haiti's psychology: a sort of inferiority complex. It is problematic that many Haitians consider Haiti as a small country not just in size but in its capability compared to others in the region. Individuals often and pejoratively call one another Haitians as a diminutive epithet to say that they are up to no good; they are supposedly not capable of doing anything valuable or positive. Paradoxically, the same people were able to defeat the Napoleon army and overthrow the French brutal slavery system to open the door to freedom for all oppressed people in the Americas and the rest of the world. That was extraordinary.

During the first few decades after independence, they were able to build great monuments that are highly valued and renowned internationally, such as the Citadelle Laferrière, the Sans-Souci Palace, and the Palace of 365 doors in northern Haiti. The country has developed a rich culture of music, dance, arts, and crafts, and produced different generations of movie producers, actors, artists, intellectuals, philosophers, scientists and professionals of all trades—men and women alike—useful to people around the world. Education, literature, liberal arts, and medical science are among areas where Haitians excel, and their contributions are notable in different parts of the world. Europe, Canada, France, the United States, Latin America, and African countries have long been the beneficiaries of important works from native Haitians, particularly as teachers, professors, nurses, doctors,

63 Jean De La Fontaine, 17th Century French philosopher, fabulist, and poet, wrote the moral tale: Le loup et l'agneau (The wolf and the sheep) to underline the dynamic between the classes in French society at the time.

and lawyers, among other professions. Haitians are not *bannann mi* (banana) nor *ravèt* (cockroach).

The opposite of the above fatalistic expressions would be others like *mwen pa pitimi san gadò* (I am not a sheep without shepherd) and *mwen gen bwa dèyè bannann mwen* (I have powerful people behind me), without a vengeful spirit. Yet, most of the time, some Haitians use these expressions to brag about how well connected they are in comparison to most people. The reason is simple. Equal opportunities are very limited. People who often succeed are not necessarily the ones that put in the most effort. So much depends on who you know, your acquaintances, your last name; whether you are from a city or a village, from an urban area or rural area, from the capital Port-au-Prince or from a province; whether you are members of a big church or a small church, or attended this school or that other school; whether you have dark skin or fair skin: or whether you have soft hair or dry, coarse, kinky black hair.

The Haitian expression *tinèg tèt grenn* (little nappy hair man or woman), often used in its plain derogatory sense, says it all. However, as grim as the situation looks, Haitians are fighters in a positive way. Many people succeed in beating the actual system by working harder, studying harder, and putting more effort into grassroots and community organizations. Many times, people recount their stories of how hard they have worked with very little or no help to achieve success in various areas of life in Haiti, such as farming, education, commerce, trades, entrepreneurship (both informal and formal), crafts, music, dance, and sports, among others.

The successes and the transcendental nature of the Haitian people are not often exposed to the world. That is one of the reasons most Haitians are usually afraid that they could be perceived in terms of their positional weaknesses when dealing with others, not in terms of their strengths. That fear has created a mentality that reflects on their interactions with foreigners and with each other, as well as on their relations with things, places, and animals.

Depending on the context, it could go either way because many Haitians do not conceptualize a level playing field in their mindset. Very often, someone is more likely to consider their interlocutor inferior or superior to themselves instead of their equal as human beings. Those in position to acquire a service are more likely to be forced to feel weak or inferior in front of those in position to provide them with that service. It works the same way in businesses, nonprofits, churches, vodou temples, schools, sociopolitical organizations, governmental institutions, etc. That is how Haitian authorities usually deal with the people they are supposed to be working for.

In contrast, they usually feel obligated to reverse their positions when dealing with foreign leaders, making the latters' reasons appear to be absolutely the best. They play the same inferior role they reserve for their own citizens locally while elevating their foreign counterparts. Sometimes they do it for flattery just to be able to get the help they are looking for. More often, they do it out of fear and a sense of insecurity.

It is that feeling of insecurity, inadequacy, and inferiority that makes Haitian leaders think small rather than big. They do not look positively ambitious enough. Their initiatives have never been big enough to shape a framework capable of social, political, and economic transformation. This is how most of the Haitian society has been fixated into the vision of smallness. Everything is attributed to being small or little. Using the term small has become abusive in Haiti. Sometimes, they use it as a way to show affection toward someone or something (my little darling/girl or boy, or my little car).

More often, they use little or small to diminish the value of something or someone, or to express the fear of thinking big. If someone wants to make someone else feels inferior, they may say "that little pig," "that little dog," "that little rat," "that little girl/woman," "that little boy/man." If someone wants to degrade their aspirations, they may say "I am building a little house," "I need to start a little business," "I need to look for a little something to do," etc. It is not usual to hear someone say things like "I have a big project—I want to build the greatest company in Haiti."

Most initiators would fear that someone might steal their idea, derail their plan one way or the other, or even kill them as a result. In Haiti, as in many other places in the world, people are generally afraid of competition. But what is perhaps unique about Haiti is that instead of strategizing in a fair and constructive manner to get an edge over their competition, some people often try to deal with it in the opposite way. These people truly believe that they can exist only if they eliminate the other or prevent the other from functioning by any means necessary.

That mindset creates a major obstacle for the development of enterprises, thus limiting opportunities for Haiti's political and socioeconomic developments. More often, we find situations where two or more people, who are doing similar activities in an area, are more likely to treat each other as enemies. They do not see each other as people or businesses competing for excellence in their field of activities.

Additionally, many Haitians are often afraid of the supposedly secretive power of the vodou religion. They think that someone considered as stronger with higher supernatural or spiritual connections could hurt or help them if they are weaker. That kind of belief has been also transmitted into the practice of Christianity in Haiti. Some converted Christians still believe they can use bible verses, worship, or prayers to seek vengeance and favors.

The good news is that whenever Haitians use their sense of rationality, they quickly realize that these beliefs and practices are far from being transformational for Haiti in a good way. They do not define who we are as a people. Beliefs and traditions are acquired within society through generations. After being tested, they can be rejected, preserved, or reinforced based on their positive or negative effects.

3.3: We Are Not Lucky

Lè ou an devenn menm lèt kaye kase tèt ou (literally translated as when you are not lucky, even spoiled milk thrown at you could crack your forehead). This proverb underlines the fatalistic attitude and mindset of many Haitians. There is a belief that all events affecting the living conditions in Haiti are already predetermined simply because the Haitian people are just not lucky, and therefore those events are inevitable. The spirit of fatalism has kept the country in a state of indifference, resignation, and stagnation for so long. This preconception makes it hard for most Haitians to realize that the country has failed due in part to a lack of proper planning and implementation of knowledge.

Things cannot just happen all the time because you are lucky or not lucky. A quote attributed to Roman philosopher Lucius Annaeus Seneca defines luck as "what happens when preparation meets opportunity."[64] It means any human being can create their own luck. Many times, people get killed in flash floods during rainy seasons, for example. Some become very frantic during hurricane seasons due to mismanagement and the lack of proper planning and preparation. Many others are severely injured, even die, in accidents that could be avoided with better infrastructure and law enforcement.

The death of hundreds of thousands of people in Haiti stemming from January 2010 and August 2021 earthquakes was another example of the country's lack of proper planning. Of course, natural disasters of that magnitude can happen anywhere. The good thing is that the advancement of science and technology allows us to receive predictions and warnings. We may not be able to know exactly when an earthquake or a fault chit an area. But we can foresee it happening based on the possibility of fault lines and the intensity of movements. Preparing for the eventuality is a wise decision. Proper planning includes, but is not limited to, information, education, zoning, and respect of construction codes.

For decades, none of these has ever been a clear priority for the country's government. When you thought the January 12, 2010 earthquake would be a wake-up call for Haitians, the reckless behaviors of many in the aftermath would simply leave you speechless and deceived. People have been allowed to build homes and buildings wherever and anyway they want, without any inspection, and in most cases, without any minimum safety standard. Having experienced the worst possible nightmare on that famous January 12, you would think that people were going to modify their behavior, and the government

---

64 Goodreads, "Author and Quotes", goodreads.com, Goodreads, retrieved March 13, 2022. https://www.goodreads.com/author/quotes/4918776.Seneca

was going to pass regulations and establish mechanisms to implement and reinforce them. There were a lot of talks in that regard, but not enough concrete and consistent actions. Some people moved away from the epicenter of the scene and built new homes in worse conditions than before. Others freely rebuilt or repaired their damaged homes without modifying the previous structures. Everything had been done under the complicit eyes of government officials. Still, no one thinks they are responsible for anything.

The trials of life, catastrophes, and natural disasters are often unavoidable, universal, and inevitable . . . But only our unshakable faith, resilient creativity and imagination, prevention, planning, sound laws and management system, undivided strength, individual responsibility, and transcendental ability can help us overcome.

When it comes to the well-being and safety of the people in Haiti, you can look at any aspect of life, not just construction. This is a travesty of enormous proportion. It seems like no one has any respect for human life; hence, they believe tragedies happen because they are not lucky. "Haitians are cursed." They are predestined to suffer, some would say. You hear people say things like that, for instance, after a driver loses control of a vehicle and runs over people sitting on the side of the road selling stuff, as if the road were a marketplace. On a regular basis, drivers plow their vehicles into crowds of people, killing and injuring them in ridiculous numbers. Incidents like that occur with private and commercial vehicles almost every day in cities and towns across the country.

On top of the existing problem with the circulation of cars and trucks in a society constantly mutating on its own in order to adjust with life, an abundance of motorcycles operated by mostly immature riders abound everywhere, while laws and safety measures lag far behind. The problem of immature motorcycle operators is only compounded by the abysmal road conditions still present in Haiti, as well as the lack of basic traffic laws. There is no national system to maintain the roadways that are currently present in the country. Furthermore, there is limited access to the asphalt needed to repair roadways. Rain, especially during hurricane season, wreaks havoc on the existing roads, making them slippery and muddy, as they are not engineered to facilitate runoff. Traffic lanes are frequently undesignated and populated by pedestrians, livestock, and vendors; guardrails, stop signs, stoplights, and speed limit signs are things of the past. They used to be visible decades ago in big towns and cities. Drivers often wear headphones to listen to music instead of observing their surroundings and driving defensively, and of course many vehicles are poorly maintained, making them a hazard to their operators and others on the road.

All of these issues, coupled with immature and reckless operators, cause many otherwise preventable accidents. The transport system along with mother nature have always been a source of great danger and calamities for the Haitian people. Whether maritime or land transport, nothing is conducted in a manner that respects human dignity and human life. The only exception is flying an airplane, mainly because regulations and safety control are not 100% in the hands of Haitian authorities.

Most recently, in less than 30 years, Haiti had at least eight major catastrophes that killed and injured an incalculable amount of people. Many of those who died or were severely injured could have been spared if there were reliable infrastructure, good laws and enforcement, and a better sense of individual responsibility and accountability among the people themselves.

The first incident happened February 16–17, 1993, when a heavily overloaded ferry sank in a storm off the coastal southwest of Haiti, drowning most of the passengers aboard. Haitian authorities took about 2 days to rescue only 285 people from that incident, out of 2000+ passengers. The 150-foot refitted cargo ship (*Neptune*) went down, just 60 miles from Port-au-Prince; there were no lifeboats, life jackets, or other emergency gear, such as radios, on board. The ship could only carry about 650 passengers. But it was irresponsibly overloaded. *Neptune* was on a 12-hour voyage from the western port of Jérérmie to Port-au-Prince carrying excessive people, tons of charcoal, many animals and farm goods for sale in the metropolitan area of Port-au-Prince, the largest city in Haiti. The second boat accident happened less than five years later, on September 8, 1997. The overcrowded *La Fierté Gonavienne* (Pride of Gonave) sank off the coast of Montrouis, fewer than 50 miles north of Port-au-Prince. Most of the 700 or so passengers aboard drowned in similar fashion to the *Neptune* tragedy.

These tragic events, among many others, were a mixture of natural and man-made disasters, which we were not prepared to deal with.

Fonds-Verrettes, a town located about 41 miles east of Port-au-Prince, registered two huge floods between 1998 and 2004. On both occasions, the deaths and material damages were colossal. The city of Gonaives, the largest and historically most important city in the Artibonite department, dealt with two major floods, as well, in September 2004 and 2008. Those floods together were responsible for the death of more than 3,000 people, and a score more were missing. In addition, there were millions of dollars in infrastructural and economic damages.

As previously mentioned, within one decade, Haiti had registered two devastating earthquakes. First, there was that magnitude 7.0 quake, which struck the Port-au-Prince area on January 12, 2010, claiming well over 300,000 lives, injuring thousands more, and leaving as many as 2.3 million people homeless and without food and clean water. Haiti was still trying to figure out how to recover from January 12, and then boom! A more powerful magnitude 7.2 earthquake struck the entire southwestern peninsula on August 14, 2021. That second quake claimed the life of about 3,000 people and affected 800,000 others due to injuries or property destruction. About 137,000 homes, 1,250 schools, and 95 hospitals and health centers were damaged or destroyed.

That same year, in the middle of the night of December 13, an unimaginable but clearly predictable tragedy happened in Cap-Haitian, Haiti's second largest city after Port-au-Prince. A truck transporting gasoline exploded inside the city after the driver lost control of the tanker while trying to avoid a motorcycle rider crossing in front of him around midnight.

The tanker exploded when some residents of the city rushed to the scene of the accident and started to pillage the tanker. They wanted the gas, a consumer product that had become scarce, expensive, and precious to Haitians. As they were filling receptacles of all kinds with gasoline, the truck exploded, killing scores of people and injuring several dozen men, women, and children. The fire from the explosion went rampant in the area and travelled through the packed corridors of the city, which were packed with homes, for several hours, burning many houses with people inside who were sleeping. Haitian authorities were helpless in the situation. After the furor of the fire calmed down, they went picking up calcined bodies of human-beings at the scene.

It is not totally the fault of God, the devil, or the state. In Haiti, people often conduct many activities in order to merely survive in conditions that put their own lives in jeopardy on a daily basis. Everything is conducted under the passive and complicit eyes of the authorities, but everyone with common sense has certain responsibilities for their own sake. Too many get severely injured or killed too often in accidents that could be prevented with proper regulations, inspections, and enforcement. But no one seems to care. However, politicians, government officials, leaders from all types of organizations, the media, and particularly the people themselves have never stopped complaining about the situation. Unfortunately, everyone rallies the cry too often in the heat of the moment. Shortly after an incident or a terrible catastrophe, everyone moves on, goes about their business, and forgets about the issues causing the incident. It is as if by doing so, the root causes of the problems would magically disappear. People will argue, criticize, and condemn, and then they will be resigned fatalistically to reappear with the same rallying cry later when another tragic incident or disaster recurs to make them count more victims.

Again, we repeat and emphasize it. It is inevitable that accidents and natural disasters happen everywhere, more so in certain developing and third world countries. Haiti and its Caribbean neighbors are no exception. The only difference is that Haiti presents more vulnerabilities by its structural and organizational design. In that sense, it is a more perfect environment for all catastrophes to happen beyond our worst imagination. Geography and bad luck are only responsible for a little part of the blame for Haiti's tragedies. Of course, the government is responsible for a big part because of its cascading failures and strings of mismanagement. Reliable infrastructure, safety policies and protocols, risk assessment, and disaster management structures are so nonexistent in Haiti that whenever, whatever, wherever disaster chooses to strike, its impact on the population is magnified many times over.

For example, Haiti has only five fire stations, of which only two are fully operational for the entire country of about 11 million people. Compare Haiti with its neighbors, which are equally prone to natural disasters but are far better equipped to cope because they are far better functioning societies. For them, the picture looks brighter. Approach Haiti's border with the Dominican Republic and the lush green of the forest begins again. You will find a wealthier place and less chaos on the same island. An earthquake, a hurricane, or flood there, for instance, has less impact because construction is stronger, building regulations are enforced, the government is more stable. In nearby Cuba, hardly a country rolling in money, emergency management is infinitely more effective simply because of a carefully coordinated, block-by-block organization. Definitely, Haiti can learn positive lessons from its Caribbean neighbors' experiences to inspire hope.

3.4: They Do Not Help Us Enough

The idea that others should help more is so excessively used in Haiti that it often dominates the discourse among Haitians themselves and divides families to the extreme. The problem is not necessarily that Haitians do not get enough help. The issue is more complex than that. If anything, Haitians are generally very generous toward each other, particularly within family circles. And a number of foreign nations, through both government and nongovernment initiatives, help Haiti regularly.

A situation worth understanding is that the Haitian culture is developed mostly out of slavery, poverty, and hardship. In typical Haitian families, men are considered as the head of households and are responsible for making money to support their families, while women have the task of taking care of the children and in-home activities. But with times and social mutations, the responsibility of being the provider can fall on anyone—a father, mother, child, sibling, an uncle or aunt, a cousin, a far distant relative, friends or benefactors, etc. Basically, anyone who is more fortunate and more economically privileged.

In Haiti, the term family is generally used in a very broad sense. People could be traced back generations by others who would seek benefits or favor in claiming them as family members. Yet, a lot of times, what links a person to another is just a last name, not really blood or marriage. Many Haitians have a common last name, but no direct blood relationship that one can easily retrieve. This is a country where personal relationships are very important, especially if those relationships mean good connections. A common last name makes access a lot easier. However, most Haitians are so much in need that one may never do enough to satisfy another. On top of that, the quality of help received from others is often open for debate. That situation often creates continuous tensions between individuals, among families, and between people and governmental institutions and nongovernmental organizations alike. Haitians living overseas suffer the most from those tensions. They are often reluctant to go back home amid fear that someone, mostly members from their own families, may intend to harm them because they are unsatisfied with the level of financial support or simply out of jealousy.

At the local level, most of the time, others hesitate to do more for underprivileged Haitians due to fear. A common issue is that helping impoverished people in Haiti often results with those in positions to help receiving backlash from professional politicians. They often think that helping needy communities makes the people helping gain political attraction or a popular advantage over them, hence increasing their chance of winning in case they entertain the possibility of running for office. Most Haitian politicians do not believe someone can genuinely be inspired to do philanthropic works. In their perceptions, there must be a hidden agenda: either it is a vehicle to accumulate more wealth, or it is a strategy to satisfy political ambitions. Once you start thinking about helping to make a difference in people's living conditions, you become a political target, an enemy to many. You face persecution, intimidation, and all sorts of threats to your life.

Very recently, before the devastating 7.2 earthquake in August 2021, a young entrepreneur in Dame-Marie (a seaside town of about 30,000 inhabitants located in Haiti's southwestern peninsula, the Department of Grand'Anse) had been providing drinking water free of charge to the most vulnerable and unfortunate people in the community during dry seasons. A well-known former senator from the region would go publicly criticizing the businessman and accusing him of showboating and self-promotion for political gain. But according to the young Haitian entrepreneur, he was simply motivated by altruism in a community where he was deeply rooted and was raised. His motivation was founded on the idea of giving back and investing into his community of origin. He wanted to pour his energy into making his own community a better place for all. In contrast, the former senator had long promised to build a water dam for the population, but that promise never materialized. This scenario is one vivid example among plenty of others all over Haiti that continues to have a negative effect on mutual aid and socioeconomic progress.

As we have seen, in addition to politicizing and weaponizing community support, there is a sense of permanent insatiability among the population when it comes to receiving help from others, either because the amount of help received is inadequate in comparison to the scope of the need, or the distribution of the aid is not well-planned. More often, the politics of aid is poorly implemented in a chaotic environment where most entities involved in the distribution have been working hard enough to nourish and maintain the dependence instead of eliminating it. Another big problem that exists among humanitarian organizations is the huge lack of accountability, where they are running as a parallel state. They have no effective coordination among them in the field, nor do they work adequately with local organizations. These issues, among others, making these humanitarian organizations' efforts very wasteful and their operations very costly at the expense of change on the ground. As a consequence, the people involved sometimes face direct backlash from the very same communities or individuals that those organizations are supposedly on a mission to help.

In situations like that, people use the metaphoric expression *Ayisyen se chyen* (Haitians are like dogs). It means Haitians will bite you at some point even if you have been gracious and helpful to them, and it is used to call someone ungrateful. Another expression is *granmesi chyen se yon kout baton*, which means the dog will be beaten with a stick instead of receiving thanks for the service rendered. It is a metaphor for the more you help Haitians, the more unsatisfied they are, and the more they might come back and hurt you as a result. However, this is an exaggeration to the fullest extent. We cannot generalize it like that. This perception is not a true representation of Haitian values.

Of course, continuing extreme poverty and hardships make people more dependent on others, and those conditions seem to make people look insatiable, especially if they are not being helped in a productive way that leads them to become financially independent. But this is not fundamentally cultural among Haitians. Ungratefulness and insatiability are practices modeled over the years by the politicians, authoritarian leaders, and corrupt oligarchs, who have been so desperate in the pursuit of power, privileges, and money at the detriment of others. And those bad practices crisscross all classes, one generation after another, and have left a stain on the society. The same way Haitian leaders publicly complain about other countries for not helping Haiti enough despite mismanaging the billions of dollars received over the last and current century, individuals do just that in pointing fingers at anyone whom they think should be doing more for them.

Haitians made the most important revolution in 1804, but they have failed to build a sound nation-state for being partly captive to their own mindset when it came to shaping their destiny. Like raising a family, no one decides to create a country in hope that others will help you build it, develop it, and manage it. You would welcome all help from international friends and sister nations as long as their idea of helping is in line with your internal strategies regarding nation-building projects and your larger vision for your country. More importantly, you would take responsibility and hold yourself accountable for your own success or failure. Responsibility and accountability in Haiti? Yes. We lack these greatly.

Everyone accuses one another of being at the root causes of Haiti's dilemma. But no individual thinks that he or she is to blame for anything wrong with the country they all cherish and love. However, they blame each other, and they blame foreigners. Despite their role in the demise of Haiti, foreign powers can justify for themselves why they have not assumed their responsibilities. You cannot blame them if their motives are contrary to Haiti's welfare. But Haitians, on the other hand, are the ones in need of soul-searching for their own well-being. Not that we do not need help from the international community. International support to Haiti needs to be meaningful and conducted in complete solidarity, taking into account the Haitian culture and environmental and institutional weaknesses.

Haitians like to often say, *kabrit plizyè mèt kap mouri nan solèy* (a goat of multiple owners is dying in the sun) in reference to a sense of neglect when it comes to the state of Haiti. Haitians are generally proud of their roots. But only a few are willing to share the burden of being Haitians. Anytime situations look dire and uncertain, Haitians leave by the thousands to look for better conditions elsewhere, constituting a great proportion of human resources lost overtime. Recent data shows that about 80% of Haitians with at least a bachelor's degree live outside of Haiti. However, between real sympathy for the most unfortunate and vulnerable people in a country of generally careless leaders and the priority on the promotion of personal interests at the expense of the common good, Haitians living abroad have never forgotten their roots. They have not neglected their families back home, nor have foreigners stopped helping Haiti. The more Haiti faces crises of all sorts, the more help is flowing into the country.

In fact, during the last three decades, Haitians from all backgrounds and socioeconomic structures have been scattered around the world and have become essentially the source of the economic survival of relatives and friends living back home. Haiti stands among the top five countries in the world with about 50% of its population dependent entirely on financial support coming from nationals abroad. The other four countries are Kyrgyzstan, Tajikistan, Tonga, and Nepal. Living conditions in Haiti would be worse if it were not for remittances from the Haitian diaspora. Before 1991, money transferred from foreign countries to Haitian families directly did not reach US$50 million annually. This figure doubled in just four years by 1994, and reached $327 million average by 1998.

By 2011, the annual average reached $1.5 billion, and it almost doubled again a year later. Today, the remittances from Haitian immigrants are estimated to be between $3 billion and $6 billion on an annual basis. That accounts for about 5% to 10% of the Haitian diaspora's total income, about 80% of which come from people living in the United States. Chile, Canada, France, the Dominican Republic and Brazil rank respectively behind the U.S. with a combined amount of about 17% out of the remaining 20% of money remitted directly to Haitian families.[65] The Haitian diaspora transferred about US$20 billion to Haiti between 2010 and 2019.[66]

Let's look at bilateral and multilateral financial and technical supports, for example. Haiti has received more help than all the other Caribbean countries combined in the last three decades. Unfortunately, the more help the country has received the more dependent it has become. Haiti would borrow billions of dollars for meager or no results. When the country becomes insolvent, international lenders—encouraged particularly by the World Bank, the International Monetary Fund, and the European Union—eliminate the accumulated debts partially or totally in exchange for a commitment from the Haitian government that they would engage in institutional and structural reforms. More often, those reforms would not necessarily work for the good of the people.

Foreign powers usually help Haiti in light of their national interests, and most of the money received by the Haitian government is spent in

---

65 Gary Cyprien, "L'évolution des transferts de la diaspora haïtienne", lenouvelliste.com, Le Nouvelliste, Nov. 9, 2021. https://lenouvelliste.com/article/232581/levolution-des-transferts-de-la-diaspora-haitienne

66 Patrick Saint-Pré, "Haiti a reçu environ 20 millards de dollars de la diapora entre 2010 et 2019", lenouvelliste.com, Le Nouvelliste, October 1, 2020. https://lenouvelliste.com/article/211022/haiti-a-recu-environ-20-milliards-de-dollars-de-transferts-de-la-diaspora-entre-2010-et-2019

implementing programs and policies that have not been designed to address people's fundamental needs and priorities. The reason is simple. The country has for so long been plagued by sociopolitical instability, corruption, incompetence, unaccountability, irresponsibility, and a lack of cohesive vision and long-term planning.

We do not need to go any further than 2010. After the devastating earthquake that had destroyed most of the capital Port-au-Prince and its surroundings, many people thought that Haiti had the opportunity to be rebuilt and rethought out for real and for good. The enthusiasm manifested by the international community in flowing financial assistance was not lacking. According to official records, Haiti had received more than US$13 billion—more than four times the national budget at the time—in financial aid pledged by foreign governments, multilateral institutions, and private donors for emergency assistance and rebuilding efforts.

From 2011 to 2020 for example, the United States alone, through the US Agency for International Development (USAID), donated $1.8 billion to Haiti. And again, when a second powerful earthquake struck southwestern Haiti in August 2021, assistance of all kinds flooded the country from everywhere.[67]

Individuals, governments, and nongovernmental organizations from around the globe, once again, demonstrated outstanding solidarity and generosity toward the Haitian people, for both relief and rebuilding efforts. After the relief phase of that second quake, the Haitian

---

67 U.S. Embassy in Haiti, "United States Commits an Additional $24.4 Million for Assistance to Haiti", usembassy.gov, U.S. Embassy in Haiti, October 5, 2020. https://ht.usembassy.gov/united-states-commits-an-additional-24-4-million-for-assistance-to-haiti/

government led an international donors' conference, hoping to raise at least $2 billion for rebuilding projects in the Nippes and Grand'Anse regions. As of mid-February 2022, Haiti has already raised $600 million of that amount from other nations.

Since the first day of relief and urgent humanitarian assistance efforts, the United States was at the front line as usual with millions of dollars in aid. Through USAID alone, $32 million were donated immediately in the aftermath of the earthquake "to support humanitarian partners delivering urgently-needed aid, including health care services, emergency shelter and food, safe drinking water, hygiene and sanitation assistance, and protection services, including gender-based violence prevention and response, child protection, and psychosocial support services in hard-hit areas," detailed a press release from the agency on August 26, 2021.[68]

The Haitian government collected another $264 million from the Caribbean Catastrophe Insurance Facility (CCIF) and the International Monetary Fund through Special Drawing Rights (SDR). Additionally, The World Bank awarded a donation of $75 million on September 28, 2021 through the International Development Association (IDA) to support job creation in the private sector.[69] These figures are just a few examples of major international financial support to Haiti among many others during the recent man-made and natural disasters. The World

---

68 Office of Press Relations, "USAID Provides $32 Million to Respond to Haiti Earthquake", usaid.gov, USAID, August 26, 2021. https://www.usaid.gov/news-information/press-releases/aug-26-2021-usaid-provides-32-million-respond-haiti-earthquake

69 Radio Télé Metropole, "La Banque Mondiale approuve 75 millions de dollars pour soutenir la création d'emplois en Haiti", metropole.ht, Radio Télé Metropole Haiti. https://metropole.ht/la-banque-mondiale-approuve-75-millions-de-dollars-pour-soutenir-la-creation-demplois-en-haiti/

Bank funds were intended to support the economic transformation of 4,000 private enterprises covering 61,000 jobs, particularly in the small business sector.

But general conditions in the country have not changed. The more foreign countries, multilateral institutions, nonprofit organizations, and private donors are pouring money into different disaster reliefs and social development programs in Haiti, the more dependent most people are. And the country's general landscape has not improved. Why is that then? Again, the answer is found in a combination of impeding factors, including corruption, unaccountability, irresponsibility, incompetence, mismanagement, dependence, and a lack of proper planning. It is not always the fault of the donors.

However, Haiti has a long history of dependence on foreign assistance that often makes its government a passive spectator. From one group of leaders to another, the discourse might change, but the issue remains. The famous slogan *grès cochon an ka kuit kochon an*—slogan used in reference to the idea that Haiti could do it financially without assistance from foreign powers—by Aristide in 1991 did not even cross the Windward Passage to reach Florida. It was flatly drowned right before attaining Cuba.

And despite the heavy reliance on foreign assistance, the government institutions themselves have rarely been the direct beneficiaries of most of the financial aid provided. Usually, a small percentage of financial aid goes directly to the Haitian government; most of it goes to foreign contractors and so-called experts and covers heavy administrative and logistics costs. This problem dates back from the Duvalier era, where multilaterals and other organizations chose not to work directly with the government due to mistrust, hence creating a parallel state. As a result, many public service functions are still in private hands more apt to facilitate corruption and no transparency. The state has become more and more eroded over time, and the government has been in a permanent position of weakness—a posture of inability to respond in times of crisis.

The Haitian government's inability to respond cannot be more exemplified than by the moribund plans to rebuild the Presidential Palace, other important government buildings, and symbols of Haiti's rich history and culture in Port-au-Prince destroyed by the 2010 earthquake. More than a decade after the natural disaster, the rebuilding effort of the National Palace has been in limbo while billions of dollars destined to fund Haiti's reconstruction projects are unaccounted for.

During the first two years that followed the destructive quake, it seemed like the palace, which was completely destroyed twice before and being rebuilt in1869 and again in 1920, might be rebuilt for a third time in its history. The Haitian government has repeatedly reiterated the will to do so, and most of the population has also wanted to see that ornate symbol of pride, sovereignty, and independence rise up from the ground and stand strong again at 6110 Avenue de la République. Like they are always proud of the 19th-century fortresses La Citadelle Laferrière, Le Palais Sans-Souci, Le Palais des 365 Portes, La Cathedrale du Roi Henri built in Northern Haiti under Henri Christophe, and the ancient Cathedrale de Port-au-Prince, Haitians were so proud of Le Palais National d'Haiti (The National Palace of Haiti) that some rivaled its opulence to that of the White House and even Buckingham Palace.

Today, the grounds of that elegant symbol of pride are empty. A trailer set there with a few small buildings around to conduct government businesses is nothing compared to the 92-year-old, E-shaped, gleaming white French Renaissance palace. Unfortunately, the plans for a new palace are tangled up between the politics of aid and reconstruction. The severely damaged palace was ultimately demolished and came down entirely in a cloud of dust in 2012, as Martelly's government wanted to portray Haiti as normal and "open for business" (in former President Martelly's own words) in order to attract foreign investors. And since then, plans to build a new presidential residence have remained unclear because government communication on the matter has been either muted or minimal at the very best.

Most Haitians want the government to build a new palace with Haitian money, not with foreign aid. This is a big deal considering the lack of reliable leadership and the financial limitations in the country. In 2017, late President Jovenel Moise announced plans to rebuild the palace with the inauguration of a special commission composed of Haitian architects and historians. The commission was tasked to undertake all aspects of the palace's reconstruction. But financial obstacles and sociopolitical instability meant that the rebuilding idea did not materialize because the construction of a new palace became a lesser priority behind Haiti's real daily calamities.

For the purpose of comparison and to understand where we are as a people today, we need to look back at what had happened after the National Palace was destroyed twice prior to 2010. When the palace (where all Haitian presidents resided from Alexandre Pétion starting in 1806 to Rene Preval up to January 12, 2010) was destroyed by a violent revolt in 1869, it took the Haitian government about 12 years to completely rebuild it.

The original iteration dated back from the French colonization time. It served as the residence to the different colonial governors before the revolution. About 31 years later, in August 1912, the structures of the rebuilt palace were damaged beyond repair as a result of a violent explosion stemming from political unrest. The Haitian government wasted no time to approve a new and opulent iteration designed by Georges Baussan, a Haitian graduate from the Ecole d'Architecture in Paris. Fewer than 2 years later, in May 1914, reconstruction began in spite of the political turmoil and socioeconomic struggles at the time. By 1920, during the first United States occupation of Haiti (1915–1934), American naval engineers helped finish the construction of the new palace like they did for a number of important government buildings and public schools.

People who argue the ongoing role of the United States in shaping the possibility of Haitian sovereignty point out that it is ironic that the construction of the National Palace was completed with the help of the U.S. in 1920, and then it was demolished in 2012 with the involvement of a U.S.-based charity organization run by actor Sean Penn. In Haiti, people often say "every fire that starts with the Americans would end with them, like giving something with one hand and taking it back with the other." Partly true. But again, most of the time, Americans are made responsible for things that they have no idea of.

The perception that Americans are at the heart of everything that goes wrong or right in Haiti is mainly driven by the Haitian psychology where someone else is always the sole culprit of our problems. We do not like to take responsibility for our situation. We often try to avoid playing an important role in our events. We rarely lead. Instead, we often wait for others to take charge so that we can blame them when things do not go our way. Once a certain group of Haitians accuses you of something or blames you for whatever reason, no fact and no one can convince them otherwise.

Among all of these issues, one constant thing is that the potential to turn things around in Haiti has never been absent. Families continue to support each other, and foreigners continue to be generous toward the country. Again, what Haiti needs to foster the hope for better days is to pull all the positive forces together and establish long-term goals with the right leadership in charge.

Chapter Four

The Failure and Abdication of Leadership

"One of the burdens of leadership is that as we go, so go the people we lead. Reaching our potential sets an environment for others to reach theirs."[70] John Maxwell

This quote means if a leader fails to grow, so do the people he or she leads. Haiti is today, perhaps, one of the rare countries in the world where the majority of social and economic conditions are worse than they were before and after World War II. People have access to new technologies, they mimic lifestyles observed around the world, and more Haitians travel, study, and live abroad. But general conditions in Haiti are either in standstill mode or moving backward. Farmers and peasants are still surviving thanks to subsistence agriculture on small parcels of lands and operating mostly with the same kind of traditional tools dating back to the early 19th century.

Even though Haiti is relatively small, moving from one place to another can take hours, even days. The transportation system is chaotic. And the roads, ports, and airports are frequently in execrable conditions.

Furthermore, most people still live in rural areas under dwellings made of mud walls and floors, and roofs that are thatched with local grasses or palm leaves. Even in major cities and towns, many people live in homes constructed with plastic and other materials and roofed with corrugated metal. The windows are without panels and covered with wooden shutters, while a privileged few live like barons and lords during the feudal era. Most Haitians in Haiti are living between the poverty line and extreme poverty. Most of the advancements made in certain sectors over the years have been practically erased by instabilities

70 John Maxwell, *The five Levels of Leadership* (New York: Center Steet, 2011), p. 17.

and mismanagement. That is the leadership legacy in Haiti, which is obviously not a good one.

Looking for good leaders throughout Haiti's long history is like looking for a needle in a haystack. Most Haitian leaders have failed to follow and apply the principles of good leadership—principles that refer to effectiveness, influence, process, fail-safe compass, addition, solid ground, respect, good intuition, attraction, empowerment, connection, inner circle, buy-in, victory, momentum, priorities, sacrifice, timing, growth, and legacy.[71] Good governance and leading for the common good do not really seem to interest most people in leadership positions in Haiti. They mostly seek power for self-enrichment at the expense of others, a luxury lifestyle for conspicuousness and glamour, and women for mundane pleasure. And the last three behaviors generate an infectious disease that can be diagnosed everywhere in the country, from government to civil-society institutions. Not even religious institutions are spared from that perpetual plague.

Haiti is a collapsed state particularly due to the political malpractice of its leaders. This political malpractice that has led to malfeasance, which is their habitual and intentional conduct of wrong and unlawful doings. We cannot avoid talking about some Haitian leaders' nonfeasance attitude nor the actions characterized by their misfeasance either. While their nonfeasance attitude refers to their failure to act, to their passivity in regard to their jobs according to the law, thus causing harm, their misfeasance is defined by their acts of mediocrity, corruption, incompetence, self-seeking, and others, often resulting in great harm to the population. Due to

---

71 John Maxwell, *The 21 Irrefutable Laws of Leadership* (Nashville: Thomas Nelson, 2007), p. vi-xi.

its traditional leadership, Haiti has been suffering from the phobia and psychoses of resignation, abdication, laziness, division, egoism, paternalism, and abuses. To that list, we can add shortsightedness, mendicity, treachery, dupery, poverty, zombification, instability, blame, and more.

Similar to an enterprise, a country cannot be successful without good leadership. Leadership that can be used for public good is make or break for any country. The history of the world teaches us that the quality of a country's leadership reveals itself in the type of legacy inherited by different generations. Countries in every part of the world have faced big challenges in their past and will continue to do so in the future. But those that have elevated themselves and continue to strive and meet the challenges of their times have one thing in common: good leadership. The assumption that good leadership is needed in a country to influence social development and progress for the public good is even more relevant in the case of Haiti. As we have mentioned earlier, without good leadership it is extremely difficult for any country, not just Haiti, to meet various challenges and benefit from the opportunities arising naturally from those challenges.

In regard to Haiti, bad leadership, or the lack thereof in some instances, has been largely discussed at national and international forums. The outlook is that the failure or simply the abdication of leadership is largely responsible for the lack of socioeconomic development and political stability. In this chapter, we look at the kind of influence that leaders of all sectors have been exercising over the Haitian people throughout the country's history. And we discuss the kind of impact that influence continues to have on sustainable development in the context of good governance as it relates to the issues of responsibility, accountability, and corruption.

4.1: Influence Is Everything

Leadership matters primarily in a country because it influences people, positively or negatively. "True leadership isn't a matter of having a certain job or title," insists John Maxwell. "To grow further in your role, you must achieve results and build a team that produces."[72] We cannot stop reflecting on some rare moments in Haitian history when leaders combined common sense, action, vision, and purpose to exercise their influence for the public good. And each time, we ask ourselves some questions: What if this leader or that other leader had the opportunity to lead the country for a longer period of time? What if the whole country rallied behind this or that leader in unison? What if this or that leader was given a chance to run the country even for a short period of time? Then, today, we would be talking about a different Haiti.

Unfortunately for the country, actions resulting from good leadership have been scarce. Too many times in our history leaders failed to inspire, have the right influence, and create the necessary harmony in the society and implement the right diplomatic strategies internationally in order to lead without major nuisance.

There have been many periods when Haitian leaders failed to exercise any good influence on the direction of the country, precisely because many of them showed a low degree of emotional intelligence. According to American psychologist Daniel Goleman, "The most effective leaders are all alike in one crucial way: they all have a high degree of emotional intelligence."[73] Beyond the technical skills and knowledge

72 John Maxwell, *The five Levels of Leadership, ibid.*

73 Andrea Ovans, "How Emotional Intelligence Became a Key Leadership Skill", hbr.org, Harvard Business Review, April 28, 2015. https://hbr.org/2015/04/how-emotional-intelligence-became-a-key-leadership-skill

required as the basics to do their job, effective leaders can recognize, understand, and manage their own strengths and weaknesses, and can do the same of other people within their performing environment. They strive to understand and manage other people's feelings and perspectives, and act with empathy for the best outcome in conflictual situations.

When General Dessalines took over the slave revolt after the kidnapping of Toussaint Louverture in 1802 and led the way in building an army coalition capable of delivering the revolution about two years later, that was a good influence. But bad influences inspired some of the elites in the revolutionary army to assassinate Dessalines, their leader, in 1806 in order to establish something far different than what was intended by the revolution itself. After Dessalines's death, Haiti's leadership was divided into two opposing visions, giving rise to two different countries within the territory and using people's skin color to turn them against each other. In the post-Dessalines Haiti, the lighter your skin color was, the more likely you would feel inclined to ally yourself with the South-West region, which was the Republic of Haiti ruled by mulatto General Alexandre Pétion, who later became president. But the darker your skin color was, the more you identified with the Kingdom of Haiti run by black General Henri Christophe, who became King Henri I, in northern Haiti. Haitians bear the scars of that ridiculous racial division to this day.

Dessalines, trying to influence the high-ranking generals to allow an equitable redistribution of lands, and looking to establish an agrarian policy capable of boosting national production and stimulating the morbid economy resulting from the revolutionary war, envisioned making use of good leadership. Around 1811–1812, President Pétion seized the opportunity to help Simon Bolivar with all resources needed (money, soldiers, and weapons) in his fights for liberation of South

America against the colonial power of Spain, notably Venezuela, after England had turned him down. That was also an example of good influence. Pétion welcomed the South American hero "with great warmth.".[74] At the time, the Haitian government had more to lose than the English colonial power that had everything to gain from the defeat of Spain.

The first emerging black nation in the Americas was still worrying about its inadequately recognized independence and was struggling to revive its economy. But Alexandre Pétion understood that it was important for Haiti to exercise its leadership in the fight for freedom wherever people were oppressed. Helping Bolivar ruin Spain's colonial power on the South Americans forever, President Pétion demonstrated good influence at the international level. However, when it came to the national level, he led with policies that were unfavorable to unity and economic prosperity. Under his leadership, racial discrimination was the norm, and the gap between people in the capital and those living in the provinces was outrageous. He encouraged laziness and did not curb debauchery or vagabondage in order to prospect his popularity. Anecdotally, Alexandre Pétion's policy of laissez-faire won him the label of *papa bon kè* (literally, father with a good heart). He let people do whatever they wanted in order to keep their support.

In contrast, his political archenemy in the North, Henri Christophe, applied more stern policies in all areas of people's life. He vehemently believed in hard work, rigid discipline, magnificence, and greatness. King Henri I gloriously elevated northern Haiti with the grandiosity of his architectural projects, education policy, and

74 Joseph Antenor Firmin, English version of *De l'Egalite des Races Humaines* translated by Asselin Charles and introduced by Carolyn Fluehr-Loban, University of Illinois Press, Urbana and Chicago, 2000, p. 396-397.

enlightened nationalism. Today, his legacy is still a source of pride for people descended from the North. They often talk about the "christophian pride" in reference to their hero Henri Christophe.

After Henri's suicide, Jean-Pierre Boyer, who succeeded Alexandre Pétion, led the country, the North and the South, into reunification (1820). In fact, the whole island, including the newly independent republic Spanish Haiti, was reunited under his leadership for 22 years (1841–1843) as one country again. However, Boyer's major leadership missteps were that he was unable to maintain that reunification, and he agreed under pressure from France to pay the large indemnity in exchange for recognition.

From Boyer's presidency (1818–1843) all the way up to Magloire's presidency (1950–1956), Haiti had known few moments of good leadership. Unfortunately, the achievements from those moments, as good as they were, suffered a great deficit of continuity. In addition to not being enough, they were also overshadowed by the effects of bad leadership. Haitians owe their gratitude to Col. Paul Eugene Magloire—one of Haitian former presidents who lived the longest (1907–2001)—for the construction of the great Péligre Dam, and for overseeing the institution of women's suffrage. Allied with Provisional President Franck Lavaud and Minister of Foreign Affairs Antoine Levelt under the banner of political party Peasant Worker Movement (Mouvement Ouvrier Paysan), Magloire's influence was not without merit in granting all male adults the right to vote directly in general elections for the first time in Haiti's history on October 8, 1950.[75]

---

75 Dieter Nohlen, *Elections in the Americas: A data handbook* (Oxford: Oxford University Press, 2005) Vol. 1, p. 381.

When it comes to women's right to vote, President Magloire, nicknamed *Kanson* fè (iron pant), recognized women's suffrage equally to men in his amendment of the constitution to break with the political system of parliamentarism. In the new political system of the republic, women and men were granted their right to vote directly in local and national elections, although it was not without relentless fights and the undaunted determination of middle-class and elite women considered as pioneers from the League Feminine pour l'Action Sociale (LFAS), or the Feminine League for Social Action, and allies. Despite extensive and aggressive oppositions to women's suffrage, the movement strengthened and garnered the support of important national and international organizations.[76] The LFAS leaders organized the first national Haitian women's congress in April 1950. That national women's congress registered the participation and support of representatives from 43 Haitian women's organizations and 17 women's international organizations.

Under Magloire, emphasis was put on tourism, increasing revenue, public works, repairing towns, constructing roads and buildings, and boosting national production, notably agriculture. Standing tall at 70 meters high, the Péligre Dam remains today one of the most tangible results of Magloire's legacy. Located above the Artibonite River—a large waterway that springs from the Dominican Republic on the east and flows all the way west to Haiti's coast—the dam was conceived in 1956 as a master plan aimed at providing controlled irrigation to boost crop yields for export, particularly the production of rice, banana, and sugar cane in the vast valley of Artibonite and in rural areas of the Central

---

76 Influential leaders such as Senators Emile St-Lôt and Castel Démesmin expressed fiercely their opposition to women's right to vote during a debate in the 1946's Constitutional Assembly. Their arguments were just nonsensical general attacks on women's rights and characters.

Plateau. The construction of the dam also meant to supply reliable electricity to Haitians and mighty hydroelectric power to fuel Haiti's industrial expansion. That was a great vision.

But with political instability following Magloire's resignation on December 12, 1956, and the inauguration of a new government in 1957 that saw Francois Duvalier (Papa Doc) become Magloire's successor, more corruption, waste, and disorganization got in the way. Haiti registered not only the diversion of financial resources from the megaproject to the Duvalier regime, but also the mismanagement of a costly enterprise, which failed in its original mission to deliver a lasting self-sustainable increase in crop yields and address the unconscionable social disparity in the country.

Fast-forward to the aftermath of 1986, the period considered by many as the era of Haiti's democratic revolution, we went from good to bad in terms of leadership. And unfortunately, this is how things have been trending within every sector in the country since then. Politically, the post-Duvalier leaders have given many Haitians an argument to wonder whether the country was better off under the dictatorship. Nostalgic of a less chaotic and more under-control Haiti, people who were old enough between the mid-1960s and the beginning of 1980s often ask themselves that question rhetorically. But what they forget is that if during the Duvalier regime Haiti looked apparently stable and less disorganized and dysfunctional, it was not because of the influence of good leadership.

People were just operating under fear. They did not give the Duvaliers permission to lead them. But they were under the terror of a brutal dictatorship regime, forcing them to behave a certain way. Once they managed to get rid of the oppressive regime in the mid-1980s, the

Haitian people felt like they were liberated for the second time in their history since 1804, even more so than at the end of the U.S. military occupation in 1934. But one constant problem remains: the leaders' thirst for power and self-enrichment coupled with their incapacity to put the country above their personal interests and own ego.

No one could live up to the population's expectation; that includes particularly all presidents provisional or not, except for Ertha Pascal-Trouillot, who had the courage to oversee the first democratic, free, and fair elections in Haiti in 1990. The military leaders such as Henri Namphy, Prosper Avril, and others did probably worse to the country, but the elected leaders, contested or not, such as Leslie François Manigat, Jean-Bertrand Aristide, Rene Garcia Preval, Joseph Michel Martelly, and Jovenel Moise, also failed the country.

They did not do enough to create harmony among Haitians, root out corruption, reform and reinforce government institutions, establish the legal framework to make the Constitution of 1987 more practical, and invest in infrastructure and social development programs. Everyone was more preoccupied by fighting each other to stay relevant personally as long as possible at the expense of the country's welfare. The following statement from Lieut. General Raoul Cédras, former commander of the Armed Forces of Haiti, underlines that perpetual problem: "I am going to meet [Father Aristide] and tell him that both he and I will pass, but Haiti will not perish."

Ironically true, but both Cédras and Aristide, whom Cédras was referring to in his statement, had in fact left the military and presidential power. Since then, Haiti has continued to be a sinking ship. General Cédras made that rare declaration in June 1993 in response to a question from a reporter before departing for Governors Island, New York, where he was hoping to meet with Aristide, the president who was deposed in a coup involving the former 21 months prior. The goal of the meeting at the tightly controlled military reservation in New York harbor was to negotiate a politico-diplomatic solution that would facilitate Aristide's return to power. As he was leaving Haiti for New York, General Cédras insisted in a televised interview, "What we are attempting to do is to have a dialogue with him to see not only a proposal for his return, but to propose conditions by which he is to return, and in fact if that return can be possible."[77]

After a week of back and forth, the two Haitian leader adversaries, who sat in separate offices under the mediation of U.N. diplomat Dante Caputo, did not meet face-to-face. Cédras was trying to meet Aristide in an attempt to negotiate the preservation of his role and that of other high command members in the army in exchange for restoring the deposed president to office in Haiti. But for Aristide, the entire Haitian high command needed to be removed.

In fact, after the U.S.- and U.N.-backed coalition forces brought him back to power, former President Aristide saw not only the Haitian army high command's departure for exile at his request, but he also decreed, soon after, the dismantlement of the military institution altogether. Former Father Aristide did not seek restructuring or reforming the army as many national and international experts had recommended. He instead went with his usual hard-headed and gutted efforts to seek revenge over justice, reconciliation, and peace. The demolition of the military institution was an unconstitutional move and became a very costly decision for the country's overall security. No doubt the Haitian army was not up to a professional military standard and too costly for

77 The Buffalo News, "Haitian Leader Agree to U.N. Meeting", buffalonews.com, The Buffalo News, June 27, 1993. https://buffalonews.com/news/haitian-leader-agrees-to-u-n-meeting/article_03d2d26c-a713-5bed-a7ff-0461bc0b4495.html

its repressive actions over the population. It needed to be transformed, not demolished.

Going back to the aftermath of the 1986 victory over Duvalier's dictatorship and terror regime, Haitians could once again breathe the air of liberty, freedom, organization, and the right to elect their leaders and be leaders themselves. It was a euphoric sense of relief to do whatever without much constraint anymore. That euphoric sense of liberty gave rise to all sorts of leaders—dead or alive today—who contributed to a legacy of anarchy, vigilantism as opposed to policing, hate, revenge, violence, destruction, political desperation, self-enrichment, favoritism, inconsideration, antagonism, and authoritarianism.

From the military leaders who governed as head of state, through different provisional presidents, to the few elected presidents such as Jean-Bertrand Aristide, Rene Garcia Préval, Joseph Michel Martelly, and Jovenel Moise, Haiti never looked like a country ruled under the influence of democratic institutions. If anything, the type of leadership that was modeled by them encouraged or facilitated the ruin of all institutions necessary for strengthening democracy, favoring progress, justice, law and order, and safeguarding human rights.

Again, the rare moments or actions stemming from good leadership have been simply overshadowed by the more imposing politics of bad leadership. If Dr. Francois Duvalier initiated the assault on certain vital institutions such as the military, law enforcement, and the legislative and judicial powers by introducing all sorts of viruses into them for the perennity of his power, the post-1986 regimes, generally led by novices with the presumption of a providential mandate, have done everything they could to pronounce either the death sentence of those institutions or put them on steroids.

The kind of leadership projected by the public sector reflects on the civil society as a whole. In business, as in religious and other types of organizations, things are not too different. The results of good influence are dismal even though conditions in different parts of the country would have been worse if it was not for them. Few men and women have always been engaged in efforts aiming at having a positive influence and impact on people. No one can deny that. Media committed to reporting environmental, health, and social issues have well documented examples of some good impact-initiatives undertaken by some religious organizations and community leaders throughout Haiti.

Our viewpoint is not to minimize those efforts and results generated by some good leadership, nor do we want to discount the level of exceptionalism of the leaders involved in those initiatives. But what we need is more good influence from leaders in all areas of the country's life, not less of it and more bad influence. We need to see good leadership as an important part of a series of principles to put in place in the wake of the current disaster that the country has become. In fact, we need leaders who can elevate themselves from being just good enough, to being great leaders. That is what Haiti deserves. From top to bottom, leaders need to come together to find solutions collectively, involving all communities, because everyone must take ownership and responsibility. Using Gandhi's words in the context of Haiti, we can paraphrase to say Haitian leaders need to be not just the agents of change but also the change they wish to see in Haiti.

Too often, the same leaders who are supposed to lead in various situations criticize people's behaviors instead. They say things like "these people do not listen, they do not respect authorities, they like chaos and they abuse their own environment. They simply don't care about their own health and safety, etc. You give them an open marketplace as a solution to risking their lives on the sidewalk of the streets, they come right back to the street putting their lives in danger while selling their stuff. They spend their whole day in the middle of the garbage they have piled up themselves without thinking about the effects on their health and the environment".

These kinds of statements and responses from some leaders show how naive or plainly irresponsible they are. The fact that, for example, some people throw garbage everywhere, build homes anywhere and anyhow, or spend their days in the streets hustling to make ends meet is not a reason to believe that they do not care about a clean environment or their own safety and health. It is a matter of not having good enough alternatives or leadership to educate and instill habits that translate into making better decisions.

More often, the leaders who criticize people's behaviors do not communicate and model anything different. Sometimes, they think that people will simply obey their authoritarian rule. You cannot dictate your way and impose fear in order to produce good results. That may only work for a limited time, as witnessed by the shallow sense of order and stability under the Duvalier regime. Equally so, you cannot ask people to act a certain way, but in part, you do the complete opposite because you are in a position of authority. In other words, Haitian leaders need to start walking the walk and talking the talk. They cannot continue to govern with the kind of leadership of "the rules are for you, not for me."

The idea that Haitians supposedly need someone with an iron pant and a strong stick to govern them is simply ridiculous. Authoritarian leaders? We had had plenty of that in the past. They only left destruction and chaos behind them. What do the Haitian people need? Leaders who understand that their role is not just to seek power for self-enrichment, recognition, a lavish lifestyle, and mundane pleasure. They are entrusted for the purpose of implementing policies conducive to the realization of progressive ideals for the benefit of all. That requires being more selfless, humble, knowledgeable, compassionate, candid, honest, attentive to people's challenges for well-advised decisions, educator, attractive to talented and skillful individuals, fascinated by law and order, patriotic, and unifier. These are the kind of qualities that Haitians must be looking for in a leader.

4.2: Corruption Is Systemic and Systematic

One of the arguments people often used to explain why Haiti keeps going backward is the lack of financial resources. There is some truth to that argument. We cannot even afford our small national budget without international aid. But money alone is not enough to run a country effectively and make quality sociopolitical and economic impacts. No amount of money can save Haiti, which remains a country that money cannot lift with the kind of leadership we have witnessed over the years. Haiti as a country in the heart of the Caribbean is not poor. It is impoverished by corruption, mismanagement, unaccountability, irresponsibility, excessive exploitation, and inequity tolerated by foreign powers, notably the United States, whose policies in Haiti have only sought to nourish U.S. interests.

With regard to the U.S., its policy in Haiti has mainly been driven for decades by whether there is an important and pressing national interest at the moment. For instance, we can consider the previously mentioned economic interests, Cold War strategy, and migration concerns. In 1994, we remember the reactions of then Senator Joseph

R. Biden Jr. in a televised interview with host Charlie Rose, just a few days before the U.S. troops landed in Haiti to restore deposed President Aristide into power. Mr. Biden, who was a member of the Senate Foreign Affairs Committee, argued against a military intervention in Haiti. He said, "I think it's particularly not wise," adding, "if Haiti—a God-awful thing to say—if Haiti just quietly sunk into the Caribbean and rose up 300 feet, it wouldn't matter a whole lot in terms of our interest." [78] For Biden, who is now president, the United States had then more pressing crises to resolve, including ethnic cleansing in Bosnia, than Haiti's situation, which was not especially important to American interests.

However, the Clinton administration went ahead with the invasion anyway, and the Haitian military leaders surrendered within hours. Aristide was restored after a deal that saw the beginning of the immediate deportation of thousands of Haitians migrants who were waiting in Guantanamo Bay for political asylum into the United States. About a decade later, in 2004, the apparent constitutional order that was restored with the help of U.S. military intervention collapsed again. Aristide, who had succeeded Preval to power for a second term, had to resign amid chaos, threats of invasion of the capital from former military rebels, and pressure from U.S. officials.

The democratic process collapse meant another U.S. military intervention, and more deportations. After the events of 2004, and up to February 7, 2022 (the constitutional date for a transfer of power) Haiti had elected three presidents. Only one, Rene Garcia Preval, had fully completed his five-year term. Of the other two, Joseph Michel

---

78 Benjamin Fearnow, "Joe Biden Saying Haiti Does Not Matter in 1994 Clip Resurfaces After Moise Assassination", newsweek.com, Newsweek, July 7, 2021. https://www.newsweek.com/joe-biden-saying-haiti-doesnt-matter-1994-clip-resurfaces-after-moise-assassination-1607692

Martelly resigned without an elected successor, and Jovenel Moise was assassinated while still in office.

All of these problems stemming from a lack of good national leadership and directives are indeed the main reasons for Haiti's lack of adequate financial resources. Not only does the country continue to register a relatively low GDP and a highly negative trade deficit, mismanagement and corruption have also been swallowing almost everything. Even in times of economic growth, the country always grapples with the question of how to make use of its resources to fuel sustainable economic and social development.

International funds never stop flooding in from everywhere in the forms of donations or loans. The United States alone infused more than $5 billion in aid in the decade of 2010 and 2020, almost twice Haiti's actual national budget.[79] Even the Duvalier regime, presented itself as anti-communist to attract the support of the U.S. government, received significant American financial aid. As of 1961, Duvalier received $13 million a year in aid from Washington. This was half of the country's national budget back then.

By 1986, the United States had spent $900 million supporting the dynasty of Duvalier while Haiti was plunging deeper into corruption and poverty. Haiti lacks a robust judicial system and suffers from limited transparency and accountability in governance. Financial corruption is systemic in both the private and public sectors. According to its report published in 2013, the organization Transparency International ranked Haiti as the most corrupt country in the Caribbean region. Problems

---

79 Chris Cameron, "As U.S. Navigates Crisis in Haiti, a Bloody History Looms Large", nytimes.com, The New York Times, December 19, 2021. https://www.nytimes.com/2021/12/19/us/politics/us-haiti-intervention.html

like embezzlement of taxpayers' funds, mismanagement, and wasted resources are part of a long-established system in Haiti. And organized crimes function as the norm.

People in every part of the society practice corruption with no shame. There was a time when people used to practice corruption in the dark and under the table. Nowadays, it has become normal to do it in broad daylight. People will rub it on your face if you are not happy about it. Everything in Haiti is running through favors and powerplay. Yet, most Haitians are not looking for favors from politicians or any leader for that matter. They want organized and well-run government services and institutions, fairness, and opportunities. It is proven that any time Haitians find a place with just a few of these characteristics, they excel. Outside of Haiti, the world is filled with Haitian immigrants' success stories.

Back home, the system is organized in such a way that it entices people not to exploit the proper channel to conduct business or acquire any type of service. Those in positions will not do the jobs that they are supposedly getting paid to do. Backlogs, strong bureaucracy, absenteeism, humiliation, discrimination, and unnecessary errors are among most tactics systematically implemented to make people use and reuse informal channels—usually a middle person hired under the table by someone inside or outside of the institutions, but often well-connected individuals—to collect money on the side, on top of the regular fees and taxes for services and the normal cost of doing business as required by the law.

To obtain a passport, an identification card, a birth certificate, a driver's license, or any other official document for instance, is most of the time a headache in Haiti. It may take you months sometimes if you follow the proper procedures and processes according to the administrative laws. You may be able to receive that same document in a matter of minutes or hours in most cases using a third party or middle person commonly known as *raketè* (racketeer). But it may cost you a fortune. And the public treasury may see very little or none of that fortune. Since most public institutions in Haiti are still using outdated and uncontrolled methods of operations, fees and taxes collected are sometimes not even recorded on the books. They go straight to someone's pocket. This is very sad, but unfortunately true. Various efforts to reform the system have had mixed and spotty results due in part to a serious lack of continuity and decentralization.

On a larger scale, you never know the real cost of anything. A program or project may be reported to cost taxpayers or donors a certain amount, while in reality it may not even be half of the reported figures. To know what the real cost of a project is, you need to know how much money was pocketed by different people involved directly or indirectly in that project. The law requires the government to receive contract bids from companies for public works in order to avoid the manipulation of costs, favoritism, and corruption, as well as to encourage competition for maximum quality, efficiency, and effectiveness. However, qualified companies are not often the winners of those contract bids. A good connection may be enough for some companies to be awarded huge contracts. Sometimes, the winner of a contract bid is a company owned by a member of parliament, a cabinet member in the government, a company just created overnight by a businessperson, or a politician with ties to high-ranking government officials. Other times, contracts are repeatedly awarded to the same companies owned by oligarch families with a permanent monopoly.

There is no real transparency. But every time there is a change of government, you hear the new officials complaining about the fact that the previous government was wasteful and left no money in the public treasury. It is true for most of the time, but the problem is that, despite criticism and finger-pointing, the new government will not necessarily change the trend. As recently as November 24, 2021, Prime Minister and de facto Head of State Ariel Henry lamented the bad shape of the country's public finances.

During an inaugural ceremony to install eight new ministers in his cabinet, Mr. Henry stated that he found the government's accounts completely empty and Haiti was operating either on credit or donations. As he explained, for the 2020–2021 fiscal year, the government forecasted a spending budget of 254 billion gourdes (US$2.54 billion). The government collected less than 40% of that amount in tax revenues, leaving the country in debt, and international aid predicaments for more than 60% of Haiti's annual budget. What concerns Henry is not new to Haiti. Every government that has succeeded after the fall of the Duvalier regime used the same playbook. Things must be drastically and systemically changed.

The Haitian government is part of a highly corrupt, chaotic, dysfunctional, and wasteful system. The billions of dollars wasted or pocketed from the Petrocaribe deal, without any sort of consequence for those involved, is a prime example of that situation. It has become easier for those in government to borrow money that they will not pay back and beg for foreign donations that they will not be held accountable for. They prefer to keep Haiti in a permanent state of financial dependency. They are either not willing to make the government efficient in its structure and organization in order to maximize tax revenues for the country's basic needs, or they are simply lazy and lack creativity and imagination.

The status quo is corruption again and always. As a result, the bulk of national revenues usually come from easy and ready targets like air travel tickets, imports and exports of merchandise, passports and other necessary personal documents, telecommunications, and money transfers to impose large taxes and fees. As an example, imposed taxes and fees paid by a traveler to Haiti via airplane could be anywhere from two to three times the actual price of the airline ticket. This is without exaggeration and far more than what is imposed by most other Caribbean and Central American countries.

Chapter Five

The Missed Opportunities

We repeat and maintain that history always gives people chances to redeem themselves from misdeeds. When it comes to Haiti, in spite of our turbulent history, we have had plenty of opportunities to amend life and make the country a better place for its citizens. But we have not made use of those opportunities. People usually attribute Haiti's missed opportunities to bad luck. Mentally, it is hard for most Haitians to comprehend the fact that luck does not work without preparation or a good disposition.

As a people, we have had our chances and our moments throughout history. And there is no doubt that we will continue to have more chances in our existence. It is up to us to look for what has been lacking, which is basically the disposition to create a more favorable environment for stability, peace, and coherence, as well as preparing to profit from opportunities given to us. By disposition, we mean a broad and sincere consensus on a clear vision as a nation.

We are in agreement that disposition is not just about the consensus on a global vision for the nation's progress; it also involves the willingness of the people to accept the role delegated to the state institutions and to work together to achieve the goals resulting from that vision. When it comes to preparation, we imply a set of practical mechanisms put in place to enable people to perform at their best possible level. This involves education, both formal and informal, coherent organizational structures, building reliable infrastructures, disseminating useful information in real time, and creating a more efficient allocation and management of resources.

In this chapter, we enumerate a number of opportunities that Haiti could have profited from to build a better nation if we did not miss them either completely or partially due to a lack of good disposition and preparation. Some of those opportunities were greater than others. But they were all very important parts of our troubled past that we could have done a better job of exploiting. We do not enumerate these events based on their level of importance, but rather in chronological order. Neither do we intend to create an exhaustive list of events, as other people may find a bigger catalog of important occasions in Haitian history.

The events that we list here are purposely selected because of how they could have helped shape a different Haiti politically, socially, and economically. They are like different trains missed by Haiti at different times when the country was trying to either forge or reshape its destiny. We are talking about Haiti as dreamed first by Toussaint Louverture and Jean-Jacques Dessalines, and to a certain degree Henri Christophe, Alexandre Pétion, and Jean-Pierre Boyer. We can also think of Sténio Vincent united with other politicians and intellectuals of the Caco's movement (movement of insurgents in today's perception) to end the U.S. military occupation (1915–1934). We analyze the context created by the end of the Duvalier regime, and the opportunities presented to Haiti for rebuilding, in particular after the January 2010 and August 2021earthquakes.

5.1: The Regime of Toussaint Louverture

The French colonial power kidnapped and tortured Toussaint Louverture to death (1802–1803) to prevent the total liberation of Haitians. Even though Louverture did not live to see the day of Haiti's declaration of independence, his works had greatly paved the way to the only successful slave revolt in modern history. After consolidating the abolition of slavery, he tried to stabilize Saint-Domingue politically, socially, and economically in preparation for a step-by-step independence process. Toussaint, influenced by Enlightenment philosophers such as John Locke and Jean-Jacques Rousseau, was deeply motivated to build an inclusive and fair nation with continuous economic prosperity. From 1796 to 1801, Toussaint was the leading political and military figure on the entire island. He was highly admired by the former slaves, whom he unquestionably helped free; and he was well respected by European power representatives whom he had secured peace with, even if it was temporary.

When it came to the mulattoes, Toussaint faced their jealousy and reluctance to let go the abolition of slavery. Before the general slave revolt of 1791, the mulatto population owned lands and slaves. Many of those slave owners wanted them back. Toussaint refused to allow anyone to run a plantation with the sweat of slaves. For Toussaint, who believed in equality of mankind, the mere idea of returning to the slavery system in any form was a war worth fighting for as long as it took. With the help of Jean-Jacques Dessalines, he was able to defeat a mulatto army in 1799 after a year of battles.

He neutralized almost all opposition, at least militarily. Toussaint reiterated the abolition of slavery and was able to start thinking about building a new nation where freedom, equality, inclusion, unity, and economic prosperity aimed to be the cornerstone. After declaring himself Governor-General for life on the island, he introduced a constitution that set the parameters within which his regime would govern. Toussaint sought to install stability, reestablish and revitalize the agriculture so important to improve the economic conditions in Hispaniola after the devastating losses caused by all the different wars that the contradictory forces were engaged in. He agreed to trade deals with the United States and the British. The agreements between

Governor-General Toussaint Louverture and the Americans and the British included the supply of arms and goods to the former's military forces in exchange for sugar and a promise not to invade Jamaica and the southern part of America, so close to Haiti.

The biggest deal of all that shows how diplomatically savvy Toussaint was, was the agreement with Napoleon Bonaparte, who recognized him as Governor-General. After Bonaparte seized power in France in 1799, he issued a new constitution and declared all colonies to be running under special rules. Toussaint and his allies had the suspicion that those special rules could have meant a return to slavery. The Governor-General of Saint-Domingue, who was still technically reporting to French authority, was careful not to declare full independence right away, but instead sought to consolidate enough autonomy capable of facilitating that independence in the near future. He professed himself a Frenchman just as a deterrence against Napoleon, whom Toussaint was trying to convince of his loyalty. In turn, Napoleon confirmed Toussaint's authority as governor and promised not to reinstate slavery.

However, the temptation to have complete control was daunting to Toussaint. In spite of his diplomatic and strategic efforts, his annoyances seemed to be greater than his will. That provoked a total missed opportunity for the prospective nation, which needed for its foundation a great visionary, diplomat, and strategist in Toussaint Louverture.

Toussaint defied French revolutionary laws by allowing plantation owners of all backgrounds who fled during the general revolt to return and contribute to the prosperity of the new system. He imposed military discipline on the workforce, but he instituted necessary reforms to improve workers' conditions. He agreed temporarily with Napoleon, who forbade him from invading the eastern part of the island (Santo Domingo), where French authorities were trying to restore order after the Spanish departure. But Toussaint's armies invaded Santo Domingo in January 1801 with little to no resistance. There, he instituted French law, abolished slavery, and set out to modernize the economy.

Angry with Toussaint, but particularly offended by the boldness of the colonial governor's actions, Napoleon, in 1802, sent 20,000 French troops led by his brother-in-law, General Charles Emmanuel Leclerc, to regain control. This time, those men of experience in different war campaigns, handpicked by Bonaparte and Leclerc, would get the backing of most Europeans and mulattoes living on the island to defeat Toussaint. Misunderstood, even Toussaint's best generals in Dessalines and Henri abandoned him to join forces with Leclerc in what appeared to be an act of betrayal.

Toussaint was in the end arrested and deported to France in a plot concocted by French General Jean-Baptiste Brunet aided by people in Toussaint's own circle under the pretense of discussing peace. Toussaint's dream for the island and influence on the world stage were crushed by his calamitous death on April 7, 1803, after succumbing under the weight of torture, pneumonia, and starvation after nearly eight months in captivity inside of a prison cell. But his actions had earned him the merit of provoking a series of global events that changed the geopolitics of the Americas and set the beginning of the end for European colonial domination on the other side of the Atlantic.

Napoleon Bonaparte was so frustrated by rebellion in Hispaniola, which he could not control, that he had to abandon his quest to expand his empire into North America. He decided to sell Louisiana to the

United States in 1803, therefore facilitating the western territorial expansion of the U.S. throughout the 19th century. Toussaint was also a source of inspiration for revolutionary leaders in many Latin American countries and American abolitionists over the next century to fight for a definite end of slavery.

5.2: The Aftermath of the Revolution

It took no time after the deportation of Toussaint for Dessalines to realize how much the loss of the latter cost them. He turned his back on the French army and successfully rallied blacks and mulatto forces together. They would force France to surrender and leave the island after a series of victories, notably after the famous Battle of Vertières, a provincial city in northern Haiti, on November 18, 1803. Then came the D-Day! On January 1, 1804, Dessalines proclaimed the independence of the island largely populated by former enslaved black people.

The accomplishment of the Haitian Revolution presented a unique opportunity for social and political transformations on the island that no other event since the arrival of the Europeans had ever done. It was the possibility for the mass oppressed and enslaved people to take over and create a more just society. They could have real power over their destiny, over their own life. That opportunity could not be discounted even during invasion threats from foreign powers.

To take full advantage of all possibilities in front of them, the leaders of the new independent country failed to keep their commitment to unity and their will to make political, social, and economic fairness larger than individual power. They failed to accept the fact that a head of state's power is ephemeral. But the legacy resulting from policies and rules implemented by that head of state could have a life-long impact on the society that he or she rules. Of course, they had to make up with the limited natural and human resources and information available to them at the time. Nonetheless, as they did to overthrow the entire slavery system and establish a new world order on the island, they could have done a better job managing the individual and particular group interests for the profit of a more harmonious and prosperous country.

Dessalines did not deserve to die the way he did at the hand of his fellow countrymen shortly after the independence. Neither did the massacre ordered by Dessalines need to be so brutal and severe against most Europeans (sparing a few German and Polish families) who decided to stay on the island and blend with the Haitian population after the revolution. To Dessalines's credit, though, the decree he published ordered the execution of those suspected of conspiring in aiding the French army.

However, imagine how hard it might have been for Dessalines's rank-and-file men to define on their own what was genuinely considered suspicion of conspiracy or not before taking action in the heat of the moment. There was no way to fully examine if there was a historical well-founded reason to act as such, but by moving squads of soldiers swiftly from house to house during a three-month period to torture and kill entire families, Dessalines deprived the new nation of important human resources needed to help the building efforts from the start.

In addition to the assassination of Dessalines and the loss of important resources due to the massacre of 1804, the country faced internal divisions and a long period of insurrections that made it almost impossible to regain the economic health Haiti had prior to independence. As the island was divided geopolitically, resources were scattered and mostly concentrated into the hands of a few allied with authoritarian leaders at the expense of the majority of the population, who were struggling to survive on their own with not much means.

5.3: The Reunification of the Island

Sixteen years after the declaration of independence, Haitian leaders finally realized the negative consequences of divisions on the foundation of the new nation-state. In 1820, President Boyer reunified Northern and Southern Haiti to function as one country, the Republic of Haiti. And then about two years later, on February 15, 1822, Boyer seized the opportunity to reunite eastern Hispaniola (the Republic of Spanish Haiti) with the Republic of Haiti. The longest-serving Haitian president to date (25 years), Boyer profited from the vacuum left in the East by Spain and France to establish one nation renamed the Island of Haiti. The opportunity appeared when several regions in eastern Hispaniola officially adopted the Haitian flag. They gave the Haitian revolutionary leaders another shot at getting it right this time. Had they really learned their lessons from the past to build on the present opportunity for a better future? Not so much in certain aspects, and not at all in others. It was only if they could get rid of the old demons—the enemies of the public good that were ever-present in their heads.

Mismanaged, the reunification that presented an extraordinary opportunity, a wholesome moment for the people of the island to pull all their resources together and build a better place for all, turned out to be a political nightmare. It was a socioeconomic mess, and a waste of time and resources for both sides. In the end, and after 22 years of being mainly neglected, oppressed, suppressed, and abused by the

Haitian authorities, separatist leaders in eastern Haiti declared their own independence on February 27, 1844, under the name La Republica Dominicana (the Dominican Republic).

The eastern part of the island was dominated by Spanish speakers as opposed to the western part, which spoke French and Haitian Creole languages. The political and social scars left by that period of unification between Dominicans and Haitians had led to a permanent schism between the two sides of the island. The opportunity to build a strong and unified republic was gone and left people on both sides of the spectrum with a legacy of frustration and animosity forever. This situation led to tensions between Dominicans (largely dominated by people of European ancestry) and Haitians (who are overwhelmingly of African descent). The massacre orchestrated by Dominican police and military forces in October 1937 against thousands of Haitian laborers living near the border has remained the most notorious and brutal official incident between the two countries since 1844. Today, both Haitians and Dominicans often think of the relations between the two countries in terms of what if . . .

It did not have to end like that. After the departure of Spain, most Dominican politicians and military officers wanted to be united with the Republic of Haiti. They sought political stability and were attracted to Haiti's perceived economic prosperity and power under Jean-Pierre Boyer, which is of course the reverse today. The Haitian population was back then eight to ten times larger than that of the Dominicans, who also had a largely reduced and untrained military force and a severely undeveloped economy.

Boyer, in contrast to the Dominican military officers, looked to secure different objectives for the island he proclaimed to be "one and indivisible." He sought to maintain Haiti's independence against potential foreign powers' attack or reconquest, France or Spain in particular, and maintain the freedom against slavery. While the unification was more popular among the black population believing that Boyer's regime would usher social reforms and the permanent abolition of slavery, the white and multiracial people did not see the possibility of merging with the neighboring and largely black country as a good idea. Furthermore, the Dominicans started to drop their full support for the project when they became aware of the unilateral agreement between Boyer and France for Haiti to pay 150 million gold francs destined to compensate the former French slave owners as reparations in exchange for recognition of Haiti's freedom. Boyer succumbed to gunboat diplomacy without involving the Dominicans in the negotiations, as 14 French warships were stationed near Port-au-Prince.

After Boyer formally entered Santo Domingo, the capital, with 12,000 troops in February 1821, the island was ceremonially united from Cape Tiburon to Cape Samana under one flag, the Haitian flag, and under one government, the Boyer government located in Port-au-Prince. The unified island was divided into six departments that were divided into administrative districts called arrondissements. Of the six departments, French Haiti (one third of the island) accounted for four (Nord, West, South, and Artibonite), while in the larger geographic portion of the island, Spanish Haiti, only two departments were established (Ozama and Cibao).

The administration under the unification led to large-scale land expropriations. It was also a period of failed efforts to force the production of export crops, impose military services, restrict the use of the Spanish language, and suppress traditional customs on top of the resurgence of years-old rivalries between the governing Haitian elite (mulattoes) and the large majority, which is black throughout the country.

In addition to other problems, a huge problem to maintaining the unity was the fact that the Boyer government had imposed heavy taxes on the Dominicans in order to pay the large indemnity to the former colonists. Economic struggles also meant that the Republic of Haiti was unable to adequately provision its army. The armed forces largely survived by commandeering and confiscating food and supplies at gunpoint. The Haitian government made several attempts to redistribute lands, which was a direct conflict with the system of communal land tenure (*terrenos comuneros* in Spanish).[80] *Terrenos comuneros* had arisen with the ranching economy prior to Boyer's intervention. It was a method of land distribution people used among themselves in Eastern Hispaniola to make sure every family received a share of necessary resources such as grasslands, forests, streams, palm groves, and small agricultural plots. The inhabitants in different communities used that method to compensate for the scare population, the low value of the land, and the absence of qualified officials to survey the lands. Some people resented being forced to grow cash crops under the Code Rural instituted in 1838 by Boyer and Joseph Balthazar Ingignac, a Haitian diplomat and powerful presidential general-secretary under both Pétion and Boyer.[81]

Using their constitution, which forbade white landowners, the Haitian administration deprived families of their properties and forced them to migrate into Cuba and Puerto Rico, which were still under Spain colonization. The Dominicans were deeply Catholic. But Haitian

80 Harry Hoetink and Stephen Ault, *The Dominican People: Notes for a Historical Sociology* (Baltimore: Johns Hopkins Press, 1982), p. 83.

81 In the Haitian political system, a general-secretary to the president is similar to the present-day White House's chief of staff position in the United States.

leaders associated the Roman Catholic Church with the French slavery system and the slave masters who exploited them before independence. Thus, they confiscated all church properties, deported all foreign clergy, and severed the ties of the local clergy to the Vatican. Schools, notably the Universidad Santo Tomas de Aquino (one of the first universities in the Americas), were closed due to the lack of students and teachers, causing a massive case of human capital flight.

The Haitian government did, however, instate a constitution modeled after the one adopted in the United States. They also abolished slavery as an institution in the Dominican Republic, as it was already an accomplishment in French Haiti. But several forms of slavery remained in Haitian society. Many of the resolutions and dispositions adopted were expressly aimed at converting the Dominicans to second-class citizens as Boyer had done with the Haitian peasantry under his Code Rural: restrictions of movement, prohibition to run for public offices, night curfew, inability to travel in groups, banning civilian organizations, and the indefinite closure of the state university.

All those issues forcibly provoked the creation of different movements on that part of the island advocating for a forceful separation from Haiti with no possibility for compromise. The formation of a new government with Charles Rivière-Hérard taking over from Boyer in 1843 did not resolve any problems between Dominicans and Haitians.

The Rivière-Hérard administration persecuted the separatists influenced by Juan Pablo Duarte, who founded a secret society called La Trinitaria (The Trinity) with a group of likeminded young people aiming at seeking their independence from Haiti. Duarte, along with other founding members, were expelled from the island when the society became not so secret to the Haitian government. However, it was too late to stop a movement that was already deeply rooted and spreading among the population. Leaders such as Francisco del Rosario Sanchez and Matias Ramon Mella were undaunted in continuing the efforts in Duarte's absence. They led the fight for a free, independent, and sovereign nation on their own at the beginning of 1844 with the ideology of La Trinitaria after several high-voltage battles and much bloodshed.

5.4: The American Occupation

How can a military occupation be an opportunity for the occupied nation, even more so in the case of Haiti during the U.S. intervention in 1915? Some people could be quick and precise to answer: almost nothing other than the violation of national sovereignty, all sorts of abuses, accelerated corruption, oppression, and exploitation. The country that Dessalines and the other revolutionary fighters founded through sweat and blood was stained when some 330 United States Marines landed in Port-au-Prince on July 28, 1915. More than just a mission to rescue Haiti from political instability and social turmoil, the mission was meant "to re-establish peace and order" as claimed by President Woodrow Wilson to avoid criticism.[82]

The U.S. Marines were effectively charged to control Haiti's political and financial interests. After more than 111 years of maintaining independence without the smallest foreign military boot defiling the Haitian soil, the Haitian leaders had seen their power reduced to a rank-and-file role dictated by the now established U.S. military regime. Even

---

82 Chris Woolf, "When America Occupied Haiti", theworld.org, The World, August 6, 2015. https://theworld.org/stories/2015-08-06/when-america-occupied-haiti

though Haiti had had three presidents during the occupation period, the United States effectively ruled as a military regime led by the Marines and their creation, the Haitian Gendarmerie, through martial law. Although the military invasion did not encounter much resistance from the Haitian army other than one soldier (Pierre Sully was anecdotally reported as trying to fight and was shot dead by the invaders), Haitians rebelled in different ways.

The U.S. occupation lasted nineteen years, during which two major rebellions took place, resulting in several thousand Haitians being killed, and numerous human rights violations, such as torture and summary executions committed by the Marines with the help of the Haitian Gendarmerie. A forced labor system (the Corvée) was instituted for the realization of massive infrastructure projects that resulted in thousands of deaths. Under the occupation, Haitians were forced to replace their constitution with a new one that guaranteed ownership of land to foreigners (banned until then) and American financial control. Most of the population became more impoverished, and more power was reestablished into the hands of the minority of wealthy and French-cultured mulatto Haitians. The American occupation helped accentuate racial discrimination and prejudices, human rights abuses, torture, and inequalities in Haiti.

However, while the Haitians were right in fighting the occupation from the beginning to the end, in spite of the atrocities exercised against them by the U.S. military forces, Haiti could have benefited from it to a larger extent than the mere imperialistic structures left behind. Even in the aftermath of the occupation, Haitian leaders could diplomatically seek an apology and reparations from the United States. To date, the U.S. has not officially apologized to the Haitian people for the mass killing of its civilians, all sorts of abuses, and the negative socioeconomic legacy of the invasion. After the 1915 U.S. intervention, Haiti became more dependent politically and economically for decades.

This cycle of crisis would persist and bring in more indirect and direct interventions from the United States (1994 and 2004), depending on the context. Some of the U.S. interventions were more brutal, bloody, and abusive than others, but none of them contributed to advancing Haiti toward democracy and progress. For decades, the U.S. has been by far the country providing the most financial and economic supports to Haiti. But U.S. aid to Haiti is more a contribution to advance American economic and political interests at Haiti's expense. This is one of the reasons the American government often supports different Haitian governments that oppress and exploit the Haitian people. U.S. policies in Haiti continue to be not that of apology or reparations for damages caused in the past, but the perpetuation of those damages.

In terms of apology, we must recognize that few U.S. military members and government officials involved in the 1915 occupation had come to regret it. However, these former military members and government official had not spoken in the capacity of the United States' representatives. Their position is not a reflection of the U.S. government in any shape or form. Former military members and officials, who had spoken out against the consequences of the U.S. occupation of Haiti, generally expressed their regret through criticism of U.S. foreign policies more globally rather than looking at Haitians in the eyes and apologizing directly to them. Below is an example of how a former U.S. military leader, General Smedley Butler, who participated in the invasion of Haiti, came to regret it in 1933.

> "I spent thirty-three years and four months in active military service as a member of this country's most agile military force,

> the Marine Corps. During that period, I spent most of my time being a high class muscle-man for Big Business, for Wall Street and for the Bankers. In short, I was a racketeer, a gangster for capitalism. I helped make Haiti and Cuba a decent place for the National City Bank boys to collect revenues in. I helped in the raping of half a dozen Central American republics for the benefits of Wall Street."[83]

In addition to the lack of apology and reparations from the U.S. government, Haiti failed to capitalize on the American expertise, experiences, and financial and material resources that the country so desperately needed in all major areas for its socioeconomic development. Politically and institutionally, the Haitian leaders missed the opportunity to use the American experience—with its well-established and strong democratic institutions—to help institute, recalibrate, reorganize, and transform Haitian institutions in a more useful and adaptive way to the national population.

The Americans had the balance of power, but the Haitians could still have done a better job negotiating the Haitian American Convention that granted the U.S. security and economic oversight over Haiti. The convention allowed the U.S. to take over all of Haiti's institutions, but said very little about the type and how much investment into the country was needed. The few existing infrastructure projects were concentrated in Port-au-Prince and metropolitan areas, while the vast majority of people became more marginalized than in Haiti's pre-occupation, resulting in a massive migration of Haitian laborers (*braceros*) to Cuba.

---

83 David Suggs, "The long legacy of the U.S. occupation of Haiti", washingtonpost.com,The Washington Post, Aug. 6, 2021. https://www.washingtonpost.com/history/2021/08/06/haiti-us-occupation-1915/

Institutional reforms and infrastructural programs were established to serve the various interests of the United States. When it comes to infrastructure, we record some important realizations, such as 1,100 miles of roads being made usable; 189 bridges built, the rehabilitation of a few irrigation canals; the construction of some hospitals, schools, and public buildings; and drinking water was brought to the main cities. Port-au-Prince became the first Caribbean city to have a phone service with automatic dialing. Agricultural education was organized, with a central school of agriculture and 69 farms in the country.

Even though the first years of the occupation were very disappointing, by 1922, with the appointment of General John H. Russell of the Marine Corps as high commissioner and the election of Louis Borno in Haiti, a better page seemed to have turned. Much was accomplished in treaty services, with a series of bonds issued to fund the country's debts and public service works. One of the most important bonds was a $16-million loan issued by the National City Bank of New York. Most of the Haitian towns, which had looked so distant since the independence, were finally connected by passable roads for wheeled vehicles. Life began to be more pleasant in cities and towns, with political stability, security, and safety provided in a more organic way. Public health services made progress in controlling the endemic diseases, which particularly afflicted the peasantry.

Elsewhere, the Americans redesigned the education system to emphasize agricultural development and vocational training, similar to the industrial education for minorities and immigrants in the United States. The program aimed to build farm schools for peasant children, and vocational and professional schools in the cities. With the complicity of the mulatto elite, the United States dismantled the liberal arts education that Haiti had inherited from the French system, threatening the traditional social and economic ascendancy of the elite.[84]

Even though some Haitian intellectuals despised the American education program, believing it was discriminatory against the people, most of the minority mulattoes were supportive of it because they thought it would weaken the middle class. They feared that the creation of a strong and professionally educated middle class could lead to a loss of their influence over the majority.

Dr. Robert Roussa Moton, who was tasked to evaluate the education program established under the management of the Service Technique de l'Agriculture et de l'Enseignement Professionnel according to a treaty agreed in 1924, concluded that while its objectives were admirable, performance was not satisfactory.[85] He also criticized the excessive amount of funding it received for a dismal result at the expense of the country's public schools, which were in very poor condition.

Unfortunately for Haiti, the treaty services had just begun to come to fruition in attacking the appalling problems of poverty, ignorance, and disease when Herbert Hoover took office in March 1929 as president of the United States. The continuance of the different programs seemed to give Haitians, most importantly the masses, the best hope for the future.

Very few people imagined at the time that the new U.S. president envisaged a radical change of policy in Haiti. Many observers thought

---

84 Dana G. Munro, "The American Withdrawal from Haiti, 1929-1934", read.dukeupress.edu, Hispanic American Review, February 1969. http://read.dukeupress.edu/hahr/article-pdf/49/1/1/763052/0490001.pdf

85 Robert Roussa Moton was an experienced American educator who served as a principal at the Tuskegee Institute from 1915 to 1935. He also served as an administrator at the Hampton Institute prior to being named principal at the Tuskegee Institute.

that the new U.S. administration prioritized early withdrawal for political reasons over the fulfillment of the treaty services that were not due to run out until 1936. Hoover did not want to be represented abroad by military forces. He was also influenced by resentment among American businessmen in Haiti who disliked efforts to curtail the privileges they'd claimed before the American intervention. And he had faced strong opposition from the Haitian upper-class radical and nationalist agitators who used discontent against new alcohol, tobacco tax, and coffee standardization laws to rally support from the peasants against the Americans.

Most of the hostilities against the Americans were aroused from the elite, mostly the mulatto Franco-German oligarchs and a few literate Haitians who considered the U.S. military regime an insult to their sociopolitical influence and a blow to their economic interests. It wasn't so much about the peasants—the great mass of the population—who apparently were appreciative of what was being done for them; the many farmers were encouraged by more than a decade of peace and were moving back into fertile areas abandoned due to being in the path of revolutionary armies during different resurrections prior to 1915. The Haitian elite did not care much about the peasant women who were making good use of the new roads and trails, or the many people from the countryside who were flocking to the travelling clinics of the health service system.

5.5: The Fall of Duvalier

After 182 years of independence, the movement that precipitated the end of the Duvalier's dictatorship regime in 1986 gave Haiti high hopes and democratic aspirations. Refugees and asylees returned because they either felt the prospect of a new Haiti or they sensed that their contributions in building the new Haiti were needed and were going to be valued. Inside Haiti, in spite of sporadic scenes of pillage and violence against mainly notorious supporters of Duvalier, alleged criminals, and beneficiaries of *macoutism*, people felt enthusiastic about the country.

Haitians largely felt the need to reconcile with each other and live as good brothers and sisters to one another. Although, after Duvalier's departure, everything looked spontaneous, disorganized, disjunct, shaky, and fragile. The institutions were so dedicated to the cult of Duvalierism and personified, the transition from authoritarian to democracy was hugely challenged. Getting rid of Duvalier was one thing. But getting the country on the rails of democracy was another. The overall sociopolitical and economic situation was better described by the Haitian expression *mennen koulèv la lekòl se youn, fè l chita se de*. This saying is a way of expressing the level of extreme difficulty in making something work.

Jean-Claude Duvalier (Baby Doc) himself understood the scope of the daunting task he left behind. He emphatically made his feelings clear about the state of Haiti when, in response to a question from a reporter the day he arrived into exile in France, he insisted that he had stepped down to spare the population a "nightmare of blood". But Haiti without him was like "a cigar lit on both ends."[86]

The first test came with the difficult cohabitation of a five-member civilian-military council led by the Lieut. General Henri Namphy, who

86 Joseph Treaster, "Duvalier Flees Haiti to End Family's 28 years in Power: General Leads new Regime; 20 Reported dead", nytimes.com, The New York Times, February 8, 1986. https://www.nytimes.com/1986/02/08/world/duvalier-flees-haiti-end-family-s-28-years-power-general-leads-new-regime-20.html

was provisionally in charge as president. The mission of that council, instituted as Conseil National de Gouvernement (CNG) and composed of three high-ranking military officers and two civilians, was to organize free, fair, and democratic elections. The council was also in charge of conducting democratic reforms to facilitate the transition to elected government officials capable of providing the country with needed stability and durable socioeconomic developments. The CNG was short-lived due to clashes between its prominent figure and one of the two civilian members, Gérard Gourgue, and the military members over human rights abuse, failure to hold their promises, and a reluctance to make a clean break with the duvalierist past.

The resignation of Gérard Gourgue from the CNG meant that Henri Namphy, an uninspiring figure from the Duvalier army supported by Col. Williams Régala, who boasted a long history of abuse with Duvalier's Tonton Macoutes, along with Max Vallès, Alix Cinéas, and Prosper Avril, would assume full control of power in the country. Although the military government allowed the formation of the constitutional assembly that permitted the drafting of a new constitution in 1987, most of the energy, which was supposed to be dedicated to the establishment and reinforcement of democratic institutions capable of fostering civic and sociopolitical education in the country, was instead wasted on a permanent fight against the old order, and on the stammering and struggles among the political class and civil society to define and establish a new order for the country.

These fights and struggles gave rise to decades of governments ruled by opportunists of all backgrounds who saw politics as a cash cow for self-enrichment and power for extravagance, conspicuous behaviors, and abuses, instead of a means to serve for the common good. For all the euphoria at the dawn of 1986, the political class and civil-society organizations did not show much preparation or maturity. Thus, democratic progress and institutional reforms were inadequate and spotty.

After so much pain endured under Duvalier, Haitians did not imagine that the success of their rebellion would follow an indefinite period of transition, chaos, and lack of good leadership. After the fall of Duvalier, the vast majority of Haitians had the disposition to listen to leaders and be led in search of real democracy. Unfortunately, the very few steps made forward in that direction were largely overshadowed by bad leadership, internal divisions, and the thirst for power and wealth.

Frustrated by the overriding absence of quality changes and democratic advances, many Haitians, a large majority of whom were aged between 18 and 40, engaged in spasms of vigilante violence. Many members of popular and grassroots organizations that were peacefully doing community organizing, social and human rights activism, and valuable volunteering works, such as cleaning the streets, securing neighborhoods, and providing mutual aid, turned to violence in order to channel their frustrations, impatience, and anger. This pattern was to recur into the 21st century with the encouragement of some influential politicians who have been incapable of offering better alternatives.

From the day of Duvalier's departure, the country embraced the concept of *dechoukaj* (the uprooting of the old order), where people take matters in their own hands in the absence of competent institutions and better leadership for a nonviolent approach. But that did not translate into forcing the establishment of the rules of law, justice, and reconciliation, obviously. Conditions have worsened, and the country has become ungovernable. With the repugnant image of

Port-au-Prince as a failed state capital circulating in the mainstream media, stereotypes, prejudices, preconceived or ill-conceived notions, and shallow perceptions about Haiti among most of the international community have been reinforced and continue to be the shelter under which people who have no interest in seeing progressive changes in the country take refuge.

The elections on December 16, 1990, which saw Jean-Bertrand Aristide becoming president and many anti-Duvalierist leaders and activists elected in all parts of government, reinvigorated the Haitian hope for change once again. Despite Roger Lafontant's coup attempt to spoil the party, General Hérard Abraham reestablished order and trust, to the delight of many.

Aristide's inauguration, a massive celebration all over the country, effectively took place on February 7, 1991. Mr. Aristide was solemnly sworn in and took office at the presidential palace in Champs-de-Mars, like more than 67% of the electorate wanted it. The vast majority of Haiti, all social categories included, was ready for change. In Port-au-Prince, as it was in all major cities in the country, it looked like we had just witnessed a political transformation that Haitians had long been fighting for. Many Haitians in the euphoria of the moment felt that the only missing variables of the change equation were social and economic transformations. They thought these variables would come with the implementation of President Aristide's promise of justice, transparency, and participation.

Unfortunately, Aristide did not measure up to the challenges in front him. He could not even consolidate and reinforce his own coalitions. He polarized people, mismanaged institutions, and incited violence for more destruction and disruptions.

Despite mistrust between Aristide and several actors on the scene, in particular the economic elite, the oligarchs, the Haitian military, and the United States, he was perhaps the political leader with the most chances for something big in Haiti's history, similar to what Nelson Mandela achieved in South Africa before his death. Mr. Aristide completely blew it. No one could discount his electoral success and popular support in 1991.

Most Haitians in Haiti and abroad were ready to do anything for the success of the former priest of Saint-Jean Bosco. They saw in Aristide's success a win for the country as a whole. He did not inherit the widely divided Haiti that he helped it become. Most of the country was freshly unified and aimed at advancing toward social justice and economic prosperity.

But a series of ill-advised decisions and colorful public speeches inciting people to commit violent acts and destruction of lives and properties gave the much-needed pretext to his most sullen opponents and detractors (a powerful minority) to disrupt the democratic process. He was deposed in a coup d'état after less than a year in office. But he was restored to power after three years in exile with the support of the United States, the Organization of American States, and the United Nations, making him the first president in Haitian history to be given this type of opportunity.

Diminished by the weight of the job and his three years' journey in Venezuela and the United States, Aristide was becoming more and more a failed leader like so many others before him. He did not show any political maturity. Neither did he demonstrate any lesson learned from the backlashes of his past political endeavors. He was nonetheless able to oversee the electoral process, allowing him to peacefully transfer the power to Préval, his former prime minister. And Préval would return the favor to him five years later, on February 7, 2001.

But this time, it was in the midst of contestations, disagreements, violence, and a major electoral boycott. Aristide had lost most of his precious assets—his popularity and credibility. He wasted every date he had with history to accomplish what was expected of him. The forces opposed to him and his way of governing had become a lot stronger than those dedicated to his support. When the caravan of rebels threatened to invade Port-au-Prince and take him out of office, he called for another U.S. military intervention to shore up the security of his government. But succumbing to significant pressure from national rebellions and the Bush administration, he in the end resigned, cutting his second term short two years.

At this point, the whole lavalas movement emboldened by Aristide was in a free fall, and the hope carried out by the movement of 1986 was literally collapsing one day at a time. All the positive energies dissipated into a destructive smoking cloud. Generations of well-educated people were rejected and dusted under the rubble of history. Among many who escaped, hundreds of thousands disappeared forever, while others who were lucky enough to discover new skies had to reinvent themselves in the service of other countries. Actually, according to a 2013 research (published by Tatiana Wah of *Haiti Research and Policy Program at the Earth Institute, Columbia University*), as much as 70% of skilled and well-educated Haitians live outside of Haiti.[87]

---

87 Tatiana Wah, "Engaging the Haitian Diaspora", thecairoreview.com, The Cairo Review of Global Affairs, Spring 2013. https://www.thecairoreview.com/essays/engaging-the-haitian-diaspora/

Aristide's successors have not done any better. From the caretaker government of Alexandre-Latortue to the second version of Preval, to Martelly and then another provisional president in Privert, to Moise, and finally to Ariel Henry as de facto prime minister-president, the road for Haiti's recovery has remained long and perilous. Everyone, mostly every Haitian, has played a part in failing Haiti, although we recognize that not all sins are equal in quality and proportion. Some Haitians have more responsibility in the demise of Haiti than others.

But we are all responsible and accountable for our actions or lack thereof. Being a foreign agent by choice or by ignorance at the expense of Haiti's interests, a government official who enforces bad policies, someone who practices hate or violates human rights, a religious leader or member of an organization who exploits and zombifies a community, a political leader who has no soul in the presence of money and power, a simple citizen who is cynically watching people pile up the streets with trash without a positive influence on them, you should all have the conscious of guilt. Haiti has come so far to continue going backward in this vicious circle of regression.

5.6: The Last Two Earthquakes

When the catastrophic magnitude 7.0 earthquake struck Haiti on January 12, 2010, particularly Port-au-Prince and its surrounding areas, Haitians and foreigners familiar with the struggles on the Dessalinian soil had reasons to believe that things would finally change for the better. Not just because of the devastation worth US$7.8–$8.5 billion, well over 200,000 deaths, 300,000 injuries, more than 1.5 million people displaced, and thousands of lives unaccounted for that had put Haiti on its knees.[88] But the optimism was natural because people were almost unanimously made to believe Haitians would finally do a real soul-searching exercise and pull their strengths and good conscience together for the sake of building a better place for all.

Additionally, Haiti had the attention of the world more so than ever in the past. It was the focal point of international news in all forms of major media, including television, news agencies, newspapers, radios, and social media platforms for a long stretch. They dedicated a significant amount of their broadcasting time to the disaster and reported live from the ground in Port-au-Prince. Many reporters lived in Haiti for months and carried the sufferings of the Haitian people far from the makeshift tents that had become their shelters. The country received an extraordinary infusion of assistance of all kinds from donors around the world. Volunteers flooded into Haiti from all kinds of organizations and governmental institutions. Locally, the earthquake seemed to reinvigorate the sense of mutual aid and fraternity lost in the sociopolitical quarrels. The government agencies were looking for ways to be effective in performing their duties that had been neglected for so long.

In many neighborhoods, survivors found a way to deal with anxiety, grief, scarcity, and the law enforcement vacuum. Singing could be heard through the nights and groups of men coordinated to act as security as groups of women attempted to take care of food and hygiene necessities. During the days following the earthquake, hundreds were

---

88 Over 316,000 people died in the massive earthquake, according to statistics reported by the Haitian government. Most international organizations and agencies recorded an estimated death toll of about 200,000-250,000. In any case, the reality is that there is no way to estimate the real number of deaths resulting from that catastrophe.

seen marching through the streets in peaceful processions, singing and clapping. But as time went by, corruption, mismanagement, negligence, a lack of coordination between the distributors of aid, weakened government institutions, and the politics of aid got in the way.

All the synergy evaporated quickly. It looked like the international community had abandoned its urgent and pressing commitments to Haiti. But billions of US dollars from pledged donations for reconstruction were collected on behalf of Haiti, even though very little of it went to the Haitian government or local organizations directly. Instead, the vast majority of money was funneled through foreign contractors. The international structures coordinating post-earthquake aid used foreign contractors and subcontractors to execute relief and rebuilding efforts, creating massive overhead expenses and obscuring whether the money was spent wisely.

After January 12, 2010, a high-profile one-day international donors conference to secure pledges for the reconstruction of Haiti was held at the U.N. in New York. The Haitian government's plan—published the previous day for the first time—secured pledges of $5.3 billion over the next two years from 2010 with a further $4.6 billion to follow, making a total of $9.9 billion from over 100 national donors and multilateral funding agencies such as the World Bank and the Inter-American Development Bank.

Together with individual donations, pledges accounted for over $13 billion. Although there has been no clear indication that all the funds pledged by donors were effectively collected, we can unequivocally add to the amount received the billions of dollars generated from the Petrocaribe deal. A critical part of the problem was that most effective local organizations on the ground saw very little to none of the millions spent. Experts from different policy research and development agencies have been lamenting for years, and many pledges have been made for changes in the way financial aid is handled in Haiti. But, according to experts like Jake Johnston, there has been no improvement. In the case of USAID, for example, out of millions of dollars spent in Haiti since 2010, only 3% went directly to local organizations. After the 2021 earthquake, of the first $50 million awarded by USAID, zero dollars went to the various local groups in the field.[89]

The country has yet to recover from the ruins of the quake. Over 300 landmark buildings and monuments damaged beyond repair have not been rebuilt. January 12 has become a date of commemoration for Haitian leaders, who line up annually at a memorial service honoring the victims in Titanyen, north of central Port-au-Prince, where a mass burial site was designated. Ordinary people, religious leaders, and activists all annually honor the memory of the victims in their own way. Protestants and Catholics gather in masses and pray while vodouists perform their rituals at the memorial site by sprinkling water on a cross before the start of official services. January 12 happened just a little over a decade ago. The hundreds of thousands of victims are still fresh on the minds of their relatives and friends, but when it comes to rebuilding efforts, the disaster seems to have taken place too far back in time to be remembered.

Over twelve years later, remnants of buildings are still in ruins, and many people are still living in camps under makeshift shelters or unsafe structures with no adequate sanitation, making them more

---

89 Jake Johnston, "Haitians don't need another President chosen behind closed doors", prospect.org, The American Prospect", July 19, 2021. https://prospect.org/world/haitians-dont-need-another-president-chosen-behind-closed-doors/

vulnerable and subjects of a humanitarian crisis. Millions of people are scattered in these small camps based north of the capital and founded under biblical names such as Canaan, Jerusalem, Bethel, Nazareth, Jericho, Bethany, and Bethlehem. Some building and home owners reentered their damaged properties without permission, evaluation, or supervised repair.

There is a total absence of communication as to whether the government has implemented or ever intended to continue implementing the recommendations made by several organizations of the U.S. building industry and government, such as the Department of Homeland Security and the International Code Council, regarding the techniques to create a more resilient infrastructure to prevent future loss of life. In the aftermath of the earthquake, these organizations announced that they were compiling a "Haiti Toolkit" coordinated by the National Institute of Building Sciences. The toolkit comprised building technology resources and best practices for consideration by the Haitian government.

If a string of additional natural disasters, in particular Hurricane Matthew in 2016, which leveled entire communities and caused an upsurge in the ongoing cholera epidemic, did not budge Haitian leaders, people thought a more powerful 7.2 magnitude earthquake on August 14, 2021, would have awakened them.[90] Unfortunately for Haiti, their answer seems to be: not before, not this time either.

---

90 As of February 2019, about 10,000 had died in Haiti due to infection with cholera and about 900,000 others had shown sign of the disease, according to the Ministry of Public Health and Population. Since then, the country "has not recorded any laboratory-confirmed cases of cholera", said Dr. Edwige Michel. She has been the research coordinator in the Department of Research Epidemology and Laboratory of the ministry since 2012.

Of course, the 2010 earthquake caused more casualties than the 2021 quake. One of the reasons was because it struck the Tiburon Peninsula, a region less densely populated than Port-au-Prince. Even though the second quake was produced on the same fault that caused the first one in 2010, the epicenter was located about 93 miles west of Port-au-Prince, far enough to avoid major shocks inside the capital city.

However, about 2,300 people were confirmed dead, over 12,200 injuries were reported, 650,000 people were in need of assistance, more than half a million of children were affected, and scores of buildings and homes were damaged or destroyed. An estimated loss of $1.5 billion was reportedly added to the already massive loss from the January 12, 2010 quake.

Once again, international support for rescue and rebuilding efforts were quick and steady. But the Haitian government responded in the same helpless, unprepared, and ineffectual fashion that we have long become accustomed to. And as time goes by, it has been a total blackout on reconstruction. And in the long run, the affected populations are left to continue licking their wounds and grieving their losses on their own, without thinking of the next disaster.

Chapter Six

The Waste of Time and Resources

Haiti has continued to waste its most precious asset, which is time. More than two centuries have gone by since independence. Haiti has not grown up with time. It is still that baby that cannot hold its own. Haiti needs help for everything. In addition to time being wasted, there is the consequential loss of the country's already meager resources. This is a pattern stemming from the old tactics of insurrection, revolt, and fight dating all the way back to the revolutionary movements for independence.

As we have seen throughout this book, most Haitian leaders have managed and led the country poorly. They have used all kinds of cynical and authoritarian methods—destruction, witch hunts, lies, death, character assassinations, repression, torture, scapegoating, secrecy, sorcery—to hold on to power. Haitians have never shied away from revendicating their rights, pushing for the precipitated fall of even the most brutal regimes.

These awful methods have helped politicians and their acolytes abuse and exploit the population and stymie socioeconomic developments of the country. But they have not been useful problem-solving methods. Haitians have never stopped demanding change from the leaders. The biggest movement in that sense arose in the mid-1980s with the overthrow of the Duvalier regime. People claimed democracy without doubt. That movement for the democratization of Haiti has stalled. But this is what most Haitians continue to demand as a political system.

The different leaders in charge of Haiti keep repeating the same errors committed by their predecessors while expecting different results. Being a brutal tyrant who oppresses your own people or a weak leader who practices laissez-faire will not help you stay in power longer than the implosion and explosion of political, social, and economic contradictions in the country allow. You can cling to power and hang on for only as long as those contradictions, manipulated by national and international actors combined, do not implode or explode. Otherwise, like other leaders before, you are gone. As you are bidding your farewell, the country is left suffering from the effects of all your messes left behind. And time will still go on. Other generations will emerge from previous legacies.

This is how Haiti has accumulated all these years without much to show for it, other than problems with complex solutions. There was a time when Haiti had adequate natural and human resources to sustain its developments. But today, it looks like we had never had anything other than the spectacle of poverty and damnation. For all these years, we have been wasting time and resources. We have left a legacy of chaos, a dog-eat-dog mentality that has become part of the country's sociopolitical, cultural, and economic fabric.

In this chapter, we discuss the type of relation that Haitians have developed over the years with the concept of time, and how that relation affects the national level of productivity in general and economic growth in particular. Additionally, we report pertinent information about the type of consideration, management, and utilization made of natural and human resources in the country.

6.1: The Perception of Time, Resources, and Productivity

Impatience, procrastination, or disregard. What has transpired in Haiti in terms of people's perception about the concept of time is not something typical just to Haitians. Human beings in general tend to misuse or mismanage time, procrastinate, or think they can use shortcuts to beat the clock. This problem is in our nature as humans. It is not a matter of background, ethnicity, race, or specific culture. Everyone can drop the ball—in private enterprises as in government affairs—when it comes to making good use of the time in hand.

Many leaders around the world, all sectors included and not just in Haiti, do not often understand the potential devastation that can come with the mishandling of time. That is why people often dedicate time, money, and energy to educate themselves on how to become more effective and efficient with time. People may not have the same resources available to them to execute and achieve what they set their minds on. But the clock ticks equally for everyone, no matter where they are. Some individuals may live longer than others, but countries continue to go through the same 24-hour cycle. In fact, some people may even achieve more both in quality and quantity in a shorter period of time than others who happen to have more resources than them. This is a question of discipline, understanding, patience, priorities, structure, and organization.

In Haiti, people seem to be so overwhelmed with the complexity of these elements mentioned as they relate to making their time count, that they simply disregard them. The problem with that is, the more you ignore the building blocks that make time useful, the more time you waste without accomplishing much. People sometimes confuse speed and precipitation. They want results to move quicker than the reasonable time necessary to complete the activities that can produce those results. Being impatience is one of the factors that contributed to Haiti's counter-productivity. This infects everyone—the mayor, members of parliament, directors of institutions, government cabinet members, president, religious leaders and any other civil-society organization, and people themselves. There have been many times in the past when Haiti could have achieved better cycles if people allowed enough time and space for those in leadership to do their job. Let us take the president for example. According to the constitution, a presidential term is five years.

On paper, this looks like enough time to accomplish something and establish the priorities for the continuity of the nation. But generally speaking, since the fall of the Duvalier regime, Haitians have been very impatient with governmental institutions. Understandably so perhaps. But if you vote for someone, it is worth giving them some time to work before you can evaluate whether they can produce results. Usually, two to three months after a president takes office, people expect everything to change rapidly. Since this is a very unrealistic expectation, especially in the context of Haiti, they start going to the streets expressing their anger in the blink of an eye. And demonstrations, petitions, and protests in Haiti against the government have rarely been peaceful. They usually cause unrest, turmoil, a standstill, and a lot of human and material casualties. Therefore, we continue to waste more time and resources that we do not sufficiently have.

Another big problem in Haiti is procrastination. Some people just think they have all the time in the world for themselves. So, there is no need for a sense of urgency or immediate action. Everything takes time in the country, and it often depends on who you know in order to get something done in a timely fashion. In government offices as in businesses, more often you come for service, but no one pays any mind to you. In many places, workers don't like to be bothered. They can be slacking or joking around with their peers while you are waiting desperately on your feet for someone to even greet you—except for a few institutions and enterprises, such as banks and car dealerships. People don't understand that each job has priorities. And it's called work for a reason, to borrow the lines of the American author and personal development speaker Larry Winget.[91]

Sometimes, people act like they are doing a lot, while in reality they are wasting time by doing things that have no bearing on their success at the job and leaving the important activities aside. By the time they open their eyes, the critical time has already gone. Other times, they do not move at all. They pay no attention to the clock, thinking that they have more than enough time in front of them. Once they realize the time has gone, they start making rushed and ill-advised decisions. Some leaders often act that way for political expediency. A lot of times, they try to use hasty shortcuts, thinking that would help them beat the clock. They do not have patience for sacrifice, commitment, focus, integrity, schedule, faith, and concordant actions.

You do not need to go to a lot of social, cultural, religious, or political activities in Haiti before you understand how Haitians perceive time. People spend a lot of time talking without making any difference. Maurice Alfrédo Sixto, in his oral story-telling piece entitled *General Tikòk*, enlightens our understanding on how most Haitians usually banalize time, either through long and unimportant speeches, or ineffective and unnecessary actions.[92]

---

91 Larry Winget, *It's Called Work for a Reason: Your Success is your Own Danm Fault* (New York: Gotham Books, 2007), p. 1-240.

92 Maurice Alfrédo Sixto, known as Maurice Sixto, was a pioneer in Haitian oral literary genre known as *Lodyans.* A storyteller and entertainer, Sixto was born in Gonaives, Haiti in 1919 and died in Philadelphia, Pennsylvania in 1984.

These days, it is very rare to attend one Haitian event—a wedding, funeral, church service, birthday party, inauguration, etc.—where you do not feel that too much time is wasted for too little accomplishment. Realistically, people waste one to two hours right before they even start. And then more time would be wasted in doing irrelevant or wasteful activities, making the event appear to be a lot longer than necessary. If they tell you to be there at 6:00 p.m., their start time is really 8:00 p.m. because no one would show up at 6:00 p.m., not even the organizers themselves. Both participants and organizers would think that is the way it is with Haitians. Each party blames the other one without making any effort to break the cycle. If someone does differently, that person may be decidedly called a *blan* (meaning he or she is not Haitian but a foreigner, as if being on time were something foreign).

The waste of time and resources has created a major handicap for creativity and imagination in the country. Energies have not been sufficiently concentrated on efforts to develop a national project that values our human and natural resources. We have not worked sufficiently on developing or reinforcing resources and using them appropriately, efficiently, and effectively according to the country's needs. The government would spend millions of dollars a year in education—all three levels of primary, secondary, and post-secondary included—to see very little to no return on investment.

Once graduated from college, most young people either look for an opportunity to leave the country or are integrated into the vast market of unemployment. Those who are fortunate enough to get a job, usually through connections in government or in the private sector, are often placed in positions completely foreign to their area of expertise. It is not unusual in Haiti to find an agronomist at an important position at the ministry of education, while someone else with expertise in the science of education may be placed at the ministry of agriculture. Many times, you find people who have no preparation at all working good-paying jobs at the expense of others who are not well-connected or do not have certain superficial characteristics. Again, it all depends on who you know and whether people that you know have influence or not.

If we count the number of hours spent on average a year in protests, blockades, early closures of businesses and institutions of service, the closing of schools and government offices, and the backlogs in public service and business operations, Haiti will undoubtedly be ranked number one in the Western hemisphere as the country with the highest ratio of time consumed to productivity. With a per capita GDP of US$671 and a relatively speedy population growth rate (faster than it can keep up to provide for its current population), Haiti cannot afford the continuity of time-wasting politics.

On top of a crucial lack of infrastructure and resources to make the country functional on a daily basis without having to shut life down almost completely from every Friday afternoon to Monday morning, we have difficulty keeping life going effectively even during the short window of five days. We have wasted meaningful years in quarrelling, fighting, blaming each other, hating, killing, chopping heads off, expelling, imprisoning, torturing our own people, destroying plants and animals, polluting water and air, exploiting each other, burning houses, buildings and monuments, and making life conditions untenable. Today, it cannot be a surprise that Haiti is trailing behind other independent nations in the region. Annual economic reports published from 2014 to 2020 show that Haiti has not registered an increase in growth since 2016, with a 0.56% GDP growth rate increase that year. Every subsequent year after, the GDP growth rate was in decline and the economic growth rate was slower than the number registered in the previous year.

Looking at the level of trade deficit recorded by Haiti in its commercial relations with the Dominican Republic, its nearest neighbor with a similar population size, the picture cannot be any clearer for Haitians. And the time for urgency is now. From 2019 to 2021, the Dominican Republic accumulated a surplus of US$1.6 billion in the exchange of goods with Haiti. Between January-August 2019 and January-August 2021, the total exports of products from the Dominicans to Haitians amounted to US$1.64 billion. That is outrageous because the value of imports from Haiti was only US$7 million.[93]

Exports to the United States, which ranks as the number one country Haiti trades with at 81%, amounted to $960.2 million versus $3.621 billion in products imported by Haitians, according to an estimate dated 2020. While Haiti, the size of Maryland, cannot compete with the U.S., the level of the deficit is just not normal. Efforts can be made to reduce the difference, focusing especially on increasing the production of certain products for exports that are in high demand in the United States.

6.2: The Handicap to Creativity and Imagination

Apart from the issues of wasting time and resources, Haiti has major handicaps to creativity and imagination. Haitians are generally

---

93 Dominican Today, "Dominican to Haiti Exports: $US1.64 Billion to a Negligeable $US7 Million", dominicantoday.com, Dominican Today, October 25, 2021. https://dominicantoday.com/dr/economy/2021/10/25/dominican-to-haiti-exports-us1-64b-to-negligible-us7m/

very creative, and their imagination goes beyond the ordinary. Walking through the streets of Port-au-Prince or any other city, observing the peasants plowing their farms, the artisans working on their crafts, the spontaneous gatherings, the young artists painting on walls or sidewalks, eyewitnesses can glance at the intriguing creativity and imagination of the Haitian people. That's how they have been surviving for so long. Unfortunately, that extraordinary sense of making the minds work could have been exponentially more useful to the country if it were not for certain obstacles.

The first major obstacle that prevents Haitians from taking advantage of the country's resourceful talents of creativity and imagination is a critical lack of reliable infrastructure. That includes both soft and hard infrastructure. The education system is very dysfunctional and disjunct. Not only do the schools lack quality, the system is not uniform and is controlled by the private sector, whose main objective is to make profit. According to an estimate published in 2020 by the ministry of education and vocational training, 82.3% of schools in Haiti are private. This is even though the constitution guarantees primary and secondary education for free. Most of these schools do not meet any kind of standard and have no business being responsible for children's education.

The ministry of education lacks the necessary resources for policing and quality control. Most of its policies and regulations are outdated. The last major regulation establishing the rules under which the education system operates was in 1974 during the Duvalier regime.[94] And we also have the issue of disparity. A category of schools for the

94 Direction d'Appui à l'Enseignement Privé et du Partenariat, *Politique Nationale d'Accréditations des Écoles Privées* (Port-au-Prince: Ministère de l'Education Nationale et de Formation Professionelle, 2020), p. 7.

well-to-do, one for the working class, and another one for the large mass of impoverished people.

In addition to the problem with the education system, we can add other difficulties such as the lack of electricity, reliable roads and bridges, and insufficient port and airport infrastructure. The way telecommunications and internet service are provided in Haiti also remains a big issue. Lack of competition and accountability enforcement make quality and reliable services very expensive compared to the cost in most of Haiti's neighboring countries. The following table compares the prices of the three major providers of internet service to give you an idea of how expensive communication is in Haiti, where most people live on less than US$2 a day.

Pricing per month by download speed and provider in 2017

Download Speed (Mbps)	NATCOM	Hainet	Access Haiti
2 Mbit/s	US$50.00	US$60.00	US$54.55
4 Mbit/s	US$90.00	US$100.00	US$99.00
6 Mbit/s	US$150.00	US$150.00	US$149.00
8 Mbit/s	US$200.00	US$199.00	US$199.00
12 Mbit/s	US$250.00	US$250.00	US$249.00
15 Mbit/s	US$300.00	US$299.00	US$299.00
25 Mbit/s	US$400.00	US$350.00	US$349.00

Jealousy, egoism, fear, and entitlement. These problems are not new in the Haitian society. The social structure has made it difficult for people to avoid being jealous of others. Young Haitians have died, been stopped in their development, or forced to leave the country simply because they looked too bright in the eyes of others. There are not enough opportunities for all. The chances are so limited that a lot of people think that they have to step over someone else in order to succeed themselves. In case they cannot push you out of the way or take your place, they may look to eliminate you altogether. So, the fear becomes evident on both sides of the spectrum.

Besides the jealousy that creates fear within the society, there is also egoism, a sense of being entitled. Some people will still work hard to hold on to the status of being on top. Reputation in Haiti is important. It can affect your status in Haitian culture and determine the level of respect you gain from society. For that reason, everyone tries to make their family's name be held in high regard. Families are viewed as one large unit. Therefore, the wrongdoings of the child could affect the reputation of the whole family. This can extend to not only parents, but grandparents and other extended family members.

Others will merely feel like they just deserve to dominate everyone else. So many people cannot bear the simple fact that others will do better than them, no matter what. They see themselves at the center of the world. The whole country must bow down to them, to their families, their children, generation after generation. They will hold on to that mindset regardless of what happens to the country. Even if it means that everyone perishes, including themselves. They are so stubborn that they will not let go. Yet, we must recognize that these issues are not typical only to Haitians. You find them among people in any country. However, the problem with Haiti is that, unfortunately, people with these kinds of behaviors and mindsets have been dominating every aspect of the society for so long. It is very difficult not to feel their influence on almost everyone, to some extent, one way or the other.

As seen previously, being good or just a little bit over average is enough. In many minds, openly striving for greatness is calling for persecution and curses. Not because most Haitians deliberately want to be mediocre, but because of that fear of evil that has been cultivated and remains fundamentally sunk into people's mindsets. They are afraid of being noticed too soon or ever by others who would seek to harm them or disrupt their activities. They will not try to be bold or ambitious. They would like to survive, just so they could live. No one would like to play by the rules. In fact, people hate written rules. They prefer to deal with verbal agreements that are easier to break. However, these are acquired customs and traditions that can change with more targeted social education.

Chapter Seven

The State of the Future

Despite all of the problems and struggles that have been taming Haiti for well over two centuries, there has always been hope. The country has had and continues to have plenty of potential for progress and redemption. There is always the possibility of better days. Even though leaders in the past miserably and immensely failed to conduct business in line with the Haitian revolution, it is very possible that today's generations of all stripes can aim to change course for a better future. They can set the foundation on which future generations will continue to build for the benefit of all Haitians.

And as we have mentioned throughout this book, the ideals of the Revolution of 1804 set the pace for that foundation. Of course, there is enough argument for pessimism. However, we must choose hope over fear, unity over division, love over hate, tolerance over intolerance, life over death, fairness over inequality, ownership and responsibility over abandonment of duty, hard work over indolence or unproductivity, nation-state building over self-interest, seriousness over triviality, construction over destruction, and preservation over abuse of resources. Our faith in the possibility of redemption should run deep into our efforts—the possibility to break with the current political cycle and the long circle of regression.

Our optimism derives from the exhibition of extraordinary traits and qualities shown by Haitians on a daily basis. Being inside Haiti or abroad, particularly in North America and Europe, Haitians detest the politics of Haiti but love their country greatly, even though it offers them limited opportunities, and its structures are chaotic most of the time. This love is the prologue of strong patriotism. Haitians prioritize family ties above other associations. From immediate relatives to extended family members, everyone is tightly connected. They usually support each other despite contentions and divisions at times. Spread throughout society, the priority given to family ties has always made unity possible. The challenge has always been the fact that unity has not been given a chance to live for long stretches of time.

Haitians are typically hard workers when working for themselves, and they feel that they are not forced to work in order to enrich others. They have lived through that painful experience for far too long. It makes them rebellious and conflictual at times. Observing around the cities, towns, and the peasantry, one can witness the energy on the streets, at the marketplaces, in the farms, in the mountains, around the villages, and elsewhere. The enthusiasm exhibited by Haitians, even in their daily struggles for survival, has put Haitians among all unique groups of people in the world. In rural Haiti, which includes mostly remote and enclaved areas largely neglected by the central government, people have been using their creativity and imagination for years to survive and give their children better chances for a lifestyle that they did not have themselves.

The zeal in a multitude of political parties and grassroots organizations all over Haiti has presented and remains today a unique opportunity for real change. The only problem, as is the case for the country as a whole, is that those structures need good leadership, unity, and important reforms. Finally, the freedom of expression, liberty of association, human rights, and access to communication technologies—notably the increasing access to social media (guaranteed by the constitution)—and all the political and social events that occurred from the 1980s through the 2000s, in spite of some major obstacles, continue to be revealed as some irreversible acquisitions in the fight for a new Haiti.

Reading through this chapter, you will find out how all of these attributes, along with some other factors and progress already made, even with some undisputable limitations, can contribute to help turn the page on the discourse about Haiti. These elements present without doubt a huge opportunity for optimism.

7.1: A Nation of Resilient People

From slavery to the very struggles of today's Haiti, Haitians are known for their resilience—a strength that economic elites as well as religious and political leaders sometimes use to exploit them even more. When you see how average Haitians are working so hard to make ends meet, often in inhumane conditions to survive daily, it reminds you of the slavery epoch. In those days, only the work of humans produced the wealth for colonial powers.

As time evolved, machines and computers have replaced the humans who used to lift, push, and pull the heavy loads. But in Haiti, we are still stuck with the same practices from long ago. We observe, we live, we meet people everywhere in Haiti, and every day, who are doing the work of oxen from plantation to plantation, the work of a tractor trailer from block to block, and the work of a truck from town to town. All of that just to be able to make ends meet. Looking at what most Haitians are enduring, how in the world have they lived through this for so long? Life expectancy in Haiti is about 64 years average. This is only a testament of the Haitian resilience.

If you go to the streets of any town, you will encounter countless people who are dealing with their workloads just through resilience. You will meet the *bouretye* (cart-puller) who ensures a great deal of transportation, *chany* (shoeshine man) who "makes you shine where you stand," all kinds of merchants, including *machann soup* (soup merchant), *machann pen ak kafe* (bread and coffee merchant), among others who are ready to feed you in the morning, and *machann chabon* (charcoal merchant) who provides the country with one of its principal sources of energy. In market venues, you will observe the picturesqueness of the market women who come from great distances, the filthy, bustling venues of trade. All of that can help you cloak certain grim economic facts about Haiti and the human energy behind all of it, and particularly how that energy can serve as a catalyst to change the country.

Other times to observe the resilience of the Haitian people in actions is undisputedly during tragedies, natural disasters, and political turmoil. They have known all kinds of unimaginable catastrophes beyond the human ability to endure and handle. When you thought that they were going to be knocked down and would stay there, they have always found the strength to rise up and overcome, mainly because of their unraveling determination.

7.2: A Place of Good Hospitality

One of the characteristics of the Haitian people is their sense of hospitality. Of course, Haitians fight hard against each other at times, but they would welcome a stranger warmly. Haitians are generally warm, friendly, and generous. Their tradition of hospitality is clear in how they treat guests or go out of their way to help strangers find an address or something else they need. It is in the Haitian tradition and culture to welcome friends, neighbors, and relatives in their home at any time of day until about 8:00 p.m. It is not necessary to call ahead.

Visitors arriving during a meal may be asked to wait in another room until the family finishes eating. If it's a close friend, he/she might be invited to share the meal, and they may accept or decline politely. It is also acceptable for guests to decline refreshments. Hosts typically offer fruit juice or soda.

In addition to impromptu visits, Haitians enjoy inviting friends over for an evening of socializing or for dinner. When a visit ends, hosts accompany guests to the door. Rather than leaving, however, Haitians frequently extend their visit for a while by standing and talking with their hosts depending on how comfortable they feel with that person. Special occasions also call for visits. Guests take gifts to hosts celebrating a communion, baptism, graduation, or wedding—occasions for which many organize elaborate parties; in other words, Haitians love to party.

In Haiti, we have a lot to offer visitors. That's why tourism used to flourish greatly not too far back in the 1970s and the early 1980s. We have good music that combines a wide range of influences drawn from the many people who have settled the island. Haitian music reflects in its rhythms African, French, Spanish, and Taino elements, as well as others who have inhabited the island. Some interesting styles of music unique to Haiti include music derived from *rara* parading music, which is a processional music with strong ties to the vodou religious tradition; *Twoubadou* ballads, which is a form of music played by peripatetic troubadours playing some combination of acoustic, guitar, beatbox, and accordion instruments, and singing ballads of Haitian, French, or Caribbean origin; mini jazz and rock bands that were formed in the mid-1960s and were characterized by the rock band formula of two guitars, one bass, drum-conga-cowbell, some use an alto sax or a full horn section for the jazz part of the band, others use a keyboard, accordion or lead guitar.

We also have another style called *Mizik Rasin*, which started late in the 1970s as a movement expressing discontent against the increase in opulence surrounding the Duvalier regime. *Mizik Rasin* drew inspiration from the global movements such as black power and the hippies, Jamaican reggae megastar Bob Marley, and extensively from rural life in Haiti. Rap K*reyòl*, which is more popular among the today's Haitian youth, often communicates social and political topics as well as materialism. And the last, but not least, the wildly popular *konpa or Compas* and meringue as its basic rhythm.

To Haitian music, we can add our dance and folklore. Music and dance are part of everyday life in Haiti. They are two of the best gifts Haitians offer visitors on their arrival to the country.

We also offer our brilliant artistic talents to the world. Haitian artists and sculptors are known for their unique images and striking colors. In fact, it is one of the most popular art forms in the region. One popular art form is a sculpture made from cut, pounded, and painted scrap metal. Tap-taps, which are brightly painted pickup trucks fitted with benches and covered tops, are both a means of transportation and traveling art. Many artists choose Haitian history or daily life for their subjects. Nature is also an important theme. Painted screens, papier-mâché art, wood carvings, basketwork, pottery, and painted wooden boxes are prominent crafts.

Oral literature is abundant and includes songs, proverbs, and riddles. Storytellers carefully craft their performance, acting out the story with their voices. There is also a vibrant tradition of Haitian literature, mostly written in French, although the native Haitian language is now commonly used as well. Another huge passion in Haiti is sports, notably soccer, sarcastically labeled "real football" by many Haitians in comparison to American football, where the athletes essentially use their hands instead of their feet to move the ball. Sports commentators and journalists have nicknamed soccer Haiti's "sport-roi" (king of all sports). Most Haitians, men and women included, live soccer almost as a religion.

In addition to its people, Haiti has beautiful nature and rich historical sites. Visitors notice the beautiful beaches along the country's coastline. They can enjoy the valleys, hillsides, plains, mountain tops, grottoes, rivers, and falls all around Haiti. Among the most popular beaches we find the famous Labardee leased by Royal Caribbean Cruise Line and located in northern Haiti near Cap-Haitian, which boasts historical sites like the mountaintop fortress Citadelle Laferrière, the Palais Sans-Souci, and the Cathedrale de Milot built by King Henri Christophe, and the Cathedrale Notre-Dame du Cap-Haitian built in the 1600s during the colonization period.

Other attractive locations due to the beauty of the natural landscape and beaches are Port Salut and Les Cayes (south), Jacmel (southeast), Côte-des-Arcadins (one of Haiti's longest stretches of pure white sand beaches and located along Route Nationale-1), and Moulin Sur Mer in the district of Montrouis (an 18th century sugar plantation converted into a hot tourist beach resort).

The Artibonite Valley with Haiti's largest river is marvelous. River des Pedernales, River grise, and other major rivers in southern Haiti are worth being noted. Haiti also boasts a number of islands and isles with some wonderful beaches and endemic natural resources. Tortuga Island (northwest), Gonave Island (west), Ile-à-Vache (south), Les Iles Cayemites, and Navassa (claimed by the United States) are among the most important islands. Rivers are also considered as an important part of Haiti's landscape. Rivière des Barres, River of Jean-Rabel,

River Henne, Les Trois Rivières, and others in northwestern Haiti are important resources.

The peninsula of Môle Saint-Nicolas (northwest) is very attractive, not only for its beautiful beach, river La Gorge, which visibly flows into the ocean through a natural aqueduct, Môle Saint-Nicolas is also an important historical site that has become the symbol of colonialism on the island, in the Caribbean, and in Latin America. That was where Christopher Columbus first landed in December 1492. Môle Saint-Nicolas is situated in an inlet of the Windward Passage, just 122 miles south of Guantanamo Bay. It had been the subject of dispute between Haiti and the United States, which wanted to occupy it mainly for military strategy purposes.

The elegant castle Palais de la Belle-Rivière, commonly called "The Palace of 365 Doors", is another wonderful historical site less and less publicized by Haitian tourism officials. It was built between 1816 and 1820 by King Henri Christophe. The Palace of 365 Doors is located in the department of Artibonite in the town of Jean-Jacques Dessalines, about 77 miles north of Port-au-Prince.

In Port-au-Prince, we cannot underestimate the famous Musée du Pantheon National Haitien (MUPANAH), which opened in 1983. Located in Champs-de-Mars near the site of the National Palace, the MUPANAH is a must-see historical site that celebrates the heroes of independence. It is one of the rare important buildings and monuments in Port-au-Prince that did not get damaged by the 2010 earthquake.

Visitors can also enjoy Etang Saumatre, also known as Lake Azuéi, the largest lake in Haiti and the second largest on the island after Lake Henriquillo in the Dominican Republic. Lake Azuei has an area of

65.64 square miles. Its waters are almost brackish, and like its neighbor Lake Henriquillo, it is expanding. From Lake Azuei, located near the official Haitian-Dominican border and east of Port-au-Prince, you can drive a few miles away to reach the massive Saut d'Eau waterfall near Mirebalais. It is said that the Saut d'Eau waterfall was created in the massive earthquake that devastated northern Haiti on May 7, 1842. Like several other sites in Haiti, this waterfall cascading over large rocks is considered as a sacred place by Haitians.

Pilgrims come from across the country each July for a traditional ceremony that mixes elements of Catholicism and Vodou. Saut d'Eau is the perfect symbol of the existing symbiosis between Catholics and vodouists among Haitians. Speaking about waterfalls, we cannot forget the beautiful Saut Mathurine (water fall) in Camp-Perrin near Les Cayes, the Seguin fall in Nippes, and Bassin Zim located near Hinche in the Central Plateau department. Bassin Zim is a spectacular natural landmark in Haiti, with a waterfall, a chain of turquoise-hued pools, and a network of glittering underground grottoes.

If you want to go for some excursions, camping, and sightseeing, a host of mountains are waiting to warmly welcome you. Haiti is home to four principal mountain ranges: Chaîne de la Selle, Chaîne des Matheux, Massif de la Hotte, Massif du Nord, and Montagne Noire. From these mountain ranges, some famous mountains are formed. The Pic la Selle, Pic Macaya, Morne du Cibao, Morne Bois-pin, Morne Terrible, Morne Bois-blanc, Morne Degas, Morne Pistache, Morne Jean, and Gros Morne are among the highest mountains in Haiti, ranging from 8,793 to 3,015 feet of elevation.

Definitely, Haiti's warm culture, people's contagious smile—even in the midst of serious economic, political, and social difficulties—

natural beauty, and the various symbolic sites of its rich and troubled history are what set Haitians apart from the rest of the world. That too boosts our optimism in a better future.

7.3: A Republic of Philanthropic Organizations

From the smallest entity in the corner of a village, to the largest nonprofit organization (NGO) in the world, Haiti is fully covered with philanthropists. With over 10,000 NGOs operating on the ground, Haiti is second to none as the country with the largest per capita of philanthropic organizations in the world. Referred to as the "Republic of NGOs," and rightly so, the Caribbean nation would have fewer worries about people's living conditions if there had been more effectiveness, efficiency, coordination, transparency, accountability, and a nationally defined project. The landscape could have shown a better picture.

There have been too many NGOs for too small of an impact, after so many years of interventions. Yet, a lot of voices have been raised calling for a better coordination of aid and for establishing strong protocols and parameters within which NGOs operate on the ground. But we have yet to see the difference. The harsh criticism and mistrust shown by Haitians after the 2010 debacle, where billions of US dollars were mismanaged by NGOs and international agencies, have not seemed to change much in terms of the strategic reorganization in the distribution of aid.

One of the UN officials in Haiti coordinating humanitarian efforts, El-mostafa Benlamlih, could not put it any clearer in a statement in 2017. "Structural problems associated with multiple emergencies continue to increase the vulnerability of millions of Haitians. We must act together to enable these people to recover and to build the future they want for themselves, their children and their grandchildren," he argued. He also concluded that aid should be distributed in a way to "strengthen the resilience of vulnerable communities and maintain the gains made in recent years, but it should also allow for a sustainable exit from humanitarian challenges while continuing the country's sustainable development process."[95]

In other words, the country cannot continue to be the republic of NGOs forever. Most of the funds collected are used in diversion, corruption, logistics, salaries, and the lifestyles of foreign experts. From emergency responses to meaningful development projects, the main causes or the fundamental aspects of the country's socioeconomic problems should be impacted in a way that makes the presence of most of those NGOs needless at some point. Those organizations should have an exit plan or strategy as they are working to create an emerging environment for positive impacts on people's life and general conditions. But instead, they have long become an integral part of the problem than a solution to the problem. They are nourishing the problems instead of the people to justify themselves and increasingly make their permanent presence indispensable in Haiti. This is a disease that Haitians must be conscious of and take steps to cure. While we recognize and are grateful for meaningful efforts in support of the most vulnerable people all over Haiti, especially in healthcare and education, various humanitarian and political interventions made by many NGOs and foreign players have not changed much.

---

95 U.N. Office for the Coordination of Humanitarian Affairs (OCHA), "The Haitian Government and the humanitarian community are requesting $ 291.5 million to provide vital assistance to 2.4 million vulnerable people", reliefweb.int, OCHA Relief, February 6, 2017. https://reliefweb.int/report/haiti/haitian-government-and-humanitarian-community-are-requesting-2915-million-provide-vital

Backtrack to the years 2007 to 2010. Former U.S. President Bill Clinton became very involved directly on the ground in Haiti. The involvement of a figure of the caliber of Mr. Clinton gave a lot of people high hopes that things might improve at a time when Haiti was suffering from the effects of long political crisis, social unrest, hunger, inflation, economic desperation, killings and abuses, health problems, and issues caused by major disasters such as a series of tropical storms and hurricanes in 2008. In 2009, Clinton was first appointed as the UN Secretary General Special Envoy to Haiti. On his arrival in the land of Dessalines, he declared his intention "to work with the Haitian people and the government, not just to repair the damage of the previous year's storms but to lay the foundations for the long-term sustainable development that has eluded them for so long."[96]

As a result of Clinton's work and persuasion skills, the World Bank and International Monetary Fund canceled $1.2 billion of Haiti's foreign debt to these multilateral institutions (some 80% of the total). Likewise, many international creditors canceled most of Haiti's debt after the 1990 elections. They judged that the country had met economic reform and poverty reduction conditions. Additionally, the former U.S. president led a delegation of 500 businessmen to Haiti, proclaiming "this is the right time to invest in Haiti." In fact, by the second half of 2009, there were some tenuous signs of economic improvement and stability in Haiti. But this economic improvement was quickly scaled back by the 2010 earthquake.

---

96 U.N. News, "Former U.S. President Clinton appointed U.N. Special Envoy for Haiti", news.un.org, U.N. News, May 9, 2009. https://news.un.org/en/story/2009/05/300442-former-us-president-clinton-appointed-un-special-envoy-haiti#:

And then, being already in Haiti as U.N. Secretary Special Envoy, Clinton co-chaired a reconstruction commission together with Former Haitian Prime Minister Jean-Max Bellerive. The commission was formed to anchor a post-disaster needs assessment (PNDA), which became a glossy, comprehensive reconstruction plan. There was plenty of input from multilateral funding agencies and major donors, but Haitian civil society organizations and even foreign nongovernmental agencies at the forefront of the relief effort complained bitterly of their almost total exclusion from the consultation process. We have seen where all of this led us to.

To address and resolve Haiti's pressing problems, we need inclusion, and unquestionably transparency and accountability. A project called Haiti Aid Map was launched by InterAction, the largest alliance of NGOs and partners in the U.S., with the partnership of the U.S. Chamber of Commerce's Business Civic Leadership Center and FedEx.[97]

Launched one year after the 2010 earthquake, the project helped create an interactive visual mapping of individual aid projects being conducted in Haiti. The goal was to increase transparency, facilitate partnerships, and help NGOs and others better coordinate and allocate resources to aid relief and reconstruction efforts. A version of the interactive visual map in 2011 featured 479 projects conducted by 77 local and international organizations operating all over Haiti. Most of

---

97 InterAction was founded in 1984 to mobilize members to think collectively as to how they serve the poor and vulnerable around the world. The alliance of NGOs' mission statement read: "InterAction is a convener, thought leader, and voice for NGOs working to eliminate extreme poverty, strengthen human rights and citizen participation, safeguard a sustainable planet, promote peace, and ensure dignity for all people."

those 77 NGOs are InterAction members. While the map covers the response of the alliance's members and partners, it left out the thousands of other nongovernmental organizations' projects being conducted in the country. USAID had come up with their own map, a more updated version, showing thousands of organizations on the ground in Haiti spending billions of dollars. Still, no significant improvements can be observed in people's daily challenges.

7.4: An Undetached Diaspora

If you launch a search on Google with the two words Haitian diaspora, you will find at least 4,960,000 results within just 0.90 seconds. Haiti has a sizable and very active diaspora. As noted in chapter two, statistics recorded through 2018 by combined sources estimate the number of people with Haitian ancestry living outside of Haiti at over 3.5 million. This figure continues to grow by the thousands every year. According to the 2010 U.S. Census, the Haitian presence in the United States alone exceeds 2 million people.

The U.S. has been by far the number one destination for Haitian migrants. Then comes respectively the Dominican Republic, Cuba, Canada, France (including its Caribbean territories), Brazil, Chile, the Bahamas, and Mexico. Smaller Haitian communities can also be found in the Turks and Caicos, the Virgin Islands, Porto Rico, Jamaica, St. Lucia, Guyana, Belgium, England, Italy, Spain, and the Netherlands, among others.

Most Haitians usually leave Haiti in their quest of either better living conditions or refuge due to political instability and persecution. But it doesn't really matter what country welcomes them, how they are being treated, how well their lives have changed, Haitians never get completely detached from their roots. That attachment and love for Haiti and their culture is passed on to next generations, even if a lot of them have never traveled to Haiti. The Haitian language, culture, traditions, and values are carefully guarded and preserved at home. This makes it possible to separate themselves from other black ethnicities around them in any country. Haitian immigrants adapt to the dominant culture in the host country while retaining their distinctive lifestyle at home.

When talking to Haitians or those of Haitian descent in the United States, there is a sentiment of attachment to Haiti with a sense of patriotism manifested differently. A certain blind patriotism tends to be exhibited by someone who espouses the absolute pride of being Haitian. For blind Haitian patriots, Haiti is perfect and anything that is wrong is the fault of the *blan*. Others prefer to show more constructive patriotism. They love Haiti as well. But they see it as it is, with a mixture of pride and regret. They are proud because of Haiti's history among nations, natural beauty, and the abundant talent and intellect of its people. They feel regret because of the picture of a failed state projected to the world. A third category is the group of negative patriots. They too love Haiti, but they live with a certain anger and rage against the country. They only see Haiti negatively. Just about anything related to Haiti provokes ire, shame, blame, and culpability. The fact is that the blind, constructive, and negative patriotism categories have one thing in common. Not only do they love their country, but they would also like to see change and would be glad to be part of it. Their respective sense of patriotism is deeply rooted in their individual experiences with or exposure to questions related to Haiti.

All of these aspects of the Haitian diaspora constitute a very important asset for Haiti. The new Haiti cannot be possible if we exclude the Haitian diaspora, regardless of how a particular group of individuals feels. Many people with Haitian ancestry around the world would love to be part of a sound project in favor of Haiti's socioeconomic development. They are highly resourceful in terms of both economics and brain power, having benefited from opportunities offered abroad. They represent various resources that Haiti either lacks or suffers from the inadequacy of, including but not limited to financial, technical, and managerial.

The combined total income within the Haitian diaspora is estimated at around $50 billion to $60 billion per year. There is a huge potential for real investment back home instead of mainly remittance to families and friends, which was estimated at $4 billion in 2021.[98] Since 2010, remittances from the Haitian diaspora have registered about a 30% increase annually. Many Haitians living abroad would like to invest in Haiti. But they fear instability, insecurity, absence of law and order.

During the last two decades, several organizations aiming to connect the diaspora together and to Haiti in various ways have formed. One of the most attractive initiatives to date is the platform called Haitian Diaspora Resources World Wide (HDRWW). According to their mission statement, the founders of the platform intend to connect the Haitian diaspora in the world to empower and mobilize professionals in different Haitian communities, and to facilitate diaspora contributions in Haiti's economic and social progress.

---

98 Sam Borjarski, "Remittances to Haiti surge in 2020 as kidnappings, other crises rose", haitiantimes.com, The Haitian Times, May 14, 2021. https://haitiantimes.com/2021/05/14/remittances-to-haiti-surged-in-2020-as-kidnappings-other-crises-rose/

Through a project conceived back in 2004 in partnership with different players, including local private-sector and government entities, HDRWW envisions creating a free trade zone over 68.6 acres of land in the commune of Ganthier, about 16 miles from the international airport in Port-au-Prince. The epicenter of the free trade zone will be in the surroundings of Lake Azuéi, which is near the Haitian-Dominican border of Malpasse. This project will be called Village Sans Souci and is a very ambitious plan that includes an industrial park, an area of residential and commercial developments comprising world-class and top-notch infrastructure, as well as healthcare, educational, and entertainment facilities. The project was approved by the Haitian government in 2018. The latest updated information related to this huge development plan was posted on the organization's website at the end of November 2020.[99]

7.5: A New Generation Enlightened by Social Media

One of the actual characteristics of Haiti in terms of human resources is its youth. Based on Worldometer elaboration of the latest United Nations data on population, Haiti has a median age of 24 years. Therefore, its population is largely young. Data through 2020 shows that over 7 million of Haiti's just over 11.4 million people are aged 14 to 64. Among Latin American and Caribbean countries, Haiti has the highest share of people aged 14 or younger (an estimated 3.7 million) in 2020. This is problematic for a country in need of experience. But it is not necessarily a terrible thing. With proper training and good leadership development programs in and out of the school system, the

99 Haitian Diaspora Resources World Wide (HRWW), "Village Sans Souci", hdrww.com, HDRWW, November 29, 2020. https://www.hdrww.com/projects-page/village-sans-souci

youth can be energy and hope for the future. The opportunity for Haiti to take full advantage of its youthful population can be a strength rather than a weakness.

Social media is one important tool that can be used to prepare young Haitians for Haiti's transformation. Training young people on how to maximize the benefits of using social media in the digital age is tremendously important. Of course, social media and communication technology globally have their negative side effects on society. But people can learn how to minimize those effects and maximize the advantages, which outweigh the disadvantages. Instead of being addicted to it, using it for disinformation, using it to show off, or using it for vulgarities and the violation of human rights, social media can be beneficial in all aspects of life. This is particularly true in Haiti, where there still is an inadequate communication infrastructure.

In addition to the insufficiency of communication infrastructure, traditional media have always been challenged in disseminating information to the people. While there have been a lot more media in Haiti over the last two decades, notably radio and television stations, as well as online information networks, both the quality and quantity of information have not been improved much.[100] Part of the reason is that Haitian journalists are underpaid, and more often they lack the capacity and resources to investigate and report on issues that require in-depth analysis, time, and research. But the general population still depends on them for information to make decisions for their lives.

---

100 The Haitian media landscape consists of one daily newspaper, a few weeklies, over 300 radio and television stations legally authorized, and multiple online-news networks.

Younger generations tend not to pay much attention to traditional mainstream media anymore. Why would they? With their smartphone or any other smart device, they can access information at the tip of their finger. And the best part about it is that they can produce and publish information as well in all different forms. More and more young Haitians have created their own channels of information using social media platforms and internet domains. These channels broadcast everything, including traditionally taboo and complicated subjects in the society. They also use those channels for awareness campaigns and socioeconomic and political mobilizations. Young Haitians just need more education on social media use.

Access is not as much an issue as it used to be in the country. Even though internet connections and communication services in general are expensive in Haiti, there were 2.3 million social media users in Haiti as of January 2021. Over 4 million Haitians had internet connections, and mobile connections represented 64.3% of the total population.[101] So, the new generation is already connected to most of the social media platforms, including Facebook, Twitter, TikTok, Instagram, YouTube, among others. They are enlightened by what is going on around the world. They are also engaged with each other in that way.

The largely peaceful mobilization of young people taking to the streets to demand audits and accountability in the embezzlement and misuse of funds generated by Venezuela's discounted Petrocaribe oil alliance program is a testament of how the use of social media can inspire young Haitians to participate constructively in a new wave of revolutions in Haiti where most people suffer from glaring

---

101 Simon Kemp, "Digital 202: Haiti", datareportal.com, Data Reportal, February 11, 2021. https://datareportal.com/reports/digital-2021-haiti?rq=Haiti

social and economic inequalities. In January 2019, a report from the Superior Court of Auditors cited disastrous mismanagement and a suspected diversion of nearly $2 billion from the Petrocaribe fund. As a result, days of social unrest roiled the country. The grassroots movement intensified with a flurry of hashtags on Twitter such as #KotKòbPetwoKaribea, #PetroCaribeChallenge, #PetwoKaribe, #PetroCaribe, and messages calling out politicians and government officials by name.

So, using social media platforms, the Petrochallengers' anger over Petrocaribe burgeoned into a vast movement against widespread corruption in the country. In a blink of an eye, the grassroots movement caught the attention of the Haitian diaspora and sympathizers in cities around the world. It mobilized people from New York to Montreal, and from Paris to Miami. Thousands of people marched to demand the end of corruption and impunity in Haiti. That was the first widespread movement organized by Haitian youth on social media.

The new generation only needs more training to be able to do it right, and to make that change much more beneficial in the long term. They need support to understand how they can use social media to help reduce unemployment in the country; promote creativity, entrepreneurship, responsibility, accountability; and spread and consume more helpful information on health issues, climate change, environmental protection, and social and economic developments. Above all, they need to be empowered in a way that allows them to discuss important social and economic issues, most importantly issues that do not necessarily get good or continuous coverage in the mainstream news media. This is not something that just a few international and nongovernmental organizations should be involved in, as it is the case now.

Political and religious leaders and the Haitian government itself need to be ready to take the lead. They need to be front and center by investing in the establishment of structures to facilitate more access and training. The government particularly needs to be more actively engaged in planning, executing, and evaluating programs run in the sector for positive direction and quality assurance.

7.6: A Country Seen Through Progressive Movements

Haiti has been, without doubt, among the countries most involved in progressive movements in the history of the modern world. But unfortunately, most people in the world do not sufficiently recognize Haiti that way. Either they do not know about Haitian history, or they are too exposed by the constant negative narrative about Haiti. They might not be interested in it or simply ignore it. Yet, Haiti's revolution (1804), along with that of the United States of America (1776) and France (1789), gave birth to democracy and outlined the idea of power among the common people.

Haiti is one of the three countries in the world that paved the way to all kinds of social, political, and economic transformations that we have become accustomed to. The Haitian Revolutions led to many progressive changes in the world. However, from the beginning to a few decades ago, Western historians overlooked that. And despite efforts and initiatives led by scholars and others concerned that the achievements of people of color are being minimized, that trend of minimization continues. Maybe, just maybe . . . because the Haitian Revolution was caused largely by black people. Until recently, the Haitian history was not really taught in school settings by world history teachers and professors. Many historians had seen the Revolution of 1804 not as a real one, but as a black uprising.

The Revolution of 1804, which took place in Haiti, was indeed a major event that saw the slaves rise to power for the first time in modern history and overthrow the colonial French rule and establish the foundation for an independent country led by themselves. The movement for Haitian independence, which strived for liberty, freedom, and human dignity, needs to be revisited and seen as encouragement and inspiration to people to take on the challenges and bring about real change in Haiti.

We just need to be conscious of that. For the rest, Haiti is essentially used to it. From small to big changes, from the battles that led to 1804 to all the struggles and movements thereafter that led to today's cycles, Haiti's history has countless examples to follow and be inspired by in order to make hope come true.

It was the progressive ideals that inspired the revolutionary leaders to search and attempt for equality among the citizens of the new nation. These same ideals have continued to provide the necessary strength to the Haitian people in their struggles to maintain and reinforce the historic gains they achieved. The timeline of different progressive movements driven by the Haitian people has been well documented in this book. They have fought and will continue to fight for human rights, equal justice, equal economic opportunities, and infrastructure development, as well as against corruption of all kinds, unaccountability and irresponsibility among their leaders, exploitation, oppression, persecution, stigmatization, and prejudices.

After World War II and the national movements precipitating the end of the U.S. occupation of Haiti, tired of seeing the power of elections concentrated in the hands of a few men (the National Assembly), Haitians fought against them controlling all the power. The success of this fight had resulted in the people winning the battle for their rights to vote through universal suffrage. And the movement also led to equal voting rights for women in the 1950s.

Even though some of these advances were hampered by the brutal Duvalier regime that followed, Haitians nonetheless resisted and found resources to regain them in 1986. From the 1986 movements, Haiti would allow a woman to become president for the first time in its history—a boasted fate that the United States democracy has not yet achieved. As mentioned in chapter one, the woman in question was Ertha Pascal-Trouillot, who oversaw the most democratically fair and free elections in Haitian history in 1990.

Elsewhere, Haiti has a solid history of a labor movement. After the inauguration of President Estimé in 1946, the movement strengthened considerably, forcing the creation of the first labor bureau to resolve conflicts and protect workers' rights. Various laws were passed to regulate trade union activity, strikes, workers' protection, safety, and social security. One of the main factors for the success of the labor movement at the time was unity among the working class influenced by some political figures, particularly Daniel Fignolé, who was an ally to progressive movements. During that time, several union organizations regrouped into federations to strengthen the movement. Some of the most influential federations created in Haiti's labor movement history included the Federation of Haitian Workers (FTH), which was strongly influenced by socialism; Labor Unions and Workers (SOT), which united unions to popular leader Daniel Fignolé; and a platform of independent unions that united workers based on their profession. The rivalry between these three federations was more in terms of which one represented the democratic interests of the working class the most, rather than the kind of division we see in Haiti today where the common good has been crushed by self-interest.

Chapter Eight

The Food for Thought

When it comes to Haiti's ability to move toward progress, we recognize the size of the challenge. There is a big mountain to climb. And behind that big mountain lie so many more mountains, as Haitians usually say in their popular wisdom: *dèyè mòn gen mòn.* It would take a gigantic effort from every actor if we were to build a sound country. This is precisely because the problems are enormous and multifaceted. However, as demonstrated so many times by the courage, the determination, and the resilience of the Haitian people, we believe it can be done with the right leadership at the top.

Haiti's solution is not so much through money and the politics of those in power, who come and go; it is much more transcendent. It mostly depends on what we want to be in the future because our past and present have been predominantly shaped by turbulence, chaos, and bitterness. We must step up to make big changes of all kinds. Ironically, who leads the country matters. We are used to those leaders who love the chair more than the country, who love their self-interest more than the well-being of the collectivity, and those who are incompetent beyond belief. But we need a sound project born of the will of the legendary Haitian people, whose history has contributed greatly to change the Americas and has enlightened the rest of the world. We have recognized that the past generations failed and the current one has not done any better so far. It is up to the younger generations to reclaim and bring back the original spirit of the Haitian Revolution. Hopefully, they are the ones who build the Haiti of the future.

In this chapter, we summarize a list of areas needing the most attention to get the country on track to development. We do not pretend to be the end-all. The list, conceptualized as the four Rs of the socio-politico-economic development of Haiti, is not intended to be exhaustive either. But the purpose is to target the most important areas that warrant Haiti's endogenous development. This is merely a collection of good ideas put forward for discussions related to the future of Haiti. These ideas open the road of possibility to Haitians. Like countless people who keep the faith, we optimistically believe in the country's possible turnaround. Among the possibilities, we outline the need for Haitians, particularly the leaders of all sectors of society, to revisit and even question their understanding of the very notion of a nation-state as it relates to protecting the citizens and establishing a system of fairness and equity.

We can conclude that most Haitians need to understand the nature of human development, reassess the education system, and revalorize, revive, and expand key industries and sectors of activities to boost national production and increase the country's GDP annually. We need to reengineer reliable infrastructure to facilitate social and economic developments. These pillars, among others, constitute a roadmap for sustainable change and tenable developments. We have already come to the agreement that all of these will not happen overnight. But it is a possibility if Haitians strongly unite. If they pull their efforts together, no doubt Haiti will progress to stay relevant among other hardworking nations during the 21st century and beyond.

8.1: Redefinition of the Nation-State Project

Conceptually, Haiti is a nation-state. But considering all the attributes of a state, it is placed among the most failed states in the world. In 2021, Haiti was ranked 13th among the weakest states in the world on the Fragile States Index (FSI), formerly called Failed States Index. It was only better than the first 12 countries listed in order as Yemen, Somalia, Syria, South Sudan, Democratic Republic of Congo, Central African Republic, Chad, Sudan, Afghanistan, Zimbabwe, Ethiopia, and Nigeria. Since 2011, Haiti has been the only Latin American and Caribbean country in the top 20 of the FSI list published by Fund for Peace.[102]

Considering the indicators used in the methodology of the report, it is not surprising that Haiti appears so high up in the ranking. The FSI uses 12 indicators of fragility to determine whether a country can be considered as a failed state or not. Some of the indicators cover political aspects like autonomy, capacity, and legitimacy of a state. Others cover economic, social, and international dimensions of vulnerability.

It is inconceivable that social and economic inequalities, the lack of soft and hard infrastructure, and the centralization of means and services have made Haiti the third most urbanized country in Latin and Central America and the Caribbean behind Trinidad and Tobago and Mexico. In the last 15 years alone, Haiti has experienced such rapid urbanization that the number of urban dwellers has doubled from 3 million to over 6.6 million. People are simply fleeing rural Haiti for a different life in major cities and towns—a life of more deceptions and calamities that usually push them to emigrate from Haiti to any other port of entry by any means.

Fifty years ago, the urban population in Haiti was just about 20%. In 2021, it was about 58%. This number is expected to continue to increase annually at a significant pace until 2070, when Haiti's

102 The Fund for Peace is an American nonprofit, nongovernmental research and educational institution. Founded in 1957, FFP maintains that its mission is "to work to prevent violent conflict and promote sustainable security." Every year, it publishes its report on the level of fragility of states.

population will reach its peak of 15.72 million people, according to the projections.[103]

Saying that Haiti needs reforms to improve its ranking in the world as a nation-state is an understatement. The country needs a complete refoundation of its political, social, and economic system. Another project is needed and another order is needed in Haiti. We cannot continue the politics of patching the holes in the old system that has failed the people and expect different results. As mentioned previously, Haitians need to sit down in order to reconcile their differences and embrace what unites them in order to transform Haiti. No one else can do that for us.

Of course, any support from true foreign allies and sympathizers, those who really have the conscience that Haiti should not perish and that the Haitian people must live, would be welcome. But we can't stay still and hope that someone with providential power or a magic stick will come to the rescue. We can't wait for foreign players who supposedly "know better" to fix Haiti's problems on their own. Nor should we continue to let ourselves be influenced by foreign diplomats with policies in their back pockets aimed at undermining Haiti for their respective country's political and economic interests. If we pull all our resources together, we will be able to do it. It is a matter of will and determination to do what is right for the common good.

We must prioritize the idea of a national forum—not the type of microwave meeting (quick gathering of like-minded people with a predetermined outcome on the table) held in New Orleans, Louisiana

103 World Population Review, "Haiti Population 2022", worldpopulationreview.com, World Population Review, March 14, 2022. https://worldpopulationreview.com/countries/haiti-population

mid-January 2022 under the label "Haiti Unity Forum."[104] This was a summit held under the initiative of the Haitian Diaspora United for Haiti (HDUH) at Southern University Law Center. It was a 5-day meeting that took place January 14–19, 2022. This type of initiative, contested in advance by most stakeholders, lacks the necessary legitimacy to help sit Haitians around the table in search of reconciliation, reparations, and a large compromise around redefining and establishing the refoundation project for rebuilding our nation-state.

We need to reshuffle the cards. We need to strive for a fairer society. Haiti cannot continue with the kind of society that is based on so many inequalities in every aspect, space, and scope. We need a state that is strong enough in its attributes to protect our history, territory, and domain of activity. The state must have the administrative capacity to deliver essential public services, such as security, good governance, and a reliable infrastructure. It should have the ability to raise revenues that enable the execution of those services for the public good. A strong state should always be working to guarantee the rights of its citizens.

But none of these attributes are possible without the legitimacy of the state in the eyes of its citizens. That has always been a major factor in the context of Haiti. We have rarely had uncontested heads of state. We do not validate election results easily, and just because someone

---

104 The quick summit's goal was to find a consensus around all the proposed solutions by different Haitian civil and political parties. After just three days, the summit, sponsored by retired Lieut. General Russell Honoré, nominated Fritz Alphonse Jean as provisional president. Right after retired Lieut. General Russell broke the news on Twitter, Ariel Henry responded by saying, "The next resident of the National Palace will be someone who is freely and democratically elected by the majority of the Haitian people." In fact, the nomination of Mr. Jean as provisional president did not go anywhere.

regularly gets sworn in after an election does not always guarantee legitimacy. There are too many parties with no clear national project.

A national forum to establish a global vision for the country is a necessity. By national forum we mean a structure of consultations involving Haitians from all vital sectors of national interests, from the peasantry to the urban areas and to the diaspora. We are in need of a soul-searching discussion. Until we allow ourselves the sincere opportunity to look each other in the eyes and speak with candor and without playing games, we will not get out of the mess. Everyone needs to take responsibility for their own actions in the failure of Haiti and ask for forgiveness. We do not need a national gathering where the less powerful people get blamed and punished, while the most powerful walk away free of any responsibility and accountability.

A real national dialogue should open the doors to responsibility and accountability, as well as reparation and reconciliation as necessary for real social harmony and economic fairness. Above all, it should bring about peace of mind, serenity, and the confidence needed in a national project of a new kind of Haitian society. With that said, together, we would heal the nation and move forward with the building process of a sound nation-state.

From the late 1980s to the mid-2000s, several figures from different organizations and institutions had in fact floated the idea of a national conference among Haitians in order to definitively resolve the country's most persistent and recurrent problems. However, the advocates of that idea were marginalized by most actors within the society and often seen as being ridiculous. Former senator and political activist of all struggles, Turneb Delpé, who died on May 27, 2017, was one of the principal promoters of a national dialogue among Haitians.

Like a panoply of other valuable personalities and human resources that vanished or were wasted in chaos in Haiti, late Senator Delpé did not see the fulfillment of the dream of his lifetime. There is a list of so many political, social, business, religious, and media figures who once thought that the realization of a national conference was necessary to reconcile Haitians and define a national plan for the advancement of Haiti. Among the most remarkable leaders include Tony Cantave, Serge Gilles, René Théodore, Gérard Pierre-Charles, Gérard Gourgue, Jean Léopold Dominique, Jean-Mary Vincent, Leslie S. François Manigat, Hubert de Ronceray, Marc. L. Bazin, Turneb Delpé, and prominent evangelical leader Charles Taylor. However, all of them died without seeing that dream become reality.

After the success of the elections in December 1990, Haitians looked as if they had found the unity needed for Haiti's progress. "Main dans la main, konsa nou va mache, dans l'esprit, l'amour, l'union fait la force" was this song written and arranged by Haitian musician Michel-Ange Bazile. It was the song of the moment on every lip and remains one of the classics in the annals of socio-politically engaged music history in Haiti. Listening to that song today makes people who were old enough to remember 1990 nostalgic of a great period of missed opportunity for real change in Haiti.

The political parties were less chaotic and less divided. As opposed to today's political landscape, 10 of the 11 presidential candidates approved to participate in the elections were from 2 coalitions (ANDP and FNCD) and 8 single parties. One candidate ran as an independent. Unfortunately, Haitians, particularly the political leaders, failed to maximize the opportunity for peace and a national consensus capable of producing a plan for durable socioeconomic development.

The constitution has the fundamental basis for a new state project. We just need to use it. The adoption of the constitution on March 29, 1987, has been to date the national realization with the most support from the Haitian population. That is why Haitians have never doubted its legitimacy. It was drafted by a Constitutional Assembly of 60 members representing all the key sectors of the population. The final draft proposed by the assembly in a referendum of an overwhelming turnout was voted with 99.8% in favor. Not only did most Haitians view the members of the Constitutional Assembly as legitimate, they also were very enthusiastic about the new constitution for its largely progressive content, which is alluded to right up front in its preamble.

No need to dive any deeper into the constitution adopted in 1987 to understand why people were so upbeat about it after so much political, social, and economic sufferings for so long. The 1987 Constitution, amended in 2012, finds its main source of inspiration in the ideals of progress from the Revolution of 1804. It proclaims eight fundamental principles in its preamble that, if we put the effort forward to apply them accordingly, are capable of bringing about the necessary transformations in the society. The preamble of the Constitution reads:

"The Haitian people proclaims this Constitution:

1. To guarantee their inalienable and imprescriptible rights to life, to liberty and to the pursuit of happiness; in accordance with their Act of Independence of 1804 and with the Universal Declaration of the Rights of Man of 1948.
2. To constitute a Haitian nation, socially just, economically free, and politically independent.
3. To establish a State stable and strong, capable of protecting the values, the traditions, the sovereignty, the independence and the national vision.

4. To implant democracy which implies ideological pluralism and political alternation and to affirm the inviolable rights of the Haitian People.
5. To fortify the national unity, eliminating all discrimination between the populations, of the towns and of the countryside, by the acceptance of the community of languages and of culture and by the recognition of the right to progress, to information, to education, to health, to work and to leisure for all citizens [regardless of gender, race or skin complexion].
6. To assure the separation, and the harmonious division of the powers of the State to the service of the fundamental interests and priorities of the Nation.
7. To establish a governmental regime based on the fundamental liberties and the respect for human rights, the social peace, economic equity, the equity of gender, the concerted action and the participation of all the population in the grand decisions engaging the national life, by an effective decentralization.
8. To assure women a representation in the instances of power and of decision which must conform to the equality of the sexes and to equity of gender."[105]

However, a constitution is like a prescription to treat an illness. No prescription can be effective if it is not applied or is wrongly applied by the person for whom it is prescribed. Haitians must be willing to apply the constitution in its entirety, not when it is convenient to them. All the important mechanisms of its application need to be put in place, and necessary amendments to bring it up to date with the reality and

---

105 Maria del Carmen Gress and Jefri J. Ruchti, "The Principles Proclaimed in The Haitian Constitution", constituteproject.org, Constitute Project, August 26, 2021. https://www.constituteproject.org/constitution/Haiti_2012.pdf?lang=en

challenges of the 21st century and beyond need to be addressed with a sense of individual abnegation. The constitution gives us the tools to create unity for that new social contract without which we can't achieve peace, stability, or progress.

8.2: Reassessment of the Education System

No serious national plan to rebuild the Haitian society can be implemented without taking into account the largely dysfunctional education system. There needs to be reconsideration in its design and structure, both formally and informally. Haiti has an enormous deficit in social and civic education. We need well-informed, trained, and educated citizens to build a better nation. The kind of careless society driven by ignorance, misconceptions, and foolishness of leadership needs to be revolutionized.

Since the 1980s, various governments that have succeeded always put education as a top priority in their policy agenda. However, their efforts have not been that fruitful or match their words. The sector is plagued by several serious problems that have been accumulating for years and exacerbated by a number of disasters. Public schools account for only about 18% of the system. The education system is largely dominated by the private sector, which includes for-profit, faith-based, and other nongovernmental organizations. Therefore, with the high level of poverty in the country, most of the schools do not have the adequate resources to deliver a quality education to children. Additionally, they do not follow a specific pedagogical teaching method that is aligned with the country's defined vision and planning. Many schools use outdated curricula, while others partially implement the last reformed curriculum of the National Plan of Education and Training (NPET).

The few schools that have the means to provide a good quality of education are unaffordable and inaccessible to most families. The quality of education and enrollment rates also suffer because of economic hardship, where schools receive little financial assistance, have high repetition rates and linguistic barriers, and contend with a dearth of materials, expertise, proper management, and organization. Referring to both the formal and informal education system in Haiti, some people even talk about a "country that is intellectually bankrupt." Important investments in reorganization, restructuring, and better infrastructure are needed.

Even though most schools in Haiti are run by the private sector, the constitution requires that the state guarantee free primary and secondary education to all children equally. The different laws and decrees on the organization of the education system lay the responsibilities of regulating and managing education on the Ministry of National Education and Professional Training (Ministère de l'Education Nationale et de la Formation Professionnelle, or MENFP). The ministry's mission is to provide education to the citizens of Haiti and execute nominative and regulatory functions. Observing the situation inside the Haitian education system, we can agree with many critics that MENFP has not been able to fulfill its mandate or mission. The MENFP's functions and the education system as a whole should be among the top agenda issues of a national forum for the refoundation of Haiti.

One of the biggest challenges is the complexity faced by the MENFP in its task of distinguishing between schools that perform above or below basic quality standards. About 70% of schools in Haiti lack accreditation. The ministry of education does not have the capacity to play its role of monitoring, evaluating, and reporting on the academic performance of schools mainly because it is overstretched and without adequate financial and human resources.

According to a recent World Bank report, there is approximately one inspector responsible to provide accreditation and administrative support, and supervise pedagogically for every six thousand students in the country. And generally, there is very little cooperation between the ministry of education and the schools. Another issue is the lack of schools in rural areas, which represent 70% of the population and only receive 20% of educational expenditures. According to the World Bank report, in 2007, 23 communal sections lacked a school and 145 did not have a public school. This situation has not improved, considering how Haiti has been poorly managed generally. It is unacceptable that over 82% of schoolchildren in Haiti attend private and fee-based institutions.[106] The system needs a major reform.

On a list of different attempts to reform the education system, apart from the initiatives led by the Americans during the occupation of Haiti in 1915–1934, Haitians have conducted to date only two major efforts to overhaul the system: the Bernard Reform, initiated in 1978 (but its implementation did not start until 1982), and the National Plan of Education and Training (NPET), elaborated in 1997–1998.

The majority of well-informed Haitians did not welcome the American-led reform of their education system. In some of the U.S. education policies implemented in Haiti, racism, classism, and

106 Direction d'Appui à l'Enseignement Privé et du Partenariat, *Politique Nationale d'Accréditations des Écoles Privées* (Port-au-Prince: Ministère de l'Education Nationale et de Formation Professionelle, 2020).

repression were identified by many. Contentious policies included the following:

1. supporting technical and agricultural training over liberal arts education using money earmarked for student scholarships to pay the salaries of foreign "experts"
2. giving more money to technical and urban schools than to universities and rural and girls' schools, and
3. giving more support to primary education in states such as Puerto Rico and the Philippines, whose populations were not predominantly black.

These policies fed into Haitian wariness that the educational reforms were not so much part of a development strategy that would further them collectively as a nation, but rather an exploitative effort by yet another foreign white power that sought a partnership with the elite minority and access to cheap labor and raw materials. Many Haitians believed that the U.S. emphasis on technical and agricultural training meant that U.S. Americans viewed Haitians as intellectually inferior and wanted to keep them in a subordinate position academically and economically.[107]

Between the late 1970s and early 1980s, the Bernard Reform attempted to modernize the Haitian educational system, make it more efficient, and build its capacity to satisfy the various needs in the sector. The Bernard Reform curriculum attempted to align school structure with labor market demands by introducing technical and vocational classes in secondary schools. According to

---

107 Ketty Luzincourt and Jennifer Gulbranson, "Education and Conflict in Haiti," usip.org, United States Institute of Peace, August 2010. https://www.usip.org/sites/default/files/sr245.pdf

the 1978 project, the school curriculum was divided into academic and technical tracks. However, one of the major innovations of the Bernard Reform was the introduction of the Haitian vernacular into the school system. Until 1978, only French could be used in formal education. Haitian Creole became the language of instruction in the first four grades of primary school.

Although many people applauded the Bernard Reform, it made little headway. Some schools were still using the old curriculum in its classical model, which did not take into consideration the labor market demands and punished students (those with disabilities or who were academically slower than others would be beaten by teachers and called cretins) instead of helping them in their learning process. Here are some of the reasons why the Bernard Reform had failed: lengthy delays in implementation, and inadequate infrastructure and resources to support the changes recommended by the experts. Another problem was that the reform did not sufficiently take into account people's mindset about education.

Most Haitian parents, up to these days, would prefer to see their children going to universities instead of attending technical schools. They consider technical or vocational schools as low-prestige institutions. It remains a source of great pride for most traditional Haitian families to be able to say that their children are attending universities to become doctors, lawyers, agronomists, engineers, professors, architects, etc. Even though the labor market lacks sufficient jobs for the graduates of liberal arts programs, remuneration often lags behind expectations.

After the failure to implement the Bernard Reform, and with the support of the World Bank and Inter-American Development Bank, the Haitian government came up with the NPET of 1997. That project was even more ambitious than the Bernard Reform. It proposed a complete departure from the French education model, which was an authoritarian system designed and monitored by a highly centralized bureaucracy. In that system, particularly dominated by private and Christian schools, children were forced to learn by memorization compared to most countries in the Caribbean, thus limiting their ability to develop independent critical thinking skills outside of what is memorized from the textbooks.

The students are basically passive learners while the focus was centered on the teacher. Instead, the Reform of 1997 opted for a participatory learning model based on student-centered approaches. One of the best things about that initiative was the shift to a new model of citizenship education aimed at developing civic knowledge and attitudes that would promote unity and an appreciation for diversity in Haitian society, thus providing the very foundation for a national identity.

The Reform of 1997 was a good start. But the overall situation in Haiti has not permitted the fulfillment of its goals. Many aspects of the project are still not being implemented. Again, a lot of schools are still using the old system, as was the case during the faltering steps of the Bernard Reform. Major changes have yet to be made. Most importantly, authorities at different levels need to show the will and commitment to reach all prescribed objectives and go even beyond those prescriptions to orchestrate deeper reforms with continuity.

We need decentralization and modernization that can resolve the problem of social polarization, not fragmentation that could accentuate that problem. The goal of making primary and secondary education free should become reality in the country. No parent should be paying entry fees in public schools before each academic year, which further complicates access. Most families are forced to even pay extra under the table to get a place for their children in public schools on top of the regular annual fees that they are already struggling economically to come up with. An expansion of public schools should also ensure adequacy in both the quantity and quality of schools to inspire the population's confidence in the system that their children would be well taught.

It is time for the state to take charge of the education system of the country, not the privateers who are mainly motivated by money. Most of the private school owners are not interested in the quality of education. They are only interested in their bottom line. As the state has failed in its responsibilities, the sector has become more and more relentlessly lucrative for less quality. A symbiosis of important elements from the Bernard Reform and the Reform of 1997 reinforced with certain elements necessary to create space for communities to express their opinions through parent-teacher associations, parent-teacher-student associations, or other mechanisms might be the way to go about a complete transformation of the Haitian educational system.

Higher education and vocational and technical training have their share of responsibility in distributing a quality education as well. Technical schools and colleges are responsible for satisfying the perceived wants of the job market and guaranteeing the development of certified and skilled students to meet the variety of demands in Haiti. But the sector is not well supervised or regulated either. Additionally, despite the constant increase in the number of technical and vocational schools, especially in urban areas, there is no central supply nationwide. There are no reliable and established institutions designed to collect labor statistics and information that might be helpful in matching vocational training to the needs in the market nationwide. Job alternatives are scarce in an anemic economy where foreign investments have always been timid due to the critical lack of infrastructure and other difficulties that tend to increase the cost for conducting business in Haiti.

Vocational and professional training schools developed in the 1920s and the 1930s during the U.S. occupation. Until the 1940s, the teaching method used focused on helping mono-academic students secure a technical skill for the employment market. That system, led by American influence, was changed in the 1940s for an approach more adapted to the nation's reality. Maurice Dartigue, one of the first Haitian ministers of education after the occupation, led the charge with new approaches.

By the early 1980s, the Bernard Reform had facilitated the expansion of vocational and training schools by providing students the chance to maneuver a pathway leading into a vocational track. After the earthquake in 2010, a multitude of nongovernmental organizations launched professional training schools and supported technical colleges financially to allow more access to young people. By 2016, Haiti's National Institute of Vocational Training had registered 190 technical schools in Haiti, and another 1,010 were functioning without official recognition or permit.

When it comes to universities, the general situation is not too different in terms of access and quality. First and foremost, there is the State University of Haiti (Université d'Etat d'Haiti in French, or UEH), which comprises 12 faculties and colleges scattered particularly in Port-au-Prince. After the earthquake in 2010, the Dominican Republic government helped build a campus in Limonade, Cap-Haitian. And there is a campus of the Faculty of Law and Economics in every capital city in 8 out of the country's 10 departments.

There is no centralized campus that can host most of the demand for annual enrollments. Each faculty is separately located in a relatively small space surrounded by residential and commercial properties and has limited capacity and logistics. In total, UEH can accommodate about 13,000 students and some 700 professors at a time, all faculties combined. The demand varies between 100,000 to 180,000 students annually.[108]

Nonetheless, the State University of Haiti is one of the country's most prestigious institutions of higher education. Its origin can be traced back to the 1820s during the Jean-Pierre Boyer presidency, when colleges of medicine and law were established. In 1842, the various faculties merged into the University of Haiti. Started originally as an autonomous institution, in 1960, the dictatorship regime of Francois Duvalier brought it under firm government control and renamed it the State University of Haiti to curtail student movements and civil liberties. After years of fighting, in 1983, the university regained its independence and autonomy. And in 1987, the constitution reconfirmed that status and gave even more autonomy to the institution.

In addition to the publicly funded university, a plethora of private institutions have emerged, mostly in the last 30 years, to fill in the gap. The market of higher education is huge. It is competitive and chaotic at the same time. Recent surveys have registered over 200 private universities in Haiti, 80% of them based in Port-au-Prince. Some are more publicized and more expensive than others. Many of them do not

---

108 Wikiwand, "State University of Haiti", wikiwand.com, Wikiwand, retrieved March 14, 2022. https://www.wikiwand.com/en/State_University_of_Haiti

even have the infrastructure of a good middle school. But they exist due to high demand and disorganization at the state level. All universities in Haiti lack adequate infrastructure and resources to provide the best quality of higher education in the absence of a clear national vision, coherent, well-defined policy, and strategies of higher education.

Challenged by structural, organizational, sociopolitical, and economic difficulties, Haitian universities lose thousands of students annually. Those who can afford it or are fortunate enough to get a scholarship leave an ineffective and inefficient university system in Haiti for a better one abroad. The Dominican Republic, Cuba, Mexico, Canada, France, the United States, Russia, China, and Taiwan—the list of countries hosting Haitian students goes on. From that form of migration, not only the university system loses millions of US dollars. Haiti continues to lose important human resources. Most of the young people who leave the country to go study in foreign countries do not go back. Few students choose to return. But most of them would like to go back and put their expertise in the service of Haiti, which is something the country needs greatly. But at the same time, they want to be realistic. They need to strike a balance between opportunities in those countries where they had earned their degrees and what they left behind them in Haiti.

There are no sufficient documented records of Haitian students in other countries. But in the neighboring Dominican Republic, the picture is clear. In 2019, around 40,000 Haitian students were enrolled in different universities in the Dominican Republic.[109] This number represents an increase of 100% within just years. In 2013, the number

---

109 These numbers were reported by the Binational Observatory on Migration, Education, Environment and Commerce—a joint bilateral Haiti-Dominican Republic commission aiming at improving the relations between the two countries. It is funded by the European Union under the supervision of authorizing officers on both sides of the border.

of Haitians attending school in Dominican Republic did not exceed 400. Haitian students have brought more than US$220 million to the D.R.'s economy on average. This is more than the amount of money allocated for education in Haiti's national budget during the fiscal year of 2018–2019. And that was just the total of money recorded in transfers alone from parents and other relatives to Haitian students in the Dominican Republic. The figure is perhaps a lot more, considering the different other ways Haitian students can bring or receive money in the D.R. This is money that could be well spent in Haiti if there were proper planning and sociopolitical stability.

The sociopolitical situation that has created a climate of uncertainty and inconsistency in the operation of the Haitian universities, in addition to the economic reality of the country, is mainly responsible for the recent flight of Haitian students to foreign countries. However, this can be a profitable benefit for the socioeconomic development of Haiti. The country merely needs to position itself in order to stimulate the return of these students after their cycle of studies and benefit from their acquired knowledge and experience. They continue to study in better environments and better-equipped universities abroad.

There is an opportunity for Haiti to consider the resources lost during the time these thousands of young Haitians spent at universities overseas as an investment in the future. Haiti can exploit their expertise as an important asset to modernize and reinforce national institutions, public administration, and private enterprises. Moreover, the Haitian government and the private-sector elite need to converge their efforts in order to increase the offer and chances of success in Haitian universities, so that millions of dollars pouring into foreign countries annually can instead be spent in Haiti.

8.3: Revalorization and Revitalization of Key Industries

To propel Haiti back to an even better position than it was once upon a time—one of the world's richest and most productive places—we need to understand our key industries for their revalorization and revitalization without neglecting any of the country's primary, secondary, and tertiary industries. We need to look at sectors that give us a good comparative advantage not only in the Latin America and Caribbean region, but which also allow us to compete globally and turn our chronic trade deficit into a surplus. After the 2010 earthquake, during a conference held in New York on March 31 of that year, the international community pledged to provide speedy recovery to Haiti and agreed on the principle of long-term assistance for the reconstruction and development of the country.

Haiti was provided long-term assistance based on what they called the Plan for Action of the Recovery and Development of Haiti (PARDH). PARDH was prepared by the International Monetary Fund and the World Bank in collaboration with national stakeholders to present the major guidelines for the implementation of development projects based on new foundations. The goal was for Haiti to become an emerging country by 2030.

From PARDH's guidelines, the Haitian government developed a strategic development plan that included planning, programming, and management. The strategic plan consisted of four pillars:

1. Economic reform and reconstruction
2. Regional development and planning
3. Social reform with a focus on social cohesion, solidarity, and cultural identity
4. Reform of government institutions

As of 2022, no visible progress has been registered as a result of the vision for 2030. To understand what needs to be done in terms of revalorization and revitalization of Haiti's key industries, we need to take a deeper look into them.

Primary Industries

As part of a tropical island in the heart of the Atlantic Ocean, Haiti's primary industry inevitably consists of its agriculture, forestry, fishing, and mining and minerals. Getting out of economic stagnation means that Haiti valorizes and revamps these three sectors. This entails major investment in modernization and reforms. We can't continue with this type of subsistence agriculture. We need to develop large farms that employ people instead of everyone plowing their small parcels of land over and over to try to make ends meet under the same conditions they have been working for decades, and from one generation to the other. We need to make reforestation an urgent priority and fishing a source of sustainable revenue. Haiti's forests have been thinned dramatically, production of wood and lumber has considerably decreased, and timber exports have declined. The fishing industry needs expansion to increase catches, not just for local consumption but also for exports. In recent years, annual catches totaled 5,000 tons of fish.

As of 2004, agriculture, together with forestry and fishing, accounted for 28% of Haiti's annual GDP and employed about 66% of the labor force. It accounted for about 35% of the annual GDP in 1987. Despite the difficulties to expand the sector due to high mountains covering most of the countryside and limiting the land available for cultivation, it remains extremely important for Haiti's economic development. Enhancing techniques that would enable better exploitation of the 1.4 million acres of arable land available for cultivation would lead to revitalization and revalorization. Of the 1.4 million acres, 308,875 acres are suited for irrigation. Of those, only 185,325 acres have been improved with irrigation. Haiti's dominant cash crops include coffee, mangoes, cocoa, avocados, oranges, and coconuts. Cotton, vetiver, essential oils, castor beans, and sugarcane used to be important cash crops for Haitian peasants. Production has decreased for years now due to various factors.

When it comes to mining, available information as of 2013 records about US$13 million. Bauxite, copper, gold, marble, calcium carbonate (limestone), and aggregates have been the most extensively extracted minerals in Haiti. Among these minerals available for extraction in Haiti, gold and copper have always been the most exploited since the Spanish colonial era. In northern Haiti alone, recent estimates for the value of gold that might be extracted through open-pit mining are over US$20 billion, according to the experts.[110]

But as Alex Dupuy, the Chair of African American Studies at Wesleyan University, and John E. Andrus Professor of Sociology at Wesleyan University, put it, "the ability of Haiti to adequately manage the mining operations or to obtain and use funds obtained from the operations for the benefit of its people is untested and seriously questioned."[111] In 2012, it was reported that agreements and negotiations had been conducted between the Haitian government and some multinational companies to grant them license for exploration or mining of gold and associated metals such copper in over 1,000

110 Jane Regan, "Haiti's Rush for Gold Gives Mining Firms a Free Rein to Riches", theguardian.com, The Guardian, May 30, 2012. https://www.theguardian.com/global-development/poverty-matters/2012/may/30/haiti-gold-mining

111 Martha Mendoza, "Gold! Haiti hopes ore find will spur mining boom", *Associated Press*, May 31, 2012.

square miles across northern Haiti. The news hit Port-au-Prince like a thunder. Eurasian Minerals and Newmont Mining Corporation based in Greenwood Village, Colorado, were the two companies involved in confidential negotiations with the Martelly/Lamothe government.

In addition to bauxite, copper, gold, marble, calcium carbonate (limestone), and aggregates, many people have always been speculative about the potential existence of other significant natural resources, such as natural gas and oil. These resources have not yet been discovered or exploited in the country. According to information published on the World Atlas, Haiti is thought to be sitting on millions of barrels of crude oil and billions of cubic feet of natural gas. In his recent estimates, Haitian scientist Daniel Mathurin said that Haiti's oil reserves are a swimming pool compared to those of Venezuela, which he likened to a glass of water.[112]

Areas thought to be vastly rich in oil include the Central Plateau; the bay of Port-au-Prince, which is expanded from the gulf of Gonave to the coastline of the Artibonite department (north/northwest); Thomonde; the Cul-de-sac plain; and the coastline of Mole Saint-Nicolas, the peninsula in northwestern Haiti. To confirm the relevance of this information, scientist need to conduct more studies. And the Haitian government needs to be more involved in the research and studies.

Inevitably, a complete reorganization and restructuring is needed in activities related to the extraction of natural resources in Haiti. The Haitian government needs to stop negotiating with foreign companies

---

112 World Atlas, "What are the Natural Resources of Haiti", worldatlas.com, World Atlas, retrieved March 14, 2022. https://www.worldatlas.com/articles/what-are-the-major-natural-resources-of-haiti.html

in opacity and total darkness. It needs to elaborate a clear plan for more research, exploration, and extraction. All activities need to consider the safety of people and wildlife, and environmental protection globally. Conventions and contracts should be negotiated with more transparency, in accordance with the principles and limits established by the constitution.

Secondary Industries

Haiti's secondary industry includes manufacturing and energy. As it stands today, the leading companies in the sector of manufacturing produce beverages, butter, cement, detergent, edible oils, flour, refined sugar, soap, and textiles. A lack of steady capital investment has hampered growth in manufacturing, as has been the case in recent years in almost all industries in Haiti. Many grants awarded by the United States—especially through the U.S. economic engagement under the HOPE Act—and other countries to tackle the problem have not produced much success.

There is also the persistent issue of sociopolitical instability on top of a deficit of management and operation efficiency. The manufacturing sector has contracted since the 1980s. Due to the military coup against Democracy in 1991, the O.A.S/U.N. embargo on Haiti put most of the 80,000 workers in the assembly sector out of employment. And most of the offshore assembly plants in the free zones of the metropolitan area of Port-au-Prince were closed. The restoration of the Aristide government in the fall of 1994 breathed some air into the manufacturing sector, and improvements occurred.

Haiti's cheaper labor brought some textile and garment assembly work back to the people in the late 1990s. In 2008, the apparel sector made up two-thirds of the country's annual exports.[113] As more political instabilities and social unrest have been taking place, the gains registered in the sector were undercut and movement has slowed. In 2004, the subindustry of manufacturing amounted to 20% Haiti's GDP and employed less than 10% of the labor force.

The situation in the energy sector is much more desperate. According to data recorded in 2014, Haiti uses the equivalent of approximately 393.67 kilograms of oil per head annually. This is very low for a country of more than 11.5 million people. It is inconceivable that, in 2021, only about 40% of Haitians get access to electricity, with an average annual consumption of just 21 kilowatt-hours (KWH) per person. Even for those with access to electricity, reliability is inconsistent. This unreliability requires many businesses and larger households to install diesel generators or solar panel systems independently from the state-run enterprise Electricité d'Haiti (EDH). In 2003, the country produced 546 million kilowatt-hours of electricity while consuming 508 million kilowatt-hours. Comparing the net total consumption of electricity in Haiti to that of a list of countries in 2013, Haiti ranked 135th out of 135 countries.

The major source of energy in Haiti is burning wood (charcoal). This has had a devastating effect on the environment in terms of deforestation. Before late President Jovenel Moise inaugurated a US$10 million hydroelectric dam in Marion, a village in northeastern Haiti about 20 miles from Cap-Haitian, the Péligre Dam, which is the country's largest, was in large part responsible for providing

---

113 Index Mundi, "Haiti Exports", indexmundi.com, Index Mundi, September 18, 2021. https://www.indexmundi.com/haiti/exports.html

Port-au-Prince with electricity.[114] Thermal plants provide energy to the rest of the country.

Even with the low level of demand for energy, the supply of electricity traditionally has been sporadic and prone to shortages. Mismanagement by the government has offset millions of dollars in foreign investment targeted at improving Haiti's energy infrastructure. Businesses have resorted to securing backup power sources to deal with the regular outages. The potential for greater hydropower exists, should Haiti have the desire and means to develop it. The government controls oil and gas prices, to an extent insulating Haitians from international price fluctuations. According to data collected in 200 countries and published on GlobalEconomy.com, Haiti imports a maximum of 7,500 barrels of fuel per day as of 2018.

Haiti needs to develop a plan that enables the use of solar and wind technologies in addition to hydropower potential and thermal power. This diversification will help boost the production of electricity.

Tertiary Industries

In this sector, we find notably the banking system and tourism among other important services. According to the World Bank, the service sector is among the few sectors in Haiti that has continued to see steady, even if modest, growth since the 1990s. It represents 52% (US$1.5 billion) of the country's GDP. And it employs 25% of the labor force as of 2018.

---

114 The Marion dam was completed over a three-year period. The plant was built to primarily water soil but also to provide access to drinking water, produce electricity, protect against flooding, and breed fish.

The banking system, as a subindustry, needs to be more stable and trustworthy in order to help the economic development of Haiti. Banks in Haiti collapse too easily. Most Haitians do not even have a bank account, nor do they have access to loans of any sort. Haiti has no stock exchange to stimulate wealth creation and add more value to the economy. The banking sector is mostly concentrated in the capital city of Port-au-Prince. Haiti's central bank, the Banque de la République d'Haïti (BRH), normally oversees ten commercial banks and two foreign banks. Efforts to expand and diversify the sector and make credit more accessible to the rural populations are not sufficient and are often impeded by structural and organic problems.

The United Nations, the International Monetary Fund, the Inter-American Development Bank, and the Canadian International Development Agency have been involved in those efforts since the beginning of the new millennium. But what has been making a difference for most of the population is grassroots and informal economic activities supported by nongovernmental organizations. After Aristide was sworn in as president for a second term in 2001, he forcefully engaged in actions to remedy the situation in the sector. Unfortunately, he introduced an unsustainable plan of community banking "cooperatives" that guaranteed investors a 10–12% rate of return. The cooperatives crumbled very quickly, and Haitians collectively lost well over US$200 million in savings.

The tourism industry has become more and more neglected. It has suffered from Haiti's sociopolitical upheaval. Yet, in the 1970s and 1980s, tourism was a very important industry for Haiti, drawing more than 150,000 foreign visitors annually. After the political events of the

1990s, tourism recovered slowly. The Caribbean Tourism Organization (CTO) joined the Haitian government in its efforts to restore the country's image as a tourism destination. As a result, 141,000 foreigners visited Haiti in 2001. But major infrastructure and security concerns continue to undermine the sector. Reconstruction efforts and apparent calm in the country after the 2010 earthquake boosted the confidence of investors a little bit. Several hotels were built and opened from 2012 to 2015.

Among those hotels, a Best Western Premier, a five-star Royal Oasis hotel by Occidental Hotel and Resorts in Pétion-Ville, a four-star Marriott hotel in the Turgeau area (first Marriott hotel in Haiti), and other new hotels were built particularly in Port-au-Prince, Jacmel, Cayes, and Cap-Haitian. By the end of 2015, the four-star, all-inclusive, 400-room, beachfront Royal Decameron Indigo Resort & Spa was opened to visitors. Statistics reported for 2012 indicated that close to 1 million foreigners visited Haiti that year, generating US$200 million, most of which came from cruises.

There is no doubt that Haiti continues to have excellent potential to make tourism a major industry. To do so, significant improvements are still needed in hotels, restaurants, and other infrastructure. The country needs to invest in building new and better roads, a telecommunication infrastructure, ports and airports, as well as restore and preserve all major historical sites and create better accessibility to those sites. In addition to improvements in these areas, we need to work very hard to change, at least in the eyes of westerners, the depicted image of Haiti as a dirty, lawless, and godless land. Haiti is already naturally beautiful. We simply need to make it a much more desirable, safe, and welcoming place to tourists.

8.4: Reengineering Reliable Infrastructure

There is no viable path to development in Haiti without rethinking our approach to infrastructure. We need to think big and be creative. We need to find companies that are willing to take a bet on the country's good will that a return on their investment can be guaranteed. Haiti's infrastructure suffers from underinvestment and natural disasters. We need to invest in ports and airports in every region. We cannot continue to have most foreign trade and air travel pass through Port-au-Prince. Why can't we have a major international airport in each department? We need reliable highways, bridges, tram networks, and railways to move goods and transport people faster.

Haiti's urban areas need to easily connect to the rural areas. We can partner with the Dominican Republic in developing a railway that can connect the two neighboring countries better and faster. After all, Haiti and the Dominican Republic are just one island with a superficies of less than 30,000 square miles in total. Tackling challenges that affect both countries together a is winning strategy for both Haitians and Dominicans. The two people groups are naturally bonded to live together on the island.

There was a time when Haiti had a national rail network. The Dessalinian country was the first in the entire Caribbean with a railway system. The first tramway opened in 1876. Between 1876 and 1970s various tramways and railways ran in the country, including three rail lines and some industrial railways.[115] The tramways became nonoperational in 1932. And by the 1970s, the disoperation of most

115 Jameson Francisque, "L'histoire palpitante des chemins de fer en Haiti, ayibopost.com, Ayibo Post, December 6, 2019. https://ayibopost.com/lhistoire-palpitante-des-chemins-de-fer-en-haiti/

railroads started due to either the bankruptcy or the closure of the companies that supported railroad construction in Haiti. The last operational railroad network closed in 1991. Today, the transport infrastructure remains one of the many challenges facing Haiti's economic development. In Haiti, most basic roads are hard to come by because roads degrade faster than they are repaired or built.

In terms of roads, Haiti only has three types of networks: national roads, departmental roads, and county roads. Most of rural Haiti is connected to a paved road, and access on vehicles is very difficult. The hub network is located at the old airport that used to serve as military aviation, at the intersection between Boulevard Jean-Jacques Dessalines and Autoroute de Delmas in Port-au-Prince. That is where Route Nationale numero 1 and numero 2 commence. There are 6 other national roads connected to these two principal networks. According to an estimate from 2011, Haiti has 6,045 km of highways, of which 2,971 km are paved, and 3,071 km are unpaved. All major road infrastructure development projects took place in the country during the American occupation between 1915 and 1934. Since then, most projects have mainly consisted of road repairs and construction of short circuits financed with millions of dollars borrowed from the World Bank and other funders. Usually, millions are spent on road networks for little and very short-term improvements.

In the water transport sector, Haiti has over a dozen functional ports. But the international port of Port-au-Prince registers more shipping than any other port in the country. In general, all Haiti's ports are underused and are in poor shape. They face high competition from the Dominican Republic's ports, where fees are a lot lower, and operations are a lot faster with less middleman involvement. Most of Haiti's 150 km of navigable waterways are accessible by small ferry and sailboats. People living in most towns near the coastline use such boats as their preferred and primary means of transportation. They are cheaper and more available than public ground transportation. Major investment is needed in the sector not only to improve the existing facilities, but also to build new and modern infrastructure in all major towns near the coast.

When it comes to aviation, Haiti has only two international airports. The main international airport, known today as Aéroport International Toussaint Louverture in Port-au-Prince, was developed with grant money from the United States and mostly money collected from Haitian citizens by François Duvalier in taxes, the lottery, and other means. It was opened in 1965. The second international airport, a much smaller one in Cap-Haitian, was completely renovated from 2010 to 2013 with the financial support of Venezuela. In 2015 and 2016, the Port-au-Prince international airport underwent a major renovation and was redesigned as well. The work was undertaken by the China National Automation Control System.

In remaking the airport, 14 gates were added to the terminal and the main passenger terminal was made bigger. A taxiway was constructed to increase traffic capacity. Apart from the 2 international airports, there are about 15 domestic and communal airports in the country. Only one of those small airports, Jérémie Airport (Grand'Anse department), has a paved runway. For the rest, the runway is either an unpaved dirt field or grass. Having these airports in place is a good start. But they all need major physical and structural improvements. Most of them need complete rebuilding.

Also, more investment is needed in telecommunications technologies. Haiti's telecommunications infrastructure needs to be more developed to fare better with most countries in the regions. The country is heavily reliant on satellite and wireless mobile technology due to the poor fixed-line infrastructure. Investment boosted broadband availability thanks to the privatization of the government's Telecommunications d'Haiti S.A.M, popularly known as "Teleco," in 2010. But major challenges remain in terms of creating more competition in the market to attract adequate capital to the sector.

The sports infrastructure is another important factor of socioeconomic development. Haitians love sports and Haiti is in desperate need of better and adequate infrastructure in the sector. This includes stadiums, gymnasiums, public parks, and recreation centers. Today, beside a good education, many young Haitians see sports as a good avenue for a better future.

Thanks to the practice of sports—soccer and basketball in particular—some young Haitians have had the opportunity to change their lives by acquiring contracts to take their talents to Europe, North America, South America, and Asia. Not only does this helps them and their families financially, but it also benefits the country economically, socially, and sportively. Some of these professional athletes, in addition to those of Haitian heritage who were born in foreign countries, have been giving back to Haiti by getting involved in entrepreneurship and social activities through sports to encourage discipline, leadership, community interaction, and healthy lifestyles and habits among young people. Haitian professional athletes also find pride in representing their country at international competitions.

Building reliable and adequate infrastructure throughout Haiti can help reinforce hope, reduce delinquency, and build self-esteem among the youth. In 2019, as one of Haitian Sports, Youth and Civic

Action ministers, Edwing Charles, said "I believe that sports can pacify the country and allow us to perform miracles."[116]

Several organizations have been involved in working to achieve social development goals through sports. The issue remains that they would have been able to accomplish more progress in that sense if they had more reliable and adequate sports infrastructures. Also, their actions could have produced a lot more positive results for Haiti if they had been included in a global plan that required coordination, evaluation, and accountability. A good partnership between the government and the private sector is necessary to prepare and execute such a national plan for better outcomes by pulling financial and technical resources together.

116 Ici Haiti Sports, "Training in Sports Infrastructure Management", icihaiti.com, Ici Haiti, May 1, 2019. https://www.icihaiti.com/en/news-26580-icihaiti-sports-training-in-sports-infrastructure-management.html

Conclusion

This book was written with the primary objective to help strike a balance between despair, which is a real thing in Haiti, and hope in a better future, which people desperately need. Through our journey with Haiti's sociopolitical and economic history, we have learned to have faith and hope in the country's possibility for a positive transformation. Plenty has been said about Haiti. But the story has been mostly incomplete. Most historians, story tellers, news media reporters, and others often portray a country marred by its constant socioeconomic struggles and political instability. Of course, these problems exist.

But Haiti is more than the sum of its issues. And the fundamental causes of Haiti's main problems tend to be brushed aside, partially discussed, or completely ignored. The understanding of Haiti's long history has permitted us to conclude that the contributing causes to its major problems have been a combination of perpetual internal and external factors. As we have seen, most of Haiti's problem is mental. Not only have many people often ignored that, they have also minimized the country's potential, resources, and ability to resolve its own problems.

Many positive aspects of Haiti's past and present—exploits, successes, natural environment, traditions, and culture—and its people are often underestimated. And more importantly, some people, including Haitians themselves, tend to either forget or ignore the magnitude of the 1804 Revolution in terms of its ideals, its reflection on humanity and progress, and how these ideals can inspire Haitians today to rethink their nation-state project.

This book has allowed us to redirect the focus on these very ideals of the Haitian Revolution to inspire the realization of Haiti's future goals. Despite the contradictions that fragilized the continuity of unity among the founding fathers of the nation, and that are still daunting current generations, the ideals of the revolution were what Haiti needed to build a solid society from the beginning. And these ideals remain today the foundation on which Haiti can rebuild for prosperity, fairness, and continuity in the sense of progress.

In the end, we understand that Haiti's socioeconomic and political developments will not be possible just because the international community supports it or demands it, as it has often been the case. But with real change, hope will arise because we [Haitians] want progress for ourselves. The only missing piece in the puzzle is unity, responsibility, accountability, and good leadership. Something we as a people need to work hard together to achieve. We repeat and maintain for current and future generations, progress will primarily be possible when we [Haitians of all backgrounds], first and foremost, decide we vigorously want it, and participate effectively in making it happen. With that said, we need to pull all our resources together, including our intelligence, creativity, imagination, and sense of community, to build a country that can project a different picture in the eyes of other nations.

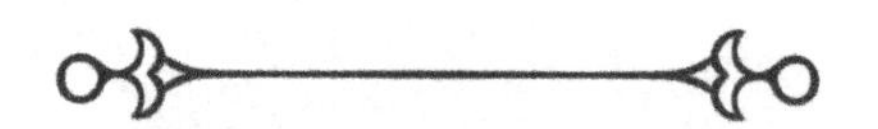

Bibliography

Abi-Habib, Maria. "Haiti's Leader Kept a List of Drug Traffickers: His Assassins Came for It". nytimes.com, *The New York Times*, December 12, 2021. https://www.nytimes.com/2021/12/12/world/americas/jovenel-moise-haiti-president-drug-traffickers.html/

Adams, David C., et al., "The Depiction of the Second Presidency of Jean-Bertrand Aristide", Alterpresse.org, June 8, 2022. https://www.alterpresse.org/spip.php?article28370&utm_source=dlvr.it&utm_medium=twitter

Alcenat, Westenly. "The Case for Haitians Reparations". jacobinmag.com, Jacobin Magazine, January 14, 2017. https://www.jacobinmag.com/2017/01/haiti-reparations-france-slavery-colonialism-debt/

Arthur, Charles and Dash, Michael. *Libète: A Haiti Anthology*. London: Latin America Bureau, 1999.

Borjarski, Sam. "Remittances to Haiti surge in 2020 as kidnappings, other crises rose". haitiantimes.com, *The Haitian Times*, May 14, 2021. https://haitiantimes.com/2021/05/14/remittances-to-haiti-surged-in-2020-as-kidnappings-other-crises-rose/

Cadet, Michel-Ange. "Dessalines' Ideals of Equality for Haiti". dadychery.org, Haiti Chery, August 9, 2015. https://www.dadychery.org/2015/08/09/dessalines-ideal-of-equality-for-haiti/

Cameron, Chris. "As U.S. Navigates Crisis in Haiti, a Bloody History Looms Large". nytimes.com, *The New York Times*, December 19, 2021. https://www.nytimes.com/2021/12/19/us/politics/us-haiti-intervention.html

Casimir, Jean. *The Haitians: A Decolonial History.* Chapel Hill, USA: The University of North Carolina Press, 2020.

Charles, Jacqueline and Weaver, Jay. "Haiti prime minister says he'd hand assassination suspects to U.S." *The Miami Herald*, Feb. 13, 2022.

CNN. "Pat Robertson says Haiti paying for pact to the devil". cnn.com, CNN, January 13, 2010. http://www.cnn.com/2010/US/01/13/haiti.pat.robertson/index.html

Colas Noel, Jocelyne. "Press Conference". Conference Episcopale Justice et Paix (CE-JILAP), December 23, 2019.

Collins, Jim. *Good To Great: Why Some Companies Make the Leap...and Others Don't.* New York: HarperCollins Publishers, 2001.

Council on Hemispheric Affairs (COHA). "The Tonton Macoutes: The Central Nervous System of Haiti's Reign of Terror". coha.org, COHA, March 11, 2020. https://www.coha.org/tonton-macoutes/

Cyprien, Gary. "L'évolution des transferts de la diaspora haïtienne". lenouvelliste.com, *Le Nouvelliste*, Nov. 9, 2021. https://lenouvelliste.com/article/232581/levolution-des-transferts-de-la-diaspora-haitienne

Dandicat, Edwige. "Haitians Are at an Impasse Over the Country's Future". *The New Yorker*, February 19, 2021.

Dandicat, Edwige. "Haitians want to know what the government has done with missing oil money". *The New Yorker*, October 19, 2018.

Davidson, Phil. "Henri Namphy: Coup Leader and Former President". *The Independent*, July 12, 2018.

Delince, Kern. *Quelle Armée pour Haiti*. Paris: Khartala, 1994.

Devereaux, Ryan. "Haiti Envoy Who Resigned: No Body Asked me about the Deportations". theintercept.com, The Intercept, October 7, 2021. https://theintercept.com/2021/10/07/haiti-migrants-daniel-foote/

Dima, Jake. "Pentagon Analyzing Haiti's request for U.S. Troops after Assassination". washingtonexaminer.com, *Washington Examiner*, July 11, 2021. https://www.washingtonexaminer.com/news/pentagon-analyzing-haiti-request-us-troops

Direction d'Appui à l'Enseignement Privé et du Partenariat. *Politique Nationale d'Accréditations des Écoles Privées*. Port-au-Prince: Ministère de l'Education Nationale et de Formation Professionelle, 2020.

Dominican Today. "Dominican to Haiti Exports: $US1.64 Billion to a Negligeable $US7 Million". dominicantoday.com, *Dominican Today*, October 25, 2021. https://dominicantoday.com/dr/economy/2021/10/25/dominican-to-haiti-exports-us1-64b-to-negligible-us7m/

Editorial Board. "Haiti needs elections and outside forces to make them safe". washingtonpost.com, *The Washington Post*, July 27, 2021. https://www.washingtonpost.com/opinions/2021/07/27/haiti-needs-elections-outside-forces-make-them-safe/

Editorial Board. “Haiti needs swift and muscular international intervention”. *The Washington Post*, July 7, 2021. https://www.washingtonpost.com/opinions/2021/07/07/assassination-its-president-puts-haiti-risk-anarchy-un-must-intervene/

Etienne, Sauveur Pierre. *La Drôle de guerre électorale:1987-2017*. Paris: L’Harmattan, 2019.

Faiola, Anthony. “Haiti’s acting prime minister Claude Joseph says he will step down amid leadership dispute”. washingtonpost.com, *The Washington Post*, July 19, 2021. https://www.washingtonpost.com/world/2021/07/19/haiti-claude-joseph-ariel-henry/

Fearnow, Benjamin. “Joe Biden Saying Haiti Does Not Matter in 1994 Clip Resurfaces After Moise Assassination”. newsweek.com, *Newsweek*, July 7, 2021. https://www.newsweek.com/joe-biden-saying-haiti-doesnt-matter-1994-clip-resurfaces-after-moise-assassination-1607692

Firmin, Anténor (Translation: Charles, Asselin and Introduction: Fluehr-Lobban, Carolyn). *The Equality of the Human* Races. Chicago: University of Illinois Press, 2002.

Forsdick, Charles and Hogsbjerg, Christian. *Toussaint Louverture: A Black Jacobin in the Age of Revolutions*. London: Pluto Press, 2017.

Gaffield, Julia. *Haitian Connections in the Atlantic World*. Chapel Hill, USA: The University of North Carolina Press, 2015.

Geffrard, Robenson. “Claude Joseph n'est pas premier minister: Il fait partie de mon gouvernement”. lenouvelliste.com, *Le Nouvelliste*, July 9, 2021. https://lenouvelliste.com/article/230284/claude-joseph-nest-pas-premier-ministre-il-fait-partie-de-mon-gouvernement-affirme-ariel-henry

Geffrard, Robenson. “Pour Ariel Henry, il n'y aura pas de President au Palais national avant les elections”. lenouvelliste.com, *Lenouvelliste,* January 17, 2022. https://lenouvelliste.com/article/233696/pour-ariel-henry-il-nyaura-pas-de-president-au-palais-national-avant-les-elections

Goodreads. “Author and Quotes”. goodreads.com, Goodreads, accessed March 13, 2022. https://www.goodreads.com/author/quotes/4918776. Seneca

Gress, Maria del Carmen and Ruchti, Jefri J. “The Principles Proclaimed in The Haitian Constitution”. constituteproject.org, Constitute Project, August 26, 2021. https://www.constituteproject.org/constitution/Haiti_2012.pdf?lang=en

Haiti Libre. “Turnaround of Core Group in Favor of PM named Ariel Henry”. haitilibre.com, Haiti Libre, accessed March 12, 2022. https://www.haitilibre.com/en/news-34260-haiti-flash-turnaround-of-core-group-in-favor-of-the-pm-named-ariel-henry.html

Haitian Diaspora Resources World Wide (HRWW). “Village Sans Souci”. hdrww.com, HDRWW, November 29, 2020. https://www.hdrww.com/projects-page/village-sans-souci

Hoetink, Harry and Ault, Stephen. *The Dominican People: Notes for a Historical Sociology.* Baltimore: Johns Hopkins Press, 1982

Ici Haiti Sports. "Training in Sports Infrastructure Management". icihaiti.com, Ici Haiti, May 1, 2019. https://www.icihaiti.com/en/news-26580-icihaiti-sports-training-in-sports-infrastructure-management.html

Index Mundi. "Haiti Exports". indexmundi.com, Index Mundi, September 18, 2021. https://www.indexmundi.com/haiti/exports.html

Jallot, Nicolas and Lesage, Laurent. *Dix ans d'histoire Secrète.* Paris: Editions du Félin, 1995.

Jean-Pierre, Karine. *Moving Forward: A Story of Hope, Hard Work and the Promise of America.* USA: Hanover Square Press, 2019.

Johnston, Jake. "Haitians don't need another President chosen behind closed doors". prospect.org, The American Prospect", July 19, 2021. https://prospect.org/world/haitians-dont-need-another-president-chosen-behind-closed-doors/

Kemp, Simon. "Digital 202: Haiti". datareportal.com, Data Reportal, February 11, 2021. https://datareportal.com/reports/digital-2021-haiti?rq=Haiti

Lamont Hill, Marc. "Foreign Intervention in Haiti". facebook.com, Aljazeera, November 17, 2021. https://www.facebook.com/watch/?v=314875216853015

Le Nouvelliste. “127 ans Pour Francoise Pascal”, lenouvelliste.com, *Le Nouvelliste*, January 5, 2022. https://lenouvelliste.com/article/233509/127-ans-pour-francoise-pascal

Le Nouvelliste. “Trop Jeune pour avoir 127 ans”. lenouvelliste.com, *Le Nouvelliste*, January 7, 2022. https://lenouvelliste.com/article/233548/trop-jeune-pour-avoir-127-ans

Lemaire, Sandra. “Haiti President’s Term Will End in 2022”. VOANEWS.com, Voice of America, February 5, 2021. https://www.voanews.com/a/americas_haiti-presidents-term-will-end-2022-biden-administration-says/6201681.html

Lynch, Willie. *The Willie Lynch Letter and the Making of a Slave.* USA: Ravenio Books, 2011.

Maxwell, John. *The 21 Irrefutable Laws of Leadership.* Nashville: Thomas Nelson, 2007

Maxwell, John. *The five Levels of Leadership.* New York: Center Steet, 2011.

McClatchy, Kevin, “State’s Sherman: Envoy wanted to send in U.S. Military”, The Miami Herald, September 30, 2021.

Mendoza, Martha. “Gold! Haiti hopes ore find will spur mining boom”. *Associated Press*, May 31, 2012.

Munro, Dana G. "The American Withdrawal from Haiti, 1929-1934". read.dukeupress.edu, Hispanic American Review, February 1969. http://read.dukeupress.edu/hahr/article-pdf/49/1/1/763052/0490001.pdf

Nohlen, Dieter. *Elections in the Americas: A data handbook.* Oxford: Oxford University Press, 2005.

Office of Press Relations. "USAID Provides $32 Million to Respond to Haiti Earthquake". usaid.gov, United States Agency for International Development (USAID), August 26, 2021. https://www.usaid.gov/news-information/press-releases/aug-26-2021-usaid-provides-32-million-respond-haiti-earthquake/

Orisma, Rhodner. *From Revolution to Chaos in Haiti.* Columbia, SC: Xlibris, 2020.

Ovans, Andrea. "How Emotional Intelligence Became a Key Leadership Skill". hbr.org, Harvard Business Review, April 28, 2015. https://hbr.org/2015/04/how-emotional-intelligence-became-a-key-leadership-skill

Parker, Sam and Anderson, Mac. *212 The Extra Degree: Extraordinary Results Begin with One Small Change.* Naperville, IL: Simple Truths, 2016.

Price, Ned. "Announcement of Daniel Foote as Special Envoy for Haiti". state.gov, U.S. Department of State, July 22, 2021. https://www.state.gov/announcement-of-daniel-foote-as-special-envoy-for-haiti/

Radio Télé Metropole. “La Banque Mondiale approuve 75 millions de dollars pour soutenir la création d’emplois en Haiti”. metropole.ht, Radio Télé Metropole Haiti. https://metropole.ht/la-banque-mondiale-approuve-75-millions-de-dollars-pour-soutenir-la-creation-demplois-en-haiti/

Regan, Jane. “Haiti’s Rush for Gold Gives Mining Firms a Free Rein to Riches”. theguardian.com, *The Guardian*, May 30, 2012. https://www.theguardian.com/global-development/poverty-matters/2012/may/30/haiti-gold-mining

Ricker, Tom. “Biden has deported nearly as many Haitians in his first year as the last three presidents – combined”. quixote.org, Quixote Center, February 18, 2022. https://www.quixote.org/biden-has-deported-nearly-as-many-haitians-in-his-first-year-as-the-last-three-presidents-combined/

Rivers, Matt, et al. “U.S. Charges Colombian man with conspiracy to kill Haiti’s president”. cnn.com, CNN, January 5, 2022. https://www.cnn.com/2022/01/05/americas/haiti-president-assassination-suspect-charged-intl/index.html

Ruiz, Jesus G. “Haiti is a source of refugees today: but it was once a haven for them”. WashingtonPost.com, *The Washington Post*, October 6, 2021. https://www.washingtonpost.com/outlook/2021/10/06/haiti-refugee-haven/

Saint-Pré, Patrick. “Haiti a reçu environ 20 millards de dollars de la diapora entre 2010 et 2019”. lenouvelliste.com, *Le Nouvelliste*, October 1, 2020. https://lenouvelliste.com/article/211022/haiti-a-recu-environ-20-milliards-de-dollars-de-transferts-de-la-diaspora-entre-2010-et-2019

Sanon, Evens and Cotto, Danica. “Haiti braces for unrest as opposition demands new president”. *The Associated Press*, January 15, 2021.

Sénat, Jean Daniel. “Jovenel appelle au dialogue et a l'organization des elections”. lenouvelliste.com, *Le Nouvelliste*, May 19, 2021. https://lenououvelliste.com/18-mai-2021-Jovenel-Moïse-appelle-au-dialogue-et-à-l'organisation-des-élections.html

Silvia, Adam M. “Haiti: An Island Luminous”. islandluminous.fiu.edu, Florida International University's Special Collections & Digital Library of the Caribbean, accessed March 12, 2022. http://islandluminous.fiu.edu/learn.html

Suggs, David. “The long legacy of the U.S. occupation of Haiti”. washingtonpost.com, *The Washington Post*, Aug. 6, 2021. https://www.washingtonpost.com/history/2021/08/06/haiti-us-occupation-1915/

The Buffalo News. “Haitian Leader Agree to U.N. Meeting”. buffalonews.com, *The Buffalo News*, June 27, 1993. https://buffalonews.com/news/haitian-leader-agrees-to-u-n-meeting/article_03d2d26c-a713-5bed-a7ff-0461bc0b4495.html

Tiralongo, Elena. “Haiti's Elections: Low Turnout Reflects Lack of Hope for Change. coha.org, COHA, November 12, 2015. https://www.coha.org/haitis-elections-low-turnout-reflects-lack-of-hope-for-change/

Treaster, Joseph. “Duvalier Flees Haiti to End Family's 28 years in Power: General Leads new Regime; 20 Reported dead”. nytimes.com, *The New York Times*, February 8, 1986. https://www.nytimes.com/1986/02/08/world/duvalier-flees-haiti-end-family-s-28-years-power-general-leads-new-regime-20.html

U.N. News. "Former U.S. President Clinton appointed U.N. Special Envoy for Haiti". news.un.org, U.N. News, May 9, 2009. https://news.un.org/en/story/2009/05/300442-former-us-president-clinton-appointed-un-special-envoy-haiti#:

U.N. Office for the Coordination of Humanitarian Affairs (OCHA). "The Haitian Government and the humanitarian community are requesting $ 291.5 million to provide vital assistance to 2.4 million vulnerable people". reliefweb.int, OCHA Relief, February 6, 2017. https://reliefweb.int/report/haiti/haitian-government-and-humanitarian-community-are-requesting-2915-million-provide-vital

U.S. Embassy in Haiti. "United States Commits an Additional $24.4 Million for Assistance to Haiti". usembassy.gov, U.S. Embassy in Haiti, October 5, 2020. https://ht.usembassy.gov/united-states-commits-an-additional-24-4-million-for-assistance-to-haiti/

Waden, Rory. *Take the Stairs: 7 Steps to Achieving True Success*. New York: Perigee, Penguin Group, 2012.

Wah, Tatiana. "Engaging the Haitian Diaspora". thecairoreview.com, The Cairo Review of Global Affairs, Spring 2013. https://www.thecairoreview.com/essays/engaging-the-haitian-diaspora/

Watkins, Eli and Phillip, Abby. "Trump decries immigrants from 'shithole countries' coming to the U.S.". cnn.com, CNN, revised January 12, 2018. https://www.cnn.com/2018/01/11/politics/immigrants-shithole-countries-trump/index.html

Wells, Jennifer. "A Dam for the People, and a People Damned". *The Toronto Star*, Nov. 21, 2010.

Wikipedia. "United States Occupation of Haiti". wikipedia.org, Wikipedia, accessed March 12, 2022. https://en.wikipedia.org/wiki/United_States_occupation_of_Haiti#American_financial_interests

Winget, Larry. *It's Called Work for a Reason: Your Success is your Own Damn Fault*. New York: Gotham Books, 2007.

Woolf, Chris. "When America Occupied Haiti". theworld.org, The World, August 6, 2015. https://theworld.org/stories/2015-08-06/when-america-occupied-haiti

World Atlas. "What are the Natural Resources of Haiti". worldatlas.com, World Atlas, accessed March 14, 2022. https://www.worldatlas.com/articles/what-are-the-major-natural-resources-of-haiti.html

World Population Review. "Haiti Population 2022". worldpopulationreview.com, World Population Review, March 14, 2022. https://worldpopulationreview.com/countries/haiti-population

Lightning Source UK Ltd.
Milton Keynes UK
UKHW040904140223
416719UK00016B/581/J